Green Spas and Salons
HOW TO MAKE YOUR BUSINESS TRULY SUSTAINABLE

Shelley Ann Lotz

SUSTAINABLE LIVING PROGRAMS
ASHLAND, OREGON

Green Spas and Salons
How to Make Your Business Truly Sustainable
Shelley Ann Lotz

Sustainable Living Programs
Box 1362, Ashland, Oregon 97520 USA
www.sustainablelivingprograms.com

Copyright ©2013 by Shelley Ann Lotz
All rights reserved under International and Pan American copyright conventions. No part of this book may be reproduced or utilized in any form, by electronic, mechanical, or other means, without the prior written permission of the publisher, except for brief quotations embodied in literary articles or reviews.

Interior and cover design: Chris Molé Design
Cover photos: Spa Moana, Natural Body, Spa Anjali/Shutterstock, Osmosis, Crystal Spa, Aji Spa
Edited by Panos Photinos, Carolyn Bond, John E. Darling, Jessica Vineyard

ISBN 978-0-9884733-2-4
Library of Congress Control Number 2012951555

10 9 8 7 6 5 4 3 2 1

This book is dedicated to all of the therapists and spa industry communities who are making the world a more peaceful and beautiful place.

A personal dedication goes to my late grandmother Mary J. Howell, who always encouraged me to write.

Acknowledgments

The following people were instrumental in helping make the book come together. A special thanks to Gina Heckley for her valuable research assistance and contributions to the green building sections. The book would not be complete without the generous contributions from the spas and salons featured in the case studies. Much appreciation to the contributors who shared inspiring words of wisdom. Additional reviewers and contributors gave essential information and feedback, including Marianne Griffeth, Lisa Sykes, and Mark Wuttke. I am grateful for the connections made through the Green Spa Network members. Thanks to the organizations who shared their valuable research.

Many thanks to my husband, Panos Photinos, for his support, and his scientific and editing expertise. Thanks to my family and friends who gave support and suggestions along the way: Janet Bocast, Heather Howell, Linda Latto, Tess Dey, Sandra Baker, and Suzanne McQueen. Thanks to Chris Molé for the beautiful book design and to Carolyn Bond, Jessica Vineyard, and John E. Darling for the valuable copyediting assistance. Additional thanks to Martine Edwards, Maria Moffre-Barnes, and the team at Milady, a division of Cengage Learning.

Contents

PREFACE x
ABOUT THE AUTHOR xi

1 REDEFINING GREEN BUSINESS MODELS 1
   What is Sustainability? 2
   What Makes a Business Green or Sustainable? 3
   Business Solutions and Initiatives 4
   What are the Benefits of Sustainability? 5
   Measuring Sustainability 6
   Green Speak 6
   Sustainability in the Beauty and Spa Industry 6
   SPA SPOTLIGHT: AGAVE SPA, WESTIN KIERLAND RESORT 9

2 FUNDAMENTAL SUSTAINABILITY PRINCIPLES 15
   What is the Difference Between Green and Sustainable? 15
   The Triple Bottom Line 16
   Using the Cradle to Cradle Philosophy 17
   Life Cycle Assessment 18
   The Natural Step 18
   SPA SPOTLIGHT: AJI SPA AND SALON, SHERATON WILD HORSE PASS 20

3 THE ENVIRONMENTAL CONCEPTS 24
   Ecology and the Ecosystem 24
   Carbon Footprints 25
   Water Footprints 26
   Natural Resource Depletion 27
   SCHOOL SPOTLIGHT: ATLANTA SCHOOL OF MASSAGE AND ITS
   DIVISION, ATLANTA INSTITUTE OF AESTHETICS 28

4 THE ECONOMIC ASPECTS OF SUSTAINABILITY 32
   Green Business and the Bottom Line 32
   The Economic Benefits of Green 33
   Sustainability Policies and Planning 37
   Accounting Practices 37
   SPA SPOTLIGHT: BE CHERISHED SALON AND DAY SPA 40

5 SOCIAL EQUITY MEANS EVERYONE BENEFITS 44
   What Is Social Responsibility? 44
   Act Locally: The Community 45
   Taking Care of the Staff 45
   SPA SPOTLIGHT: COMPLEXIONS SPA 47

6	**AN INTRODUCTION TO GREEN SPA PRACTICES**	52
	The Treatment Menu	52
	Choosing Green Products	53
	Treatment Rooms	53
	Conscious Purchasing	53
	The Green Facility	54
	SPA SPOTLIGHT: CRYSTAL SPA	55
7	**THE SERVICE MENU AND BEYOND**	60
	Stimulating the Five Senses	60
	Holistic Health and Beauty Services	61
	Highlighting Local Culture	61
	Planning the Service Menu	61
	Food Service	63
	Fitness and Gyms	63
	Spa Industry Services and Statistics	63
	SPA SPOTLIGHT: ELAIA SPA, HYATT AT OLIVE 8	66
8	**DEFINING GREEN PRODUCTS**	69
	What Makes a Product Green?	70
	Natural versus Synthetic Ingredients	71
	Organic Ingredients	71
	Toxins and Chemicals	72
	Green Chemistry	74
	Growing and Harvesting Ingredients	75
	Manufacturing and Sourcing	75
	Packaging	75
	Vendor Relationships	76
	SPA SPOTLIGHT: GLEN IVY HOT SPRINGS	77
9	**PRODUCT STANDARDS AND REGULATIONS**	82
	Natural and Organic Standards	82
	Certifications and Ecolabels	84
	SPA SPOTLIGHT: NATURAL BODY SPA AND SHOP	86
10	**CHOOSING PRODUCTS AND INGREDIENTS FOR THE SPA**	90
	Choosing Green Products and Ingredients	90
	Green Criteria for Products	92
	Personal Care Ingredients	94
	SPA SPOTLIGHT: NATUROPATHICA HOLISTIC HEALTH	100

11	**PURCHASING AND GREEN MATERIALS** 104
	What Is a Green Material? 104
	What Criteria Make a Material Green? 105
	Ecolabels Everywhere 108
	SPA SPOTLIGHT: OSMOSIS DAY SPA SANCTUARY 110

12	**WASTE REDUCTION AND PURCHASING** 117
	Green Purchasing Guidelines 117
	Green Packaging 119
	Waste and Recycling 120
	SPA SPOTLIGHT: SPA ANJALI 122

13	**HEALTHY INDOOR ENVIRONMENTAL QUALITY** 126
	Design for Health 126
	Indoor Air Quality(IAQ) 129
	Chemicals and Toxins 130
	Feng Shui Design 132
	SPA SPOTLIGHT: THE SPA AT CLUB NORTHWEST 133

14	**ENERGY CONSERVATION** 138
	Benefits of Energy Conservation 138
	Energy Conservation Practices 139
	Energy Concepts 140
	SPA SPOTLIGHT: SPA MOANA AT HYATT REGENCY MAUI 143

15	**WATER CONSERVATION** 148
	Benefits of Water Conservation 148
	Water Concepts 149
	Global Water Impacts 149
	Water Conservation Practices 150
	Bottled Water Issues 151
	SPA SPOTLIGHT: SUNDARA INN AND SPA 153

16	**STAFF NEEDS AND GREEN TEAMS** 158
	Happy Employees 159
	Green Teams 160
	Staff Training 160
	WEIGHT LOSS AND WELLNESS HAVEN SPOTLIGHT: THE NEW WELL 162

17	**EXPLORING GREEN STEPS AND PRACTICES** 165
	TABLES:
	The Service Menu 166
	Retail and Service Products 167
	Purchasing and Supply Use 168
	Purchasing Spa Equipment 169

	Waste Reduction	170
	Packaging	172
	Green Materials for Interiors	173
	Indoor Environmental Quality (IEQ)	174
	Energy Conservation Steps	175
	Water Conservation Measures	177
	Landscaping	179
	Food and Beverage Choices	180
	Sustainable Transportation and Travel	180
	Staff Care	181
	Clients and the Community	181
	SPA SPOTLIGHT: VDARA SPA AND SALON	182
18	**GREEN PLANNING AND ASSESSMENTS**	185
	Define Your Goals and the Vision	185
	Planning Steps	186
	Evaluate the Spa's Current Practices	188
	Energy Tracking Sheets	190
	Water Assessment Sheets	194
	SPA SPOTLIGHT: WATERSTONE SPA	196
19	**CREATING YOUR GREEN ACTION PLAN**	200
	Creating Sustainability Goals	200
	Sustainability Planning Tables	202
20	**IMPLEMENTING YOUR GREEN PRACTICES**	208
	Implementing Sustainability Practices: Action Steps and Tables	208
21	**MARKETING GREEN**	213
	Marketing and LOHAS	214
	Business Trends for Today's Marketplace	215
	Demographics and Different Generations	216
	Ethics and Greenwashing	218
22	**PLANNING YOUR MARKETING COMMUNICATIONS**	220
	Marketing Assessment Worksheet	220
	Green Marketing Ideas	221
	The Social Media Revolution	222
	Marketing Tools	222
	Marketing Review Checklist	223

23 BUILDING GREEN ... 225
- The Green Building Process ... 226
- Site Design ... 228
- Energy Systems ... 229
- Green Building Materials ... 231
- Indoor Environmental Quality ... 233
- Water Conservation ... 233
- Green Building Trends ... 234
- Green Building Certification and Standards ... 235

24 GREEN BUILDING PRACTICES ... 238
- Planning for Green Building ... 238
- Site Design ... 240
- Energy Conservation and Practices ... 240
- Green Materials and Interiors ... 244
- Indoor Environmental and Air Quality ... 245
- Water Conservation ... 247
- Landscaping Design ... 248
- Green Building Worksheets ... 249

REFERENCES ... 252
RESOURCES ... 258
INDEX ... 260

Download online Planning Worksheets and additional resources at
www.greenspasandsalons.com

Preface

This guidebook focuses on developing smart, sustainable practices for long-term business success. You will learn how to implement green business practices, sustainability, and green building components, which are simply explained all in one book. Use this resource as a planning guide and use the personalized action plans, how-to steps, and worksheets included here to help you efficiently track and achieve your sustainable goals.

You can evaluate your services, products, supplies, operations, facility management, and green building elements. Staff engagement, client needs, and marketing ideas are all important aspects covered here. Even if you are already using green practices, this guide can help you stay on track and assess your policies and procedures. These practical tools go beyond the spa/salon industry and most are applicable to any business.

Inspiring spa case studies and real world examples are included to give you creative ideas and showcase what others in the industry are doing to make their businesses more sustainable. It's essential to keep up with the fast-paced changes in society and the beauty industry, which are discussed here. You can review the educational and scientific aspects of sustainability so you are knowledgeable and articulate about why green practices are important. You can also gain the knowledge to monitor your green operations, construction, and remodeling projects.

Connecting all of the green dots can be challenging. It is helpful to have a foundation to understand sustainable policies and to be familiar with the lingo before going into the greening process. The range of topics integrated here will provide a comprehensive picture of sustainability. Chapters are divided into short theory and practical sections.

The case studies in this book have been chosen to offer diversity. There is a broad range of businesses across the country included here, from small salons to large resorts. The examples show that you do not have to be the greenest spa in the land in order to make a positive difference. The case study interviews were conducted in 2011 and 2012. Each spa, school, and hospitality business has its own focus and unique green features.

The questionnaire format used in these interviews is incorporated into the assessment phase of green planning found in Chapter 18 and in the online Planning Worksheets. Case study facts and figures were not available for every category, so not every case study is identical. There are many more green spas and salons that deserve recognition, but space does not make that possible in this first edition.

The book is designed to help you, the reader, by sifting through the "green hype" and presenting useful practices that can make a real difference in your business. Since the book covers sustainability, the spa/salon/wellness industry, and green building, it is like three mini books in one. My hope is that the book is useful and inspiring for businesses of all shapes and sizes.

Thank you for your green efforts in making our industry more sustainable and beautiful. Please share your own green efforts by sending comments, questions, or suggestions to lotz.shelley@gmail.com. More information and resources are available at greenspasandsalons.com.

---

* Note: The author makes no representation regarding the products, services, or business practices of the companies or organizations named in this book.

About the Author

Photo by Judith Pavlik

Shelley Lotz's lifelong passion for both sustainability and the spa industry has naturally led her to focus on green practices in the beauty industry. She feels that green spas/salons are a complementary blend of green business and holistic beauty—the two go hand in hand. Shelley has over 25 years of experience in the spa industry as an esthetician, educator, and business owner. She enjoys the hands on work as a therapist, as well as the business aspects of the industry.

Shelley has an extensive business background in marketing, management, staff training, and retail. She is a contributing author of *Milady's Standard Esthetics Fundamentals,* a core textbook for esthetics students. She started an institute of esthetics and taught for many years. She consults for spas and schools on esthetics, spa procedures, and curriculums.

The green side of Shelley's career includes working as a Certified Sustainable Building Advisor and as the former director of the Sustainable Building Advisor Institute in Southern Oregon. Shelley loves the travel/hospitality industry and travels extensively while doing spa research and studying industry developments. She has a bachelor of science degree in biology, geography, and communications from Southern Oregon University, with a focus on environmental education. Her website is greenspasandsalons.com.

CHAPTER 1

Redefining Green Business Models

INTRODUCTION

The spa and salon industry has an exciting opportunity to bring together beauty and green business. It is a natural extension of the holistic, healing nature of the beauty and spa world to take better care of the planet and people through sustainable practices. Sustainability balances three aspects: people, planet, and profit. While the industry is known for its focus on caring for others, it uses a large amount of packaging, water, supplies, and other resources. This guide will help you to sift through the green hype and focus on useful, real world practices that make a difference in your business.

Green practices bring an abundance of positive results. It is not just about jumping on the bandwagon or Greenwashing. It is the new way of living and the new definition of prosperity. For example, reducing energy and water use has many positive benefits beyond saving money. Customers today expect businesses to use green practices and to be more socially responsible. People are willing to pay more for green products and services. Additionally, the cost of green products is becoming more affordable as sustainable business models become mainstream.

The conscious movement to improve the way we live and lessen the impact on the world is at the forefront of today's culture. "The ***Lifestyle of Health and Sustainability (LOHAS)*** consumers are forward thinking individuals who consider the impact on the environment and society when making buying decisions. The LOHAS market comprises a significant percentage of the adult population and is a $290 billion dollar market that is expected to grow annually" (lohas.com 2010). This is only one piece of the green market, and businesses are rushing to keep up with the demands of green consumers.

Greening the way we do business is imperative not only because it is the right thing to do, but also because it helps to sustain our business. The demands for these changes are moving at a fast pace as new technology designed to help save resources is also advancing. Everywhere you look, education is more focused on sustainability. At home and in the workplace, buildings, schools, and government offices are all going green. Even small steps make a difference in achieving your goals.

Managing a business is more challenging in today's ever-changing world. Keeping up with everyday operations and making complex marketing choices is a demanding job. Businesses that strive to be sustainable are more balanced, healthy, and successful. This book is designed to help businesses improve their bottom line and become more sustainable without having to wade through complex models and assessment methods.

How do we take care of the business, people, and the environment in a healthy way? How do we define what green is and communicate that to our clients? Why should we care? Since a significant percentage of our customer base expects responsible practices, it is now part of our culture and is a necessary part of our business.

WORDS OF WISDOM

Going green is no longer a trend, it's a lifestyle. We are consuming less, but we are reading labels more, and we're much more aware of making our purchases count. We're also factoring in a value differential that encompasses fair trade, sustainability, and giving back (corporate social responsibility programs).

When it comes to beauty, not only are organic and natural products healthy, they are stylish, sophisticated, and luxurious, and they really work. The granola-crunchy days of green beauty are gone. The question now becomes: "Why wouldn't I use them?" As consumers eat healthier foods and embrace more sustainable lifestyles, it's inevitable that they are drawn to natural and organic beauty, because they are thinking, big-picture, in terms of what is safest and healthiest to put in and on their bodies.

On a global scale, consumers are beginning to connect the dots, think about their beauty products, and ask, "What is that washing down my drain, and how does that impact my health and the health of the environment?" When we apply moisturizer–if the molecule is small enough–it penetrates through the skin and directly into the bloodstream. In fact, penetrability has been a selling point in the industry for years.

It's important for me to say that a few occasional ingredients in your moisturizer are not necessarily going to cause you harm. But when you think about the cumulative effects of these ingredients entering your bloodstream along with all of the other pollutants, pesticides, synthetic preservatives, hormones and antibiotics, etc., in our food, our environment, and the air we breathe, over a lifetime, it is a wake-up call.

~ RONA BERG, bestselling author, beauty and wellness expert, contributing editor of *SPA Magazine* and Executive Editor of *Organic Spa Magazine,* www.ronaberg.com

---

Green Spa Business Concepts Address the Following Areas:

- Beauty Services
- Products and Supplies
- Green Material
- Operations
- Resources and Utilities
- Facility Management
- Green Building
- Staff Engagement
- Client Expectations
- Marketing

WHAT IS SUSTAINABILITY?

Everyone may have a different idea of what sustainable means, but there is one universal definition. The global definition of **Sustainability** is "meeting the needs of the present without compromising the ability of future generations to meet their needs." For simplicity, *green* and *sustainable* are used interchangeably in this book unless the distinction is needed. While the terms have different meanings, they are both commonly used as lay terms for environmentally responsible practices. The **Three E's of Sustainability** are the three pillars of sustainability (Figure 1-1).

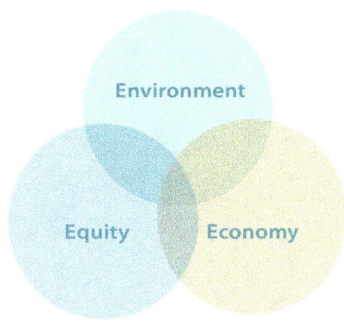

Figure 1-1: The Three E's of Sustainability.

 Equity/Social Benefit: Benefits everyone in society and globally—think about the effects of our actions on everyone in the community and beyond.

 Environment: Protect the environment: minimize the use of non-renewable resources and use renewables at a sustaining rate.

 Economy: Develop a healthy economy integrated with environmental goals.

The Three E's are also known as the three P's: *People, Planet, and Prosperity, or Profit.*

WHAT MAKES A BUSINESS GREEN OR SUSTAINABLE?

A sustainable, *green business* can be defined as a "business conducted in a manner that is environmentally, socially, and economically responsible." This is a high standard to live up to, but how is it defined and who defines it? What is the motivation for being sustainable? One definition of a green business is that it "solves environmental and social problems, rather than creating them. Adopting policies and practices that improve the quality of life for customers, employees, communities, and the environment" are the key green ingredients (Green America 2012).

Sustainable practices are being weaved into organizational culture and strategically integrated into companies of all sizes. A green salon can offer healthier beauty services, sell natural products, practice recycling, reduce the use of supplies, utilize more efficient operations, monitor energy and water use, have conscious facility management, and buy green building materials. Considering the needs of both the staff and clients is part of this overall equation.

Making choices based on the impact we have is considered the basis for a green business model. There is a global mindset brought on by recent experiences and knowledge that we need to slow down our consumption as it may exceed the resource supply. So how do we sustain both our lifestyle and the world that supports us? Conservation is the best place to start.

We have a long way to go, but every little step helps make a difference on the impact we have on the world. Personal and corporate choices such as using recycled products are becoming common practice because they are easy changes to make. Recycling, turning off lights to save energy, using less water, and eating organic are now daily habits. Are these conscious decisions for a healthier environment or are they based on saving money or for personal health?

Most businesses are going green to become more economically sustainable. There is no downside to using green practices. There is also a growing need for a green economy with green jobs. This is part of the public's awareness and discussion. Even in the recent economic challenges, green is still growing because of today's culture and the positive impacts in business across the board. It is no longer an expensive threat, but the smart thing to do.

Long-term sustainability incorporates a business plan focused on saving and conserving resources for a lighter footprint, or impact, on the world. Thinking in terms of long-term costs, not just immediate costs, is more sustainable. You can save money, save resources, and increase revenue all at the same time.

WE ARE RIDING A WAVE OF INNOVATION.
Many industry professionals say that sustainability is a current wave of innovation.

BUSINESS SOLUTIONS AND INITIATIVES

Interwoven in business mission statements are sustainability principles addressing such issues as water and energy conservation, recycling, purchasing nontoxic products, and caring for staff, customers, and the community. Local and global green business programs are everywhere. Many companies have attempted to calculate their carbon footprint. That is a big shift in business philosophy.

According to the website Environmental Leader, *The State of Sustainable Business Poll* in 2011 conducted by BSR/Globescan, shows that "8 in 10 respondents are optimistic that global businesses will embrace **Corporate Social Responsibility (CSR)** as part of their core strategies and operations in the next few years." CSR is now part of business accountability and the sustainability business model. CSR includes sustainability reporting and carbon management.

Creating innovative products and business models designed for sustainability, as well as measuring positive social and environmental impacts, are major focal points for companies. There are big investments in green product development, green chemistry, and better packaging. Social issues, climate change and water issues are cited as significant priorities in sustainability efforts (BSR.org 2011). Sustainability is a key to achieving long-term business success.

Best Practices are industry guidelines to achieve high standards in specific areas such as energy and water conservation (Figure 1-2). There are best practices to use among all categories, including green manufacturing, packaging, energy use, water, operations, recycling, and waste management. Green initiatives are everywhere. Large corporations such as hotel chains have implemented sustainability initiatives, as shown in the case studies.

Figure 1-2: Best practices are guidelines for high industry standards.

To support these business initiatives, educational courses in sustainability are available in many fields of study. Business schools are adding sustainability management courses and degrees to their programs. Environmental studies programs and educational certificates are also popular. Classes such as *Sustainable Hospitality and Spa Management* and *Green Spas, Hotels, and Resorts* are becoming more universal.

What is your vision of green?
Take a minute to think about what being green means to you.
Is it saving energy? Is it recycling? Is it a lifestyle?

Green businesses:
- Are aware of the sustainability issues
- Use goals and plans to achieve green practices
- Take initiative and action steps
- Conserve resources and recycle
- Measure their impacts
- Are innovative and efficient
- Analyze their eco footprints
- Focus on their customers' needs
- Support their staff beyond just a paycheck
- Are active in the community
- Demonstrate the core organizational values
- Have active leadership
- Practice Corporate Social Responsibility
- Use Sustainability Reporting
- Practice carbon management
- Use Best Practices
- Make green investments

WHAT ARE THE BENEFITS OF SUSTAINABILITY?

There are many benefits to living sustainably. What do you feel the main benefit is? Here is a quick introduction of the benefits to adapting sustainable business practices. Sustainable Building Advisors (2011) note the following benefits:

Equity, or Social Benefits, for People
- Better quality of life
- Improved employee productivity
- Staff and customers valued
- Holistic focus on health and wellness
- Healthier Indoor Environmental Quality (IEQ)
- Less dependence and strain on natural resources
- Higher standard of living
- Better jobs and worker benefits
- Healthier environment

Ecological Benefits for the Planet
- Natural resources conserved
- Improved potable water quality
- Cleaner streams, rivers, and oceans
- Better air quality
- Less pollution and toxins
- Land, soil, and trees protected
- Greenhouse gases and climate change slowed down
- Forests and wildlife benefited

Economic Benefits for Prosperity
- Cost savings
- Resource savings
- Bottom line margins/profits
- Increased market share
- Customer loyalty
- Positive reputation and public relations
- Better employee morale and productivity
- Increased efficiency
- Reduced risks from less reliance on natural resources
- Protection from inflation and future costs
- Increased values and revenues for owners, businesses, and buildings
- Eco-competitiveness

What do your clients want?
What sustainable practices would they like to see you use?

> **How is Sustainability Measured?**
> Life Cycle Assessment, Triple Bottom Line (TBL) accounting, and carbon footprints are three of the ways to measure sustainability.

MEASURING SUSTAINABILITY

Life Cycle Assessment (LCA), Triple Bottom Line (TBL) accounting, and carbon footprint calculations are three models businesses can use to measure how green they are. *Triple Bottom Line (TBL)* accounting is an accounting method that takes the three E's of sustainability into consideration. These concepts are discussed in the next chapter.

The sustainability assessment process takes into account all of the environmental, social, and economic effects. For example, what is the resource use and the carbon footprint of the company? How are employees treated? The *Return On Investment (ROI)* is the third part of the green triangle—is the investment economically feasible? ROI calculates the payback for the amount of money invested. This approach can be adapted to any industry or product.

Global Reporting Standards (GRS) are another set of business standards used to measure sustainability. While some companies use these methods, you can go green with simple practices that are even easier. To measure sustainability and implement green practices, many companies use green teams, sustainability coordinators, and *Chief Sustainability Officers (CSOs)*.

GREEN SPEAK

Business as usual has many new descriptive words associated with it: sustainable, eco-friendly, holistic, natural, authentic, transparency, lifestyle, and engagement. The sustainable lingo now carries over to regular business terms and practices. Does your business use these terms to describe how you operate or relate to customers? *Conversational marketing* and *social media* are the current marketing trends. Marketing is discussed in Chapters 21 and 22.

Green marketing strategies and sales pitches have been over used in marketing. Nevertheless, green practices still need to be promoted and publicized. It is still an important part of the business model. Misleading consumers with false claims is known as *Greenwashing*. This has given green a bad name, so make sure your claims and statements are indeed true. Products with recycled content are not necessarily enough to be labeled sustainable in today's world, but many companies capitalize on one small aspect regardless of their other detrimental practices.

> **"Eco-Friendly"** generally means the product or company practices are less harmful to the environment by meeting criteria such as conserving resources or being less toxic. This term and many others are vague and can be misleading.

Green certifications are becoming more common, but these are not always regulated. Third party certifications have more validity when making claims about green products. If you are not sure of a product's greenness, do not promote it as green. Subsequent chapters include Greenwashing, certifications, and labeling of green products and buildings.

SUSTAINABILITY IN THE BEAUTY AND SPA INDUSTRY

Green spas, salons, and businesses are predicted to become the standard model in the next five years (Figure 1-3). When discussing salons and spas, the term *spa* will be primarily used to include beauty salons, cosmetology schools and spas. The spa movement in the last decade has seen major growth.

According to the *International Spa Association* (ISPA), there are over 18,000 spas in the US and there is a consistent annual growth rate. Historically, the beauty industry is resilient. Even in a bad economy, the industry typically does well or even better. The industry has had major growth as salons have evolved into day spas, while medical spas have become part of the health and wellness business. The hospitality industry, hotels, and resorts are a large part of the spa business. With billions of dollars in sales, this beauty/wellness industry continues to expand. The marketplace is always shifting with new technology, products, and trends. Businesses must adapt quickly to keep up or they will be left behind.

It is only right that the "makeover" business is getting its own makeover as the shift to green continues. The beauty industry is all about change and growth. We naturally embrace this fluidity concept, so we can adapt more quickly with today's moving green target. Many spas are returning to their natural roots, which are focused on health and wellness.

With so much information overload, health and wellness services offer a much needed retreat from daily stress. The aging population is also looking for genuine evidence-based health and therapeutic treatments. Another service that spas offer is giving people a chance to connect in person in a meaningful way. There is discussion of spa memberships that could be promoted like gym memberships and become a place to visit on a regular basis. This leisure industry has a positive impact on people's lives in many ways beyond offering beauty services.

Do the words green and spa seem contradictory? Promoting products and consumption is part of the beauty business. Can we promote less consumption and still thrive? The beauty industry has obvious impacts on global resources such as energy and water. Waste, numerous chemical ingredients, an excess of containers and packaging, and laundry are major industry concerns. It is also a service industry with few employee benefits and a huge amount of money spent on marketing. On the other hand, the beauty and spa business is about nurturing, giving, health, and wellness. Expanding those concepts to consider the health of the ecosystem outside the salon is a natural step.

The Beauty Industry Evolution

There are many positive examples of beauty industry innovations. Initiatives to make more sustainable packaging and new regulations and certifications for natural products are in the works. Product manufacturers and suppliers are implementing sustainable practices and offering greener products. A few years ago there were only a handful of organic product lines. Today there are many and the availability is growing quickly. Green chemistry technology is also advancing in many industries.

Current US spa business trends complement the green market. A focus on offering simple, well-priced products and services, engaging clients, using social media, and supporting local products are part of the new business

Sustainable Business Models
Aveda and Kiehl's are commonly mentioned as two prominent companies that report using the *Cradle to Cradle* philosophy and consider *Life Cycle Analysis (LCA)* in their core values and practices.

Figure 1-3:
Green will soon be the standard business model.

model. Healthier products and natural practices are also in vogue. An industry overview is discussed in Chapter 7.

Many service and product companies have a sustainability philosophy and mission statement that are prominent on their websites. A prime example of how green has become prominent in the industry is that the *International Spa Association* (ISPA) has a sustainability statement and global best practices for sustainability using the 3 P's of sustainability: Planet, People, and Prosperity.

Other examples of industry changes include professional trade journals and websites that include green sections. *Skin Inc.* has a sustainability section on their website and a green section in the journal. *American Spa* magazine and *Day Spa* magazine discuss sustainability on a regular basis. The journal *Les Nouvelles Esthetique* (*LNE*) also has informative articles and now has a green pavilion at their conferences. *Spaclique* is an online professional resource that features green business practices and conferences. The *Green Spa Network* (GSN) is a growing green trade association. Another organization, *Organic Monitor,* tracks organic industry news and research, and hosts a sustainable products summit. *Spa Finder* for consumers now lists green spas in their publications. *Organic Spa* magazine is another successful publication that has become very popular with the public.

2010 ISPA Statistics
- There were over 150 million spa visits in 2010.
- Over $12.8 billion of revenue was generated by the US spa industry.
- Annual growth of visits and new locations increased steadily from 2000–2008 then declined in 2009 and 2010 to 19,900 locations in the US. (This does not include the number of salons and schools in the US and North America.)
- US spa employment exceeded 330, 000 employees (full-time, part-time, and contractors).
- The natural products industry is projected to grow annually.

(Courtesy: ISPA)

The Green Spa Network

Green Spa Network (GSN) is a not-for-profit trade association. The goals of GSN are to bring sustainable operating practices to the spa industry; facilitate education, research, and alliances in sustainable business practices; and promote the natural connections between personal wellbeing, economic sustainability, and the health of our planet.

GSN.org notes the benefits of green spas and facilities:
- Green spas are naturally healthy.
- Green spas are more relaxing.
- Green spa treatments are more effective for long-term health and beauty.
- Green spas put the body in harmony with nature.
- Green spas are good business.

(Courtesy: GSN)

How sustainable is your business?
Is it dark green or light green?

CHAPTER 1: Redefining Green Business Models   9

SPA SPOTLIGHT

AGAVE SPA, WESTIN KIERLAND RESORT
An upscale, luxury resort experience with low impact living practices

Contact: Carol Ford, Spa Director (2012)

Westin Kierland Resort
6902 E Greenway Parkway
Scottsdale, AZ

www.kierlandresort.com

Facility size: 16,400 sq. ft.

Number of employees: 81

Number of treatment rooms:
20 treatment rooms

Established in: 2002

Facility Description
The Westin Kierland Resort & Spa is a four-diamond resort located in Scottsdale. The resort features over 800 rooms; 208,000 square feet of indoor and outdoor function space, eight food and beverage venues, a full-service spa and fitness studio, a water park, Westin Kids Club®, and the 27-hole Kierland Golf Club. In 2010, The Westin Kierland Resort continued to enhance their "Be Greener" efforts, becoming an Energy Star Partner, a member of the Phoenix Green Chamber of Commerce and named a "Green Certified" hotel by the Arizona Hotel & Lodging Association. The resort's "Be Greener" program, launched in early 2007, was initiated to help set an example and lead the way in the hospitality industry for the state.

SPA GOALS AND VISION

What is your green business mission statement?
The Westin Kierland Resort & Spa's Environmental Policy: The resort is committed to protecting our environment and preserving our precious natural resources. We believe being green is not a definitive objective, but understand it's a process of being "greener." We are dedicated to the process and promise to promote a lifestyle that ensures our environmental impact on the world around us is minimal and as positive as possible.

What is your spa image?
A transformative retreat inspired by the healing and life-giving nectar of Arizona's indigenous agave plant. Treatments are effective, cutting-edge, and valuable to guests' health, beauty, and well-being. We do not subscribe to "gimmicky" treatments and services. By blending an upscale, luxury resort experience with low impact living practices, Agave offers guests the peace of mind of knowing they are doing business with an organization that has the environment in mind.

What is important to you regarding sustainability?
We have integrated various methods of greener living into our daily lives and encourage our guests and

team members to do the same. We reduce, reuse, and recycle where possible. We support our vendors, neighbors, and local merchants and do our best to promote the work they are doing. We are in the midst of great change and look to our customers, associates, and partners to help us navigate through this change and support us in our efforts.

What business practices or areas would you like to make more sustainable?
Director of engineering, Bob Cisco, notes, "We've been actively researching and implementing operational change for a few years now and we've made great strides with what we've done so far. We still have a long way to go, but every day we are finding out new, smarter, 'greener' ways of operating."

Is the staff interested in greening the facility?
Yes, they are active participants in daily green and recycling efforts.

What business practices do you think your clients want to see concerning sustainability?
They want greening efforts without compromising quality or their experience.

Do you promote your green practices?
The environmental policy statement is promoted on the website. We ask guests if they would like a bag, rather than just assuming. Recycle bins are used for plastic goods in the spa for plastic cups and bottles. We provide refillable Agave Spa water bottles for hikes rather than plastic water bottles. Promotions with "Bring your own robe/slippers" to receive a discount on a pedicure or spa service reduces water and electric usage.

SPA ELEMENTS

The Treatment Menu
- The menu is printed on recycled paper.
- Most services have a green component via local vendor supplies or certified organic products.
- The Eastern Essence is a series of treatments combining traditional Chinese medicine and other holistic modalities; these include acupuncture and Thai massage.
- Agave therapies include desert plant and mud extracts in treatments.

Products
- Recycle plastic bottles from professional products.

Skin care products
- Eminence Organics: The farm is 100% powered by solar and wind energy and uses only natural compost during planting and harvest. Planting and harvesting are done by manual labor compared to traditional mechanical means. Eminence packaging is made from 30% post-consumer recycled paper and is recyclable.
- Packaging chips are made of corn and dissolve harmlessly under running hot water.
- Paperless ordering and invoicing.

Body care: Organic aromatherapy oils and massage oils.

Hair care: Certified organic extracts; NO: sulfates, parabens, phthalates, DEA, TEA, or artificial colors; recyclable/reusable packaging. Prive's empty containers from the Concept Vert line can be turned back in to the salon and sent to the manufacturer to be reused.

We use the Zerran Vegan Hair Smoothing System in lieu of the Brazilian Blowout. The Zerran System is 100% vegan, botanically based, paraben-free, and sulfate-free.

- *Nail care:* Vegan nail polish.
- *Makeup:* Advanced Mineral Makeup is 100% vegan, paraben-free, talc-free, no perfumes or dyes.
- *Retail:* Yoganastix clothing: local vendor; Lotus Wei: local vendor and member of the Green Spa Network, paperless ordering and invoicing; Olreka: local vendor with green packaging practices, paperless ordering and invoicing.

Supplies

- The spa works with vendors and partners whose businesses are either completely organic or environmentally conscious for more than 75% of its business.
- The spa also recycles all of its plastic, glass, and paper from all of the products it uses for treatments.
- Non-toxic products are used for cleaning.
- Offer an environmentally friendly, 100% recyclable and reusable Westin Kierland "GREEN" retail bag.

Treatment Supplies

- Living Earth Crafts (massage tables and chairs): FSC® certified manufacturing facilities, low-voltage factory lighting, intensive recycling, managed forest hardwoods, water-based lacquers and glues, CFC-free cushioning systems, and biodegradable fabrics are some of the many ways EarthLite and Living Earth Crafts demonstrates its commitment to environmental sustainability.

Energy

- Central Energy Plant upgrade to reduce electrical consumption.
- The resort reduced electrical consumption by 12.9% year over year by upgrading the resort's heating, ventilation and air-conditioning systems.
- Participation in the 2009 and 2010 global "Earth Hour" efforts to conserve energy.
- Guest room sensors regulate temperature according to activity in the room.
- Meeting room temperatures centrally controlled in accordance with meeting schedules.
- Computer and lighting are shut down each night.

Type of lighting

- Most light bulbs have been switched out with CFL bulbs and LED light fixtures.
- Six Sigma Energy Reduction Project resulted in reduced electrical usage by 4%.

Water

- A new pilot program also offers guests the option to purchase a reusable water bottle that they can refill an unlimited number of times at dedicated water stations (with a special filtration system).
- Conserving water in the desert is vital! Linen and towel reuse program available in all guest rooms.
- "Make a Green Choice" program allows guests to decline housekeeping services in return for a $5 gift card available to use at the resort.
- *Hot water:* We are currently considering a new system that introduces ozone into our laundry washers. If we decide to move forward, hot water would no longer be required during our washing

process, which will result in substantial energy savings.
- **Fixtures:** We have low-flow aerators as well as 1.6 gallon-per-flush toilets.
- **Landscaping:** We just received approval to install a WeatherTrak irrigation control system. We estimate a 30% reduction in water consumption as a result of this "smart" system.
- **Green materials:** The Westin Workout floor is made of recyclable materials (recycled plastic water bottles etc).
- **Indoor Environmental Quality (IEQ):** Standard filtration in all HVAC equipment.

Purchasing

- Vendors are local, when possible, to support the local economy and to reduce our carbon footprint.
- Vendors that belong to the Fair Trade guidelines and are truly organic are preferred.
- Corn-based disposable cups and products for food and beverages.

Waste Reduction

- Key programs include recycling for cardboard, paper, plastics, aluminum, and food waste.
- Only work with printing companies that are certified as responsible companies with reforestation and rehabilitation projects in place, and we print on recycled paper.
- Vendors that do not pre-package in boxes for back bar items are preferred.
- Paperless systems are implemented to minimize paper waste.
- Paper recycling bins in each spa office with the main recycling bin in the back of the resort.
- Plastic recycling bins in the Westin Workout, juice bar, and spa prep room.
- Cardboard boxes received from shipments are taken to the recycling bin for pick up.
- Use filtered water tap instead of bottled drinking water. This is a less expensive alternative and limits the usage of plastic water bottles. A reverse osmosis system is used in all the resort outlets to eliminate the use of plastic water bottles.

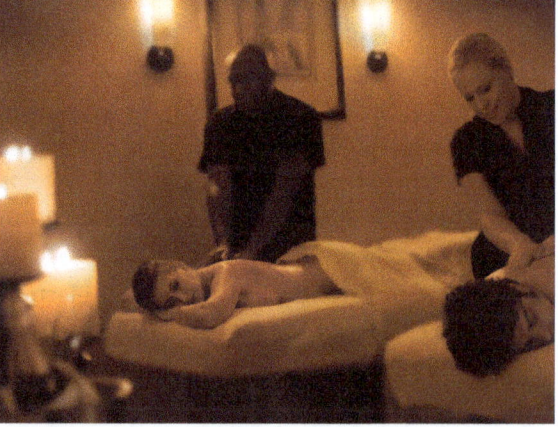

- Biodegradable corn-based cups at all water stations, bottled water given only upon request.
- Back-bar product containers are repurposed by refilling for usage.
- Collectively, the resort has reduced what they send to the landfill by more than 55%.
- Landscape waste is being recycled at 100% with all of these materials being used at local compost fields.
- Associate newsletter is printed on 100% recycled paper.
- Installation of a trash monitoring system on the resort compactor has resulted in reducing pulls by 40%.
- Recycle all computers and monitors through certified computer recycling.
- A guest room recycling program is in place in all guest rooms and meeting spaces.
- Green office supplies are used when the option is available.
- Elimination of Styrofoam from the associate cafeteria.
- Recycle cooking oil in outlet's kitchen operations.

- Reusable dishes, cups, and cutlery in associate cafeteria and banquet functions.
- Donation of old lost and found items to local charities.
- Sale clothing from the spa retail boutique that doesn't sell will be marked out of stock and donated to either a local charity (Fresh Start Women's Foundation) or our Adopt-A-Family during the holiday season.
- Worn and tattered linens and robes are donated to a local animal shelter.

Year-to-date for 2010, The Westin Kierland has recycled a total of:

52.4 tons of paper, 56.4 tons of cardboard, 5.1 tons of shredded paper, 1 ton of plastic materials, 5.4 tons of metal materials, 0.8 tons of aluminum materials, and 860 tons of landscape compost.

In the first year alone, the "Be Greener" program the resort recycled more than 760 tons of recyclable material. That is the equivalent of more than 13,000 trees saved, 2,200 cubic yards of landscape space that wasn't used, three million gallons of water saved, and six million kilowatt hours of electricity saved.

Food and Beverage
- Implemented an eco-culinary program, completely eliminating trans fats from all food served.
- Incorporation of superfoods into menu offerings and vegetarian options for all meals.
- Installed and currently utilize a reverse osmosis system to bottle glass water bottles.
- The resort completed a 2-week pilot program in partnership with Global Green Integrators, a zero landfill company that specializes in food recycling.
- Each kitchen and associate cafeteria contains a recycled signature trash can just for food waste.
- Waste is taken to a pig farm where the food waste is transformed into food for the pigs. This pilot program resulted in 5.51 tons of food scraps being recycled.

Marketing
- Green features are shared with staff and clients.
- Pending member of the Green Spa Network.

Individual Staff Contributions
- Associates make an effort to print less paper and work more digitally.
- Bring their own coffee mug or water container to reduce the use of water bottles.
- The associate cafeteria eliminated Styrofoam and paper cups completely.
- Turn computers and lights off when not in use.
- Recycle all paper and cardboard.
- Tips on green living at home.

Transportation
- Utilize online resources and webinars for continuing education, when possible. Most recent webinar resulted in 100,000 lbs of reduced carbon footprint by not traveling.
- Carpooling program encouraged and discounted bus passes are available.
- Participate in Trip Reduction Program through Arizona Department of Transportation.

Education
- The resort implemented an environmental policy and named a sustainability council that meets on a regular basis to discuss operational opportunities and implement changes that will further enhance the resort's environmental policies.
- The committee also takes the initiative in training staff and promoting awareness.

- The Westin Kierland associates have made a very considerable impact just in the way they do business, get to and from work, and take their knowledge home with them for changes in how they operate in their personal lives and their homes.

"Greener Meetings" Program

- Provide meeting planners a meeting impact report, upon request, that provides them with statistical data on their recycling efforts for the duration of their meeting.
- Clutter-free meetings allow attendees to utilize meeting space to the highest potential. All necessary supplies for a successful meeting are conveniently located at a supply station.
- Recycling services available in meeting rooms; digital copies of meeting materials.
- Eco-friendly bottled water alternatives with water stations throughout meeting space with biodegradable corn-based compostable cold cups.
- Clients are provided with several options to customize their meetings with other green practices.
- Paperless meeting planning: kierlandmeetings.com provides electronic versions of meeting materials for planners to view at their convenience.
- Flip charts and paper products made out of recycled materials.
- Green transportation services available to large groups upon request.
- Sustainable disposable food and beverage packaging and reduction of individually packaged condiments.
- Options available to meeting planners to organize programs that benefit the local community.

FUN Department and Education

- Work with the Phoenix Zoo to educate their smallest guests on how to preserve wildlife and have respect for their habitats, including lessons in the environment.
- Programs that are currently planned and underway are lessons in the environment educating the younger traveler.

Kierland Golf Club, Landscaping

- Kierland Golf Club is an Audubon Cooperative Sanctuary Program (ACSP) golf course and maintains a partnership with Audubon International.
- Implemented a recycling program throughout the course.
- Minimizing turf that needs to be watered and turning it into a natural preserve.
- All grass, plant, and tree green waste from the golf course is collected in "roll-offs" and recycled. The green waste is separated for effective composting. This one meaningful act saves approximately 1,000 tons annually from entering a landfill.
- Recycled over 500 tons of yard waste through a local compost plant that turns it into fertilizer.
- We use a lot of natural preserve landscaping and have been transitioning what used to be watered and maintained turf back to a natural desert terrain.
- We have been looking for new ways to use solar power to run our golf carts and beverage carts, and several other ways we can contribute, such as environmentally friendly packaging for our food.

CHAPTER 2

Fundamental Sustainability Principles

INTRODUCTION

There are different principles and ways to measure sustainability. Understanding these philosophies and terminology are good starting points into the world of green. The principles help with the planning process so you can implement and communicate your green practices. You can base your sustainability plan on one of these models or just go straight to the checklists and practices that naturally incorporate some of these principles.

WORDS OF WISDOM

With my 25+ years in the spa industry in USA and abroad, it is refreshing to see in this century how our world is working together to become more eco-aware and is taking action to help the planet. Each day, simple actions of recycling, reusing, and re-purposing are making a difference, one person at a time. In our service industry, evaluating the products and resources that are used daily in all aspects of our work makes a difference one property, one spa, one salon at a time – customers notice. I encourage all spa and salon owners to put eco-actions and green initiatives into their business models today and let the customers see the progress they are making for a positive reaction to inspire others!

~ Kim Collier, LMT, Esth, HHP, Founder, JAMU
Organic Spa Rituals, www.jamuspa.com

WHAT IS THE DIFFERENCE BETWEEN GREEN AND SUSTAINABLE?

Green and sustainable are often used interchangeably, but green does not always mean sustainable. Many green practices are not necessarily sustainable. *Conservation* is a component of both green and sustainable practices. **Green** is a component of sustainability and could be defined as being environmentally friendly, or healthy for the planet, or for people. *Sustainable* is a broader definition that includes green practices. The three pillars of sustainability (economy, environment, and equity) each share an equal part in sustainable practices.

Note: For simplicity, however, the terms sustainable and green are sometimes used interchangeably in the text.

Take one example of using water in your facility:

Level 1: Conservation is the first level of being green. Low-flow fixtures, automatic shut-off valves, water efficient appliances, and using less water are initial conservation steps. Conservation is typically based on cost savings and is not hard to achieve because changing traditional habits is not a big sacrifice.

Level 2: Green is the second level of saving water. This includes all water-saving devices as well as a filter for water quality. This is healthy for drinking water and saves resources. This is a conscious choice to save water for environmental reasons.

Level 3: To become even more sustainable, add a solar thermal hot water heater to save both energy and water. This cuts resource use and saves money for years to come. It achieves more of a lifetime impact.

Greywater systems that use reclaimed water and rainwater catchment are even more sustainable and address the fact that fresh, potable water is a finite resource. If you reclaim and catch all of the water used on site, this is the epitome of sustainable. This sounds far-fetched to most, but there are facilities that are now trying to achieve this *net zero* goal.

THE TRIPLE BOTTOM LINE

Developed by John Elkington, *Triple Bottom Line (TBL)* measures the bottom line of profits, environmental, and social performance (Figure 2-1). The TBL is also known as people, planet, and profit. Many companies are using this approach to measure their bottom line. With TBL, the three E's are referred to as the three P's to describe sustainability.

"TBL is considered full cost accounting, which includes natural and human capital. TBL is the eco-budget standard for reporting the ecological footprint.
- *People* are the human capital in the TBL equation that relates to fair and beneficial practices toward labor and the community. The social structure is seen as reciprocal, interdependent, and includes the well-being of the stakeholders as well as the corporation.
- *Planet* is the natural capital in the TBL. Sustainable environmental practices mean "do no harm." This considers energy, resources, pollution and waste. The *life cycle assessment* is the true cost of manufacturing products, from harvest, distribution, use and post-use recycling, or waste, to landfills. Disposal, toxicity, chemicals, and other potentially destructive aspects are measured, not ignored.
- The third pillar, *Profit,* is the eco bottom-line. This represents eco-capitalism. If a company is not financially sustainable, it cannot survive, let alone thrive" (johnelkington.com 2012).

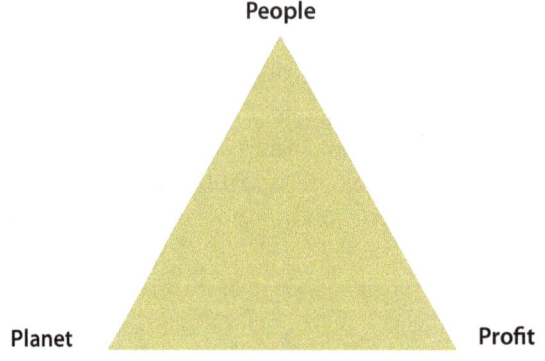

Figure 2-1: The Triple Bottom Line measures sustainability.

USING THE CRADLE TO CRADLE PHILOSOPHY

One of the most inspiring and innovative perspectives around sustainability comes from architect William McDonough and Dr. Michael Braungart, who created the Cradle to Cradle® Philosophy (Figure 2-2). This is described on mbdc.com and in the Cradle to Cradle book.

Cradle to Cradle (C to C) means that "a product or material will have a continuous life cycle. Instead of a product going from cradle to grave (being thrown out as waste at the end of its life), it can be reused indefinitely if it is designed correctly to be reused, recycled, or composted.

- The first point in the C to C philosophy is that eliminating waste is following nature's cycle of all waste equals food. There is no waste—everything has a purpose at the end. Ideally, products would break down and be food for the soil or be recycled to flow back into the industry.
- The second point is to use solar and renewable energy, using the free abundance of the sun's energy. For example, passive solar design for buildings uses no energy.
- The third point is to respect humans and natural systems: conserve resources, promote healthy ecosystems, and respect local impacts; use social responsibility to guide operations.

McDonough says, "With intelligent design, both nature and commerce can thrive and grow." The *C to C Certification*^{CM} is an ecolabel that assesses a product's safety to humans, the environment, and is designed for future life cycles. Safe materials can be disassembled and recycled or composted. In manufacturing, the materials and processes are evaluated and assessed in five categories: material health, material reutilization, renewable energy use, water stewardship, and social responsibility. Some of the companies embracing the C to C philosophy are Patagonia, Nike, and Shaw Carpet. In 2008 alone, American consumers doubled their spending on sustainable products and services to an estimated $500 billion, according to a survey by Penn Schoen Berland Associates, a market research firm that studies the green economy" (McDonough 2012, mbdc.com 2012).

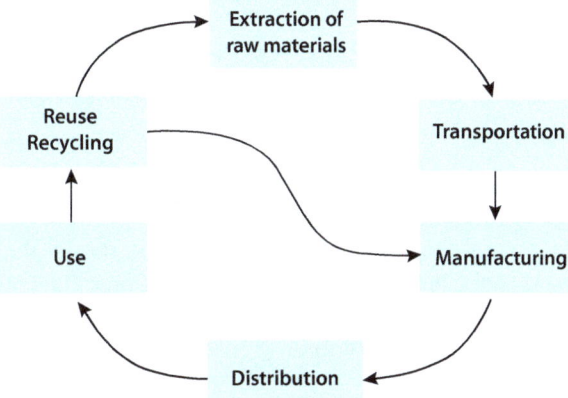

Figure 2-2: Cradle to Cradle designs products and materials for a continuous life cycle.

Different Sustainability Methods and Tools

- The Three E's
- Triple Bottom Line
- Cradle to Cradle
- Life Cycle Assessment
- The Natural Step
- 360° Sustainability

LIFE CYCLE ASSESSMENT

Life Cycle Assessment (LCA) "measures the environmental impacts of extracting, manufacturing, transporting, constructing, using, repairing, and disposing or recycling a product or material. LCA is a scientific method that measures the entire life cycle of a product by systematically assessing the impact of each step from the birth of a product to its disposal (Figure 2-3). This includes the amount of energy, water, and other natural resources used for the product" (athenasmi.org 2012).

Life Cycle Assessment (LCA) is also known as *Life Cycle Analysis or Ecobalance*. There are software models for calculating these LCA figures, such as the *Athena Sustainable Materials Institute* software and *Building for Environmental and Economic Sustainability* (BEES) assessment tools found on the internet. *ISO 14044:2006* is an International Standard that specifies requirements and provides guidelines for life cycle assessment (epa.gov 2012).

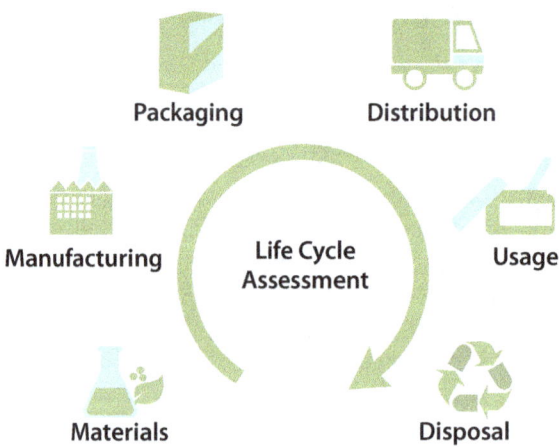

Figure 2-3: Life Cycle Assessment measures product life cycles, impacts and resources.

THE NATURAL STEP

The Natural Step (TNS) is "a non-profit organization founded in Sweden in 1989 by scientist Karl-Henrik Robèrt. The Natural Step has pioneered a "Backcasting from principles" approach to advance society toward sustainability. The Natural Step Framework is a scientific model that helps organizations make decisions to move toward sustainability by using four system conditions: The Four Principles of Sustainability.

To become a sustainable society we must:
1. Eliminate our contribution to the progressive buildup of substances extracted from the Earth's crust (for example, heavy metals and fossil fuels).
2. Eliminate our contribution to the progressive buildup of chemicals and compounds produced by society (for example, dioxins, PCBs, and DDT).
3. Eliminate our contribution to the progressive physical degradation and destruction of nature and natural processes (for example, over-harvesting forests and paving over critical wildlife habitat).
4. Eliminate our contribution to conditions that undermine people's capacity to meet their basic human needs (for example, unsafe working conditions and not enough pay to live on)."

The TNS planning approach uses a concept called *backcasting from principles*. We usually backcast whenever we think about some future possibility, whether it be a new job or a sustainable society. Backcasting is a way to plan for the future that starts with a vision of what sort of future we want. What would success look like for us if we achieved what we wanted? What would that job or that society really look like?"(naturalstep.org 2012)

> **360° Concept of Sustainability**
>
> Some companies use the *360° Concept of Sustainability* to measure their progress. A 360° evaluation analyzes four resources for sustainability: the organization, the human resources, the community/society, and the environment (Hollingworth 2009).

SPA SPOTLIGHT

AJI SPA AND SALON, SHERATON WILD HORSE PASS
An authentic spa embraces its local culture.

Contact: Shane Bird, Spa Director (2012)
Aji Spa and Salon
5594 West Wild Horse Pass Blvd., Chandler, AZ
www.wildhorsepassresort.com
Facility size: 18,000 sq. ft.
Number of employees: 63; most are part-time
Number of treatment rooms: 18
Established in: 2002

Facility Description
Aji spa has a café, retail area, fitness center and studio, private pool, and jacuzzis. The Starwood resort is designated a GeoGreen Resort that is culturally sustainable and environmentally responsible. The authentic Native American atmosphere has a relaxed, at home feeling.

Aji means "sanctuary" in the local native Pima language.

 ### SPA GOALS AND VISION

What is your business mission statement?
To create a luxurious sanctuary that enables our guests to discover serenity and fulfillment. Our authentic journey honors the rich culture of the Pima and Maricopa peoples by providing an indigenous spa experience.

What is your spa image?
We are culturally sustainable. We share culture and luxury.

What are your sustainability goals?
To install solar hot water, go off the grid, and have solar power in stages (3–7 years).

What is important to you regarding sustainability?
Less waste, giving back, and leaving everything/everyone better than we found it/them.

What business practices or areas would you like to make more sustainable?
It is a dream for the spa to be as self-sufficient as possible.

What are the challenges in being green?
The cost.

Is the staff interested in greening the facility?
YES.

What business practices do you think your clients want to see with regard to sustainability?
The ongoing efforts to incorporate our garden plants into our café and service products.

Have you seen any positive effects from green practices you have implemented?
Yes, a larger sense of awareness and education for our guests.

What positive benefits do you offer your staff?
Staff is encouraged to use the facilities when possible to make sure we are "walking the talk."

Do you promote your green practices?
Yes, we have literature that speaks of our efforts and how our guests can participate at the spa and at the resort.

SPA ELEMENTS

Culture
- Gila River Indian Tribes: Pima and Maricopa cultures are showcased throughout the spa design, artwork, architecture, and legends.
- The products, décor and services were all approved by the tribes.

The Service Menu
- Focuses on healing and holistic health.
- The authentic Native American spa menu offers signature indigenous treatments.

- Only licensed tribal members can perform the indigenous services.
- The Thoachta is a healing massage that incorporates polarity and Pima doctrines.
- The Pima Medicine Massage incorporates ancient medicine healer techniques.
- Native Herbs Cleansing Wrap, Sacred Salt Wrap, and the Four Directions are examples of the treatments.
- Designed to stay true to the community and the environment, yet still a Forbes 4-Star spa that meets guest expectations.
- Brochure printed on FSC paper.

Products
- The products are performance products.
- Enzyme peels are natural.
- The spa promotes sunscreen, good nutrition and skin care.
- Local ingredients are used for body services.
- The salon uses L'Oreal's Nature line.
- Arcona is a California boutique natural skin care line that contains aloe and yucca.
- Jane Iredale is the makeup line.

Building
- Designed similar to a traditional Pima home facing east and designed for natural light.

Décor
- Beautiful attention to detail using indigenous materials.
- A comfortable living room atmosphere in the reception area with doors out to the pool.
- The local Devil's Claw plant is used for weaving and décor.
- The entrance is built to face the sunrise to the east. A sky mural dome graces the entryway.
- Mosaics with native legends: the four directions: east is in white for illumination, west is red for the sunset, north is blue for rains, south is desert brown.
- The skeleton of cactus wood is used for light fixtures.
- Pima people are known for their basket weaving; Maricopa people are known for their pottery.
- Traditional calendar sticks on the walls depict the Journal of Life.
- Community high school art hangs in the lobby.

Treatment Rooms
- Traditional blankets are used and medicine pouches hang on the walls.
- "Saging" for cleansing and indigenous plants are used in select treatments.

Building Materials
- Low-VOC paint and glues were used with the refurbishing.
- The lounge area has a beautiful traditional fireplace design.

Energy
- The resort is moving toward LED lighting, and dimmers are used.
- The fireplace is not turned on until services are scheduled and is only used during the colder months.

Water
- We do not use bottled water anywhere in the spa.
- There are private Jacuzzis and courtyards in the women's and men's lounges.

Indoor Environmental Quality (IEQ)
- HVAC filters are on scheduled maintenance.
- Cleanliness is important for IEQ.

Green Materials
- ProClean monitors standards for low toxic cleansers. Tea tree and eucalyptus oils are also used.

Waste Reduction
- Recyclable cups are used instead of bottled water. The spa promotes that clients bring their own bottles.
- Paper, plastic, and metal are recycled. The bins located in the café and break room are collected and sorted at the hotel.

Food/Beverage
- Indigenous food is offered (Sage panini is a specialty).
- An organic garden is grown on-site with native herbs and spices, squash, tomatoes, eggplant, and peppers.
- Organic waste is composted for the gardens.
- There is a special local flavored spicy snack mix and local flavored teas available.

Nature/Outdoors
The Grounds
- The peaceful pool area is for spa guests only. The organic pool design reflects the original Gila River (as it was before the dams).
- The traditional home, or roundhouse, "Olas Ki," is made from willow and arrowweed and is used for meditation.

Landscaping
- Indigenous desert plants such as yucca, cottonwood, and grasses meet tribal standards.
- Wildlife lives on the grounds.
- Many green, multi-use practices are used in the garden at Aji.

Fitness
- The gym overlooks the pool area.
- There is a motion studio for classes, yoga, and Pilates.
- The fitness equipment was purchased for cleaner lines and fewer distractions.

Marketing
- Green features are mentioned throughout the resort and in some of the marketing pieces.

Education
- We have a cultural concierge who leads a cultural induction for all new employees.

CHAPTER 3

The Environmental Concepts

INTRODUCTION

Before going into the business aspects, here is an overview of the broad environmental concepts and the impacts on the world's resources and society. Understanding the issues can help motivate and educate others on why green practices have positive effects. Statistics are not always pretty or fun, but deserve our attention. Being aware of the issues is the first step in finding solutions.

There are many facts on the impact of development and our daily living habits. The web resources will lead you to this vast amount of information. The resource areas that are pertinent for spas and salons are categorized by topics in each chapter. Taking positive steps is the focus here in greening your business.

Why should we care about the effects to the environment? While not always evident, the ecosystem costs are enormous when you consider the extraction, manufacturing, transportation, use, and end-of-life cost of products. The ecosystem is not traditionally considered part of the cost equation because the effects are absorbed by society. This externalization of costs has a domino effect on the ecosystem. The ability of finite natural resources to sustain us is limited. Keeping the ecosystem healthy sustains our ability to survive and thrive.

WORDS OF WISDOM

We are the children of Nature. Nature feeds us when we are hungry; she gives us warmth when we are cold, and cures us when afflicted by illnesses. If we listen to her advice, Nature teaches us how to live in love, peace, and harmony. Organic skin care lines are built on this philosophy.

~ Szilvia Hickman, Sr. Vice President, Szép Élet – exclusive distributor of ilike organic skin care and Purée Organics, www.szepelet.com

ECOLOGY AND THE ECOSYSTEM

The *ecosystem* is "a natural community of plants, animals, and other living organisms and the physical environment in which they live and interact. The variety of life on Earth, its biological diversity, is referred to as *biodiversity*. The number of species of plants, animals, and microorganisms, the enormous diversity of genes in these species, the different ecosystems on the planet, such as deserts, rainforests, and coral reefs, are all part of a biologically diverse Earth. Appropriate conservation and sustainable development strategies recognize biodiversity as being integral to any approach. Almost all cultures have recognized the importance of nature and its biological diversity and have understood the need to maintain it" (biodiversity.ca.gov 2008).

Climate change, deforestation, overgrazing, fisheries collapse, food insecurity, and the rapid extinction of species are all part of a single, over-arching problem. Today the global population requires "the equivalent of 1.5 planets to provide the resources we use and to absorb our waste" (footprintnetwork.org 2012). This means it now takes the Earth one year and six months to regenerate what we use in a year. This is a strong incentive to use sustainable practices in our everyday life.

What is the Ecological Footprint?

The Ecological Footprint is "a resource accounting tool used to calculate how much of the biological capacity of the planet is required by a human activity or population. This is used for education, management and communication purposes. The *Ecological Footprint* measures the amount of biologically productive land and sea area an individual, a region, or a human activity requires to produce the resources it consumes and absorb the waste it generates, and compares this measurement to how much land and sea area is available" (footprintnetwork.org 2012).

Figure 3-1: The eco footprint measures all resources needed to support our lifestyle.

"Most people in the US need over five planets of resources to support their current lifestyle" (Figure 3-1). This is a high ecological footprint (sustainableschools.org 2012). Businesses use their estimated Ecological Footprint to strategize, manage operations and communicate their progress. Businesses that assess their ecological impacts and implement best practices are also more successful.

What is your Eco footprint?
Find out at footprintnetwork.org

CARBON FOOTPRINTS

A *carbon footprint* is "the amount of carbon (usually in tons) being emitted by an activity or organization (Figure 3-2). This is the total amount of *greenhouse gases* (GHG's) that are emitted into the atmosphere each year by a person, family, building, organization, or company" (footprintnetwork.org 2012). Carbon dioxide is the primary GHG. "A person's carbon footprint includes emissions from fuel that he or she burns directly, such as by heating a home or riding in a car. It also includes GHG's that come from producing the goods or services that the person uses, including emissions from power plants that make

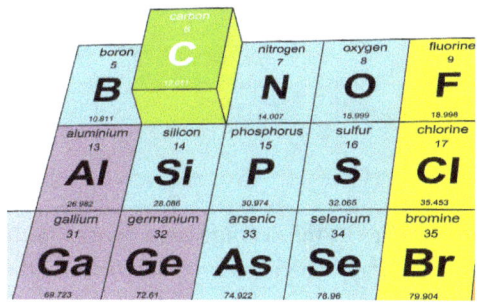

Figure 3-2: Carbon footprints are measured by carbon emissions and greenhouse gases.

electricity, factories that make products, and landfills where trash gets sent" (epa.gov 2012).

Climate change is "a significant change in the Earth's overall climate. The Earth is currently getting warmer because people are adding heat-trapping greenhouse gases such as carbon dioxide to the atmosphere. The term *"global warming"* refers to warmer temperatures, while "climate change" refers to the broader set of changes that go along with warmer temperatures, including changes in weather patterns, the oceans, ice and snow, and ecosystems" (epa.gov 2012). Increased natural disasters, floods and risk of food supplies from changing weather patterns are results of climate change. The choices we make in our homes, our travel, the food we eat, and what we buy and throw away all influence our carbon footprint and can help protect the environment for future generations (nature.org 2012).

***

What is your carbon footprint?
Find out at carbonfootprint.org

WATER FOOTPRINTS

The **water footprint** is a calculation to measure water use. Your company "can reduce its operational water footprint by saving water in its own operations and by decreasing water pollution. Key water practices are to reduce use, recycle, and treat water before disposal. For most businesses, the supply-chain water footprint is much larger than the operational footprint. It is therefore crucial that your company addresses that as well. Achieving improvements in the supply chain may be more difficult—because it is not under your direct control" (waterfootprint.org 2012). Your company can cut its supply-chain footprint by specifying certain standards with suppliers or by changing to another supplier. Among the various tools that can help improve practices are setting quantitative reduction targets, benchmarking, and water footprint reporting as discussed in the *Water Footprint Assessment Manual* available at waterfootprint.org.

***

What is your water footprint?
Find out at waterfootprint.org

> In the US, the average person uses 1800 gallons of water per day, which is 2485 m^3 (cubic meters) annually. This is approximately twice the world average of 1385 m^3/year. That's equivalent to an Olympic-sized swimming pool, or 2.5 million liters per year (waterfootprint.org 2012). This number is interesting to contemplate, and is of course only an estimate and includes the water used to produce our goods and services.

NATURAL RESOURCE DEPLETION

The resources we consume are energy, water, wood, and other raw materials (Figure 3-3). Land use and air quality are additional concerns with respect to the environment. While the economy and people benefit from environmental programs, this is not always clear without considering the true costs of extracting resources or the impacts on the global society. It is estimated that it would take several planets of resources to supply everyone equally. Every decision we make impacts the amount of resources we use. For example, cutting back on retail shopping bags may seem insignificant, but when you factor in billions of people using them, that adds up to a lot of water, energy, and other resources saved by not using as many disposable bags.

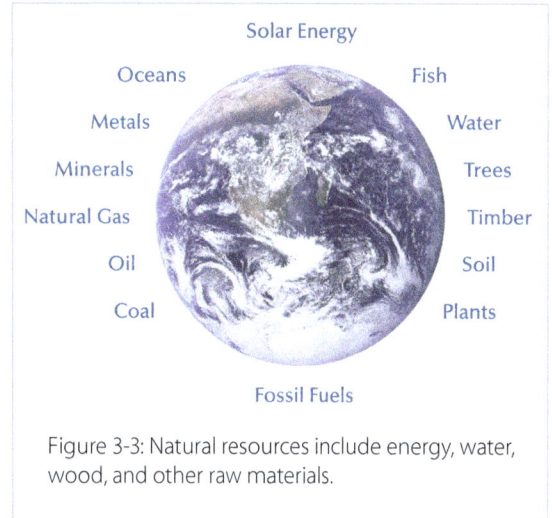

Figure 3-3: Natural resources include energy, water, wood, and other raw materials.

[**For more information on Global Ecosystem Statistics check out nationalgeographic.com, fao.org, or greenfacts.org .**]

SCHOOL SPOTLIGHT

ATLANTA SCHOOL OF MASSAGE AND ITS DIVISION, ATLANTA INSTITUTE OF AESTHETICS
Teaching Sustainability.

Contact: Edie Morton, Assistant to the President, Eco-Champion (2012)
Atlanta School of Massage
2 Dunwoody Park South, Atlanta, GA
www.atlantaschoolofmassage.com
Facility size: 28,000 sq. ft.
Number of employees: 50
Number of treatment rooms: 18
Established: Atlanta School of Massage was established in 1980.

Facility Description
Our facility includes a massage and aesthetics school in addition to a teaching clinic.

 ## SPA GOALS AND VISION

What is your green business mission statement?
As a Silver Sponsor of the Green Spa Network, Atlanta School of Massage pledges to promote and cultivate the vital connections between personal well-being, economic sustainability, and the health of our planet.

What is your spa image?
Our clients continue to visit our teaching clinic because our students have a reputation of being highly skilled and professional. Our teaching clinic has a clean, eco-friendly and spa-like atmosphere. It is unlike many teaching clinics that can be industrial and clinical. We are also known for our very reasonably priced spa services.

What are your sustainability goals?
We will contract with a green cleaning company and purchase green janitorial supplies.
We will provide green education and resources to students, "the children of the spa industry."
A future goal is to establish a green team. If feasible, we would like to install sensors on fluorescent lighting fixtures in public spaces throughout the facility.

What is important to you regarding sustainability?
Education about sustainable food is most important to me because the commercial food industry imposes a huge environmental impact. Not only does the commercial food industry contribute to high environmental costs, but also is contributing to the rise of health problems.

What business practices or areas would you like to make more sustainable?
I would like to see the areas of energy and transportation become more sustainable in the Atlanta business community. Atlanta has a serious air quality and traffic problem with too many cars on the road at the same time (business commuters). Our public transportation is not accessible or practical in many cases. More people working from home and carpooling could make a simple and significant impact.

What are the challenges in being green?
Challenges in being green can be finding the best way to communicate about environmental issues to a broad group of people.

Is the staff interested in greening the facility?
Staff members have been inspired by our green initiatives and education about environmental challenges. Staff interest and participation is growing.

What business practices do you think your clients want to see with regard to sustainability?
Our clients like services that get results while providing health benefits to people and the planet.

Have you seen any positive effects from green practices you have implemented?
Staff and students have increased their knowledge regarding green practices and environmental issues. *"The Story Of"* videos are always great tools, informative, and deliver a substantial impact.
Cost savings with decreased water usage has been positive.

What positive benefits do you offer your staff?
We offer yoga classes on-site 2 times a week. If staff members attend 9 out of 12 classes, they are reimbursed half of the fee. Each staff member gets one free treatment (skin care or massage) per month. We offer health insurance that includes free preventative screenings.

Do you promote your green practices?
We promote our green practices through websites, social media, and signage.

SPA ELEMENTS

The Menu
- ***Esthetics:*** Students use an organic skin care line, Lotus Moon, when giving our signature and advanced facials.
- ***Massage:*** Massage services are performed with Sacred Earth Botanicals made of certified organic ingredients, have environmentally friendly packaging, and implement sustainable business practices.

Products
- ***Face:*** Lotus Moon philosophy: "We are dedicated to developing high quality products based on our on-going research into Mother Nature's plants and enzymes, and true science with a reverence for all life. We are committed to manufacturing

products in a gentle manner to preserve the integrity of the natural ingredients using ecologically sound and cruelty-free practices.

We use recyclable plastic and glass, support fair labor practices, print brochures and other informational materials locally and on recycled paper using vegetable-based inks.

- *Body:* Coola Mineral Sun Care Collection, 100% PURE Bath and Body products, and Sacred Earth Botanicals are available in our retail store.
- *Makeup:* We carry Jane Iredale Cosmetics.
- *Retail:* Additional eco-friendly retail products include Comphy sheets, RaRaw soy candles made locally, *Not Just Another Pretty Face* books, Chico reusable bags, and Eco Vessel reusable water bottles.

Supplies

- Supplies for treatments or operations are purchased with green considerations whenever possible.
- *Single-use items:* The Georgia Board of Cosmetology has restrictions regarding reuse of certain supplies.
- *Cleaning:* We use a green cleaning company and purchase as many green janitorial products as possible.
- *Client lounge:* The client area has sustainable furnishings and carpet. High quality filtered drinking water is available for our clients.

Energy

- Our energy consumption is electric with a gas water heater.
- We have installed timers on hydroculators and aerators on faucets.

Building

- We lease a brick building remodeled in 2002; there was an energy audit conducted in 2010.

HVAC system

- The thermostat settings are 70° for offices and 72–73° for treatment rooms and classrooms.
- Ventilation Systems are maintained by management.

Appliances

- We have Energy Star clothes washers, dryers, and freezers.

Equipment

- We have timers on our hydroculators.

Type of lighting

- We have mostly fluorescent fixtures with CFL's used wherever possible.
- Treatment rooms and some classrooms have dimmers.

Water

- We discontinued our Vichy shower class, which saves 4500 gallons annually.
- We installed aerators on 40 water faucets, saving approximately 80,000 gallons annually.

Green Materials

- Furniture, décor: In 2010 our clinic was redesigned using sustainable furnishings, Interface carpet (recycling the old carpet), and new paint containing no VOCs.

Purchasing
- Green aspects are considered when purchasing products.
- We have an exclusive relationship with Earthlite tables, sustainably built and built to last a lifetime.

Waste Reduction
- Glass, paper, and plastic are recycled. We have recycling bins throughout the school and signage that describes what is recyclable. We recycle equipment including computers and ink cartridges. We discourage printing documents.

Landscaping, Exteriors
- Landscaping includes minimal maintenance without the use of chemicals.

Transportation
- We have a bus line nearby. We also sell public rail line passes at a discount.

Food Service
- We have worked with two food trucks that deliver foods made with organic ingredients. This has been challenging, as both businesses were inconsistent and their prices are higher than what students are willing to pay.

Marketing
- We primarily utilize digital marketing.

People: What green practices benefit employees, students, or clients?
- We provide 3-stage filtered water coolers and request that students and staff refrain from purchasing bottled water. Staff members are given reusable water bottles.
- Students and clients benefit from our organic skin care and massage lubricant lines.
- Our green cleaning protocol benefits employees, students, and clients.

Education
- Please visit our website for our sustainability information.
- Our *Introduction to Sustainability* class goes into more depth, covering the topics noted in our sustainability section of our website.

CHAPTER 4

The Economic Aspects of Sustainability

INTRODUCTION

What are the advantages and rewards of sustainable practices? Adding green factors is a sound investment. From LEED building certification to green hotel programs, there are many ways to add sustainable measures to your policies and increase revenues. Certain changes can be expensive and time consuming, but the alternative of lost revenue and higher costs from no action can have even more adverse consequences. Various accounting methods and software are used to calculate the savings of sustainable practices, such as the Triple Bottom Line (TBL). It is good to be familiar with the tools used to calculate sustainability even if they are outside of your daily business needs.

WORDS OF WISDOM

Green, eco, sustainability, call it what you like, everyone has an opinion. I've been a firm believer in balance and that includes how we treat our planet. For some it may be every ingredient in every product including the clothes you wear… good for you. For others, it's the net profit on running a business; we need to make profits while we sustain and protect the environment as part of our mission to grow our business. Balance!

~ Allan Share, Day Spa Association, International Medical Spa Association, www.dayspaassociation.com

GREEN BUSINESS AND THE BOTTOM LINE

Financial savings is the primary reason businesses implement conservation practices. Energy and water savings can add up to thousands of dollars annually for small businesses to millions of dollars for larger companies. Add to that the increased market share from customers looking for green businesses to support, and the return on investment is significant. On a larger scale, securing our future is the ultimate objective of sustainability.

Measuring the savings versus costs can be challenging. It is not always clear exactly how much money you save from certain practices, and for small businesses it is not always worth taking time to calculate it. Larger corporations often measure savings, and have more resources and the staff to track the numbers. *Chief Financial Officers* (CFOs) need to know the *return on investment* (ROI). Small businesses may not monitor or track the savings very closely, but that does not mean the business is not benefiting from its conservation measures.

Upfront costs can hinder the decision to invest in items that have an initial cost. Water aerators and light bulbs are minor costs and these are what is called *"low hanging fruit"*—the easy inexpensive changes that can be made (Figure 4-1). These are typically the first of the prioritized actions. On the other hand, it is harder to justify the cost of solar photovoltaic panels because it may take up to 20 years to recapture the upfront costs. Solar thermal hot water systems, however, are a good investment and have a faster payback of about 3–5 years. After that, the hot water cost is minimal for years to come. A few examples of the economic benefits are included below by category. Best practices and action steps for each topic are covered in corresponding chapters.

Ecosystem services and natural capital provide water and climate regulation valued at trillions of dollars (NaturalCapitalDeclaration.org 2012).

Figure 4-1: The easiest, most inexpensive action steps are called the "low hanging fruit."

THE ECONOMIC BENEFITS OF GREEN

Each spa has areas where they can save money from using green practices. Each of these areas are discussed in more detail throughout the chapters.

Saving Energy

By utilizing best practices for energy conservation, the long term costs are greatly reduced (Figure 4-2). In addition to real-time savings, conservation helps insulate the business from the rising utility costs in the future. This also reduces reliance on energy resources. Energy is expensive and has many external costs. The source, production, transportation, and international issues are all costs associated with energy. In a bigger facility and for resorts and hotels, the costs are even more of a consideration. Hospitality groups are reporting thousands to millions of dollars saved annually from increased conservation measures.

A good place to start saving on energy costs is with an energy audit. This is free in many states and offered by power companies or state agencies. Many helpful web sites give information on saving energy, rebates and incentive programs. Unfortunately, the information can be confusing because the programs change constantly. Energy concepts and conservation steps are listed in Chapters 14 and 17.

Water

Water costs will continue to rise as pure water becomes more scarce. This is one area where conservation measures will become even more necessary in the future. Water use impacts all industries. Critical issues today are the natural limits and maximum stress on our fresh water supply known as "peak water." Water footprints are becoming as common as carbon footprints. Calculating water use in both our products and services is part of the new business model (waterfootprint.org 2012).

Figure 4-2: Best practices for energy conservation reduce long term costs.

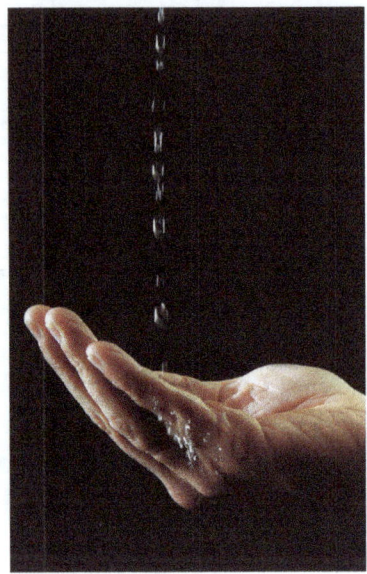
Figure 4-3: Low-flow fixtures are easy changes that save water.

Corporate water strategies can help with water stewardship. It's important to educate and engage all stakeholders in water management solutions. Tax rates and repair costs will continue to rise for water systems. The public and private sectors need to value water more accurately and integrate water stewardship into policies and actions. Water conservation reduces storm water and infrastructure costs, which are very expensive.

Another huge issue is bottled water. Bottled water impacts go beyond the bottle cost. The plastic waste, production, and drain on resources is extreme. Weaning ourselves off of the plastic water bottles is imperative for many reasons, including the adverse health effects from ingested plasticizers, and impact on the ecosystem and oceans. The cost is enormous and the savings to the business is worth the effort.

For spas, installing low-flow fixtures and aerators on faucets are easy changes that save water (Figure 4-3). Offering body treatments that use less water can yield significant savings. Other practices such as reducing outdoor water needs save labor, materials and time. See Chapter 17 for more on water conservation practices.

Convenience is Expensive

If you are buying and giving out bottles of water instead of filtered water in reusable containers, the cost is at least 50 cents per bottle plus the cost to recycle them. If you have 50 clients per day, that is $25 per day, $175 per week, $700 per month, and $8400 per year. You do have to figure in the cost of filtering water and washing or buying recyclable cups to offset this. Many companies and spas are encouraging staff and even clients to bring their personal water bottles (stainless steel BPA-free bottles are best). This reusable bottle habit is becoming similar to bringing our own shopping bags.

Indoor Environmental Quality (IEQ)

Costs from poor *indoor air quality* (IAQ) are not always visible. A healthier atmosphere and better air quality for the occupants has many benefits. A healthy building increases staff productivity and satisfaction. Ventilation is especially important in salons where nail care products and hair chemicals are used. Gone are the days when we ignored these strong toxic odors.

Good indoor environmental quality and air quality are important for occupant comfort. A nice atmosphere attracts employees who want to be there, not to mention the clients who come for the relaxing atmosphere and quality services. We cannot afford to have the staff out sick from working in an unhealthy building, because the service business relies on these individuals. Evaluate the indoor air quality and atmosphere for unhealthy elements using the checklists in Chapter 13 and 18.

Employee Satisfaction and Productivity

While it is the highest expense of most businesses, employee productivity is not always calculated in the bottom line. In the spa industry, the technicians are the most valuable asset we have. We cannot serve clients without the staff. Paying the staff well and offering benefits is smart for business. People want to be in a place with others who have shared values (Figure 4-4). Green-minded individuals will want to stay with a company that shares those values. Employee retention leads to less turnover and training, which is very expensive and time consuming.

Other economic components are benefits and wellness programs. While benefits can be expensive, weigh in the cost of happy employees, reduced sick leave, and turnover rates. Wellness programs could start with something as simple as having staff members give a talk on their areas of expertise such as nutrition, fitness, or aromatherapy. In a small business with one owner, the staff may not realize that the owner gets paid last from a small profit margin. Share some of this profit and loss information so the staff does not think they are being slighted or underpaid. Without profits, benefits are not possible.

A common purpose and positive atmosphere where people feel valued and share in the prosperity builds a solid team and collaboration. Share conservation information with your staff and educate them on the bottom line. More savings in one area equals more pay for the employees. Staff issues are discussed in Chapter 16.

IEQ and Work Performance

"The quality performance of office and school work is affected by indoor environmental conditions and by the features of buildings that influence those conditions" (epa.gov 2012). Work performance, test scores, and attendance have been shown to improve by providing healthy indoor environmental quality (IEQ), ventilation, appropriate temperatures, and balanced humidity levels. The economic benefits of the work performance improvements will often far outweigh the costs of providing better IEQ.

Products, Purchasing, and Supplies

Buying green products and materials can cost more due to the manufacturing costs of the niche market compared to the larger mass production. Reducing inventory, along with product and supply usage, is good for long term cash flow and efficiency. Additionally, using fewer paper and disposable items saves upfront costs and reduces waste. Ordering bulk items and using refillable dispensers for your client locker room saves money and limits throw-away single-use items. You could then offer more amenities from the cost savings.

Purchasing organic products may cost more, but clients will buy more natural and organic products to support their values. Additionally, buying local and a vendor's use of lighter packaging saves on shipping costs. Streamlining purchasing is efficient and cost effective. Buying more items from one source saves staff time and transportation/shipping costs. See Chapter 11 for purchasing considerations.

Green Materials

This area is interwoven with all purchases and overlaps with indoor air quality and health. Green materials are anything that is less harmful to people or the environment such as natural fabrics, low-VOC paint, and recycled packaging. These materials are preferred for products and goods we buy. Using green material purchasing criteria also reduces waste. Chapter 11 covers green materials.

> Greening the business strengthens relationships between employees and customers who share the same values.

Waste Reduction

We all know the mantra *reduce, reuse, recycle*. Now reject and repair are being added to the original 3 R's. Generating less waste from packaging and disposables is more efficient and reduces trash hauling and landfill costs. Using recycled and double-sided paper can save money by reducing paper costs. The 'e' (electronics, computers) society has already saved significant paper use. Another benefit of reducing waste is saving on environmental cleanup costs and the increased cost and scarcity of goods. See Chapter 12 for more on waste reduction.

Transportation

Cars, parking, and land use have external economic impacts beyond the business logistics. Planning efficient trips and scheduling save gas and time. Mass transportation options and carpooling save employees money. Buying local goods or from vendors with closer locations also reduces shipping costs and pollution from transportation. For example, island resorts can benefit from exploring alternatives to current shipping practices.

Figure 4-4: People want to be in a place with others who have shared values.

Designated bike and electric car parking spots are popping up all over (Figure 4-5). Being located near a bus route or subway earns points in green building certifications. Urban mixed-use development complexes that reduce driving are good locations for visibility and convenience. This helps clients get to their appointments and reduces the parking stress. In remote locations, grouping airport pickups is a helpful service to offer guests. Additionally, switching to golf carts and electric vehicles on large properties cuts down vehicle costs, saves gas, and may qualify for tax credits.

Business Investments and Public Relations

Sustainable capital investments increase the value and success of the business for long term growth and resale value. Sustainable practices can show stakeholders, investors, and potential buyers that the business is sound. Green investments make capital assets more valuable. Taking advantage of green building incentives, rebates, and tax credits is a great return on investment. Adding interesting features to your business also attracts clients and generates marketing and public relations opportunities.

Stakeholders

Who are the stakeholders? *Stakeholders* are defined as "a person, group, or organization that has a direct or indirect stake in an organization because they can affect or be affected by the organization's actions, objectives, and policies" (businessdictionary.com 2012). Key stakeholders in a business organization include creditors, customers, directors, employees, government, owners (shareholders), suppliers, unions, and the community from which the business draws its resources. The environment can also be considered a stakeholder, but is not part of the traditional definition.

Figure 4-5: Designated bike and electric car parking spots are becoming more popular.

When making business decisions, stakeholders such as the staff and customers are considered in the mix. Looking at how decisions affect everyone on a broad scale is better than just looking at the bottom line without considering the impact on stakeholders. Taking time to think decisions through and weighing the pros and cons is the essence of wise planning.

Involve the Stakeholders
- Staff: communicate and educate.
- Consumers: communications and public relations.
- Environment: show the facts and figures on the impacts.
- Community: use public relations and charitable investments.
- Suppliers: share the plan and ask for support on green policies.
- Investors: show the cost benefit analysis and savings.

[SMART goals are Specific, Measurable, Attainable, Realistic, and Timely (goalsettingguide.com 2012)]

SUSTAINABILITY POLICIES AND PLANNING

It is well known that owners and managers have a better chance of implementing change by getting everyone on board with the project. Businesses first need to see the math and cost-benefit analysis. What's the payback? A sustainability team can gather the information, have planning meetings, evaluate current practices, and set goals and timelines. Communicating and educating the employees from the bottom to the top of the organization is a vital piece of the plan's success.

Include all departments in the plan: operations, accounting, marketing, human resources, and purchasing. You can improve efficiency, performance, and environmental goals by each department or company-wide. Effective goals are "specific, measurable, attainable, realistic, and timely/scheduled" (goalsettingguide.com 2012). Goals and checklists are included in other chapters.

Sustainability Planning Steps:

- Form or hire a team.
- Hire professionals for more complex data analysis.
- Establish an initial baseline and starting point to measure from.
- Determine challenges and opportunities.
- Review and decide on priorities.
- Set goals and timelines.
- Start with the low hanging fruit.
- Get buy-in from the staff and stakeholders.
- Monitor progress.
- Calculate the Return On Investment (ROI).

ACCOUNTING PRACTICES

There are various accounting tools and methods available to determine the sustainable bottom line. Full cost accounting, simple payback, life cycle analysis, triple bottom line all have their own systems for calculating profit and loss information. These methods have become more complex as sustainability principles expand. All of the detailed methods are beyond the scope of this book, but it is good to be familiar with the concepts.

Simple Payback

Simple payback is straight profit and loss. The payback time is calculated by dividing the initial investment by the net savings per year. The cost of an item minus the savings equals the net return on investment. This does not include other factors such as long term savings, inflation, or other accounting considerations (net present value or cash flow analysis).

Full Cost Accounting

Full cost accounting includes the costs and benefits of externalities. Hidden and liability costs, and weighing less tangible costs and benefits, are part of this model. Externalized costs are costs that are not directly paid for by a company. Pollution, environmental damage, and infrastructure are types of external costs. Internal and external impacts include positive social investments such as charity gifts and community investments. Savvy accountants can provide support and information on this method and other options.

Triple Bottom Line Accounting

Triple Bottom Line (TBL) is a globally accepted accounting method to measure a company's bottom line where profits go side-by-side with environmental and social performance. At its core, TBL embraces the concept of People, Planet, and Profit. The company is responsible to all stakeholders, rather than just shareholders.

Life Cycle Assessment

"Life Cycle Assessment (LCA) is a technique used to evaluate the environmental aspects and potential impacts associated with a product, process, or service. This evaluation is based upon a product's entire lifespan from raw material acquisition, to manufacture, use and maintenance, to its final disposal. It's a system of inputs (raw materials, energy) to outputs (atmospheric emissions, waterborne wastes, solid wastes, coproducts and other releases)" (epa.gov 2012).

> *Multidimensional accounting* includes the 5 capitals of business: manufacturing, financial, human, social, and natural (nbis.org 2012).

LCCA, Life Cycle Cost Analysis

Life Cycle Cost Analysis (LCCA) evaluates the full costs of acquiring, installing, owning, operating, and disposing of a product or building system (Figure 4-6). According to the National Institute of Building Sciences *Whole Building Design Guide* (wbdg.org 2010) areas of focus may include "the investment/initial cost, fuel costs, replacement cost including labor, residual values (resale or salvage values or disposal costs), finance charges, operating, maintenance and repair costs, and non-monetary benefits or costs."

Based on what is being evaluated, the methodology can be extremely complicated, or simple, depending on the ultimate goal. While both LCA and LCCA methods are based on the entire life cycle of a product, building or system, LCA measures environmental impacts, while LCCA evaluates the financial costs.

Up-Front versus Long-Term Costs

To consider only the initial cost of a product, or an entire building for that matter, is a short-sighted approach to acquisition. Many additional factors impact the value beyond the initial cost: efficiency, durability, impact on health, and serviceability. For example: when evaluating the cost of a new HVAC system, it is important to know its efficiency rating so that energy costs can be included in the decision-making process. It is also important to evaluate the seasonal needs of the facility to determine the correct capacity of the system.

Sustainability Reporting Guidelines

The *Global Reporting Initiative's (GRI)* mission is to provide "a trusted and credible framework for sustainability reporting that can be used by organizations of any size, sector, or location....The GRI Reporting Framework is intended to serve as a framework for reporting on an organization's economic, environmental, and social performance" (www.globalreporting.org 2011).

International Organization for Standardization (ISO)

International Organization for Standardization is the world's largest developer and publisher of International Standards for many fields and products such as building materials. Due to many international languages used, the acronym is not IOS. It is ISO , which is derived from isos, Greek for "equal." "ISO is a non-governmental organization that forms a bridge between the public and private sectors. Many of its member institutes are part of the governmental structure of their countries, or are mandated by their government" (iso.org 2012).

Figure 4-6: Life Cycle Cost Analysis (LCCA) evaluates the full costs of a product.

ISO 14000 addresses environmental management and ISO 26000 is for social responsibility. ISO's are helpful for sustainability and environmental impact documentation. Other ISO's include environmental management systems and occupational health and safety.

B Corporations and Benefit Corporations

A *B corporation* is a certification of a C corporation or an LLC, given by *B Labs*. B Corps are "certified by B Lab to meet rigorous independent and transparent social and environmental performance standards. A *Benefit Corporation* is another new class of corporation available in several states of the United States, required by law to create benefits for society as well as for shareholders" (bcorporation.net 2012). Note that B corporation and benefit corporation are similar, but are two separate designations.

SPA SPOTLIGHT

BE CHERISHED SALON AND DAY SPA
An Aveda Concept Salon that reflects responsibility and integrity on an individual, environmental, and professional level.

Contact: Susan Zastoupil, Owner, Stylist (2012)

be cherished LLC
393 E. Main Street
Ashland, Oregon

www.becherishedashland.com

Facility size: 1890 sq. ft., leased

Number of employees: 8 total; 4 full time, plus the owner is a stylist.

Number of treatment rooms: 3 hair stations, 1 mani/pedi, 1 massage, 1 esthetics room.

Established in: September 2010: The owner felt that it was necessary to open the salon to continue to use the natural Aveda product line, especially the hair color. Most of the staff worked at a former Aveda Day Spa that closed.

Facility Description
The salon is located right on Main Street in a remodeled historical building shared with other businesses. The facility includes a large retail and front desk area, 1 client comfort zone lounge area, large dispensary/break room/classroom, and 1 bathroom.

SPA GOALS AND VISION

What is your green business mission statement?
We are committed to providing personal care, services, and beauty products that reflect responsibility and integrity on an individual, environmental, and professional level.

What is your spa image?
An Aveda Concept Salon; also that we care, and that clients will be cherished during their service.

What are your sustainability goals?
To continue to reduce waste and water use.

What is important to you regarding sustainability?
To care for the world we live in, using our natural resources with responsibility and integrity. The salon resonates with Aveda's mission and philosophy.

What business practices or areas would you like to make more sustainable?
Use less water and recycle more.

What are the challenges in being green?
The inherent nature of using resources such as water and products in the salon.

Is the staff interested in greening the facility?
Yes, they are all on board with the concept.

What business practices do you think your clients want to see with regard to sustainability?
The Aveda philosophy; practicing responsibility and integrity, recycling, and purchasing recycled products.

Have you seen any positive effects from green practices you have implemented?
- The salon has a good, healthy feeling and atmosphere.
- Additionally, hair color clients have a healthy option for their hair with Aveda color, otherwise they would not be able to color their hair.
- Product usage has been reduced by measuring the hair color product amount in grams for each individual client, so this saves product and cost.
- Instead of taking tips, the owner has a jar on the front desk to take donations for the Columbia Riverkeepers, a nonprofit that supports the health of the Columbia River in Oregon. Be Cherished raised $1,400 in one year to support the clean water efforts. Susan says that she feels like it's helping give back to offset all the water the salon uses.

What positive benefits do you offer your staff? (health, wellness, incentives)
- Health insurance is a goal once the new business is more solid.
- The owner took the entire staff to Disneyland in 2011 to honor their hard work and the success of their first year.
- They will also be offering more education beyond the standard Aveda training.

Do you promote your green practices?
The Aveda concepts are naturally green and this is the primary focus. We use education to explain the importance of plant-based ingredients that are sustainably sourced.

SPA ELEMENTS

The Menu
- Printed on recycled paper.
- All the services use *Aveda* products and protocols.

Products
- Aveda is the original "green" line in the industry. The company has always been green and products are now close to 90% organic.
- The packaging and bottles are glass and plastic. The plastic is post-consumer recycled PET and soy ink. Also the bottles are now lighter for less shipping weight.
- The hair color is close to 99% plant-based. The quality is excellent and lasts.

- *Nails:* Switching to Zoya polish.
- *Retail:* The retail area is large and the displays are organized and accessible with eco-friendly signage.

Supplies
- *Treatment supplies:* Organic cotton linens are laundered on site.
- *Cleaning products:* Simple Green™
- *Private treatment rooms:* The cotton flannel sheets are from the New Life catalogue.
- *Client lounge and reception:* Uses vintage furniture.
- *Office area:* Reclaimed and recycled pieces/furniture.
- *Retail area:* Aveda bags and Aveda collateral and signage.

Energy
- The salon had an energy review in 2011 from the Southern Oregon Sustainable Business Network.
- Music is Pandora over the Internet, which saves energy (no CD players needed).

HVAC system
- Gas, manual temperature controls.
- Thermostat settings are typically held at 74°F in the summer and 69°F in winter, which saves energy.
- *Ventilation system:* Filters are regularly maintained and changed every 6 months; ceiling fans circulate air.
- *Appliances:* All Energy Star efficiency rated: washer/dryer, refrigerator, microwave, dishwasher.
- *Hot water heating:* Electric.

Type of Lighting
- *Fixtures:* Flood, fluorescents, and lamps.
- *Bulbs:* Full spectrum fluorescent, and CFL bulbs as they need replacing.
- Occupant lighting sensors in the bathroom.

Water
- Drinking water is filled from Pur® filters and then put in a standing water cooler unit.
- *Hot water:* New electric hot water heater (chosen because gas is not as much of a renewable resource as electricity).
- Sinks and faucets have natural low pressure so no low-flow fixtures needed.
- Installed a dual flush toilet.
- *Laundry:* A high efficiency washer/dryer.
- Pedicure station has a pipeless foot bath so water is not recycled (Sanijet).

Green Materials
- *Interiors, furniture, décor:* The majority of the interiors and décor are reused, repurposed, and second

hand finds from thrift stores. The quality is beautiful and does not compromise the look at all. This saved money and resources.
- The owner tries to buy only what is necessary and is creative in decorating.
- *Reception:* The front desk and retail area shelves are made of rubber wood from the company Etopa.
- Floors are recycled vinyl tiles. The bathroom floor linoleum was salvaged in the remodel.

Indoor Environmental Quality (IEQ)
- Paint used for the remodel is low-VOC paint.
- Sound dampening metal roofing material was used in treatment room ceilings and painted to match the walls.
- *Ventilation, fans:* Installed a screen door for fresh air.
- *Air fresheners:* The Aveda aromatherapy diffuser is used.

Purchasing
- If the quality is there, we always choose recycled products.
- *Glass:* The client and staff cups are washed in the dishwasher with a sanitation cycle, no disposable cups are used.

Waste Reduction
- Recycle bins are in back of the building for cardboard and comingling.
- We also recycle plastic lids, returning them to Aveda.
- *Paper:* Most is recycled, printed on both sides, and reused for more copies or notes.
- *Printing:* The salon refills ink cartridges.

Landscaping, Exteriors
- The city maintains the outside plants on the sidewalk.

Transportation
- Downtown pedestrian location.

Marketing
- Green features are shared with staff and clients as we are often asked about this.
- The Aveda concepts are the selling points: plant-based formulas and sustainably sourced.

People
- Service trades are encouraged; staff pays a small product cost charge for services.
- Drinking water is filtered.
- The staff is just as important as clients and the owner treats them as coworkers, not employees. This is why there is such a long term, harmonious staff that have positive relationships with each other.

Green Education
- One staff member acts as a mentor and keeps us on our toes.
- The Aveda training includes green aspects.
- There are reminders in monthly staff meetings to conserve product and to recycle.

Social Equity Means Everyone Benefits

INTRODUCTION

Social Equity means "to benefit everyone in society and globally." Thinking about the effects of our actions on everyone in the community and beyond is the equity part of the three E's of sustainability. Corporate Social Responsibility (CSR) is now part of business ethics. CSR is a win-win for everyone.

WORDS OF WISDOM

I often go back to one of the fundamental principles that Organic Spa Magazine was founded on– and that is, by bringing these two worlds together, the spa/wellness world with the green/sustainable world, we reinforce the need that in order to look after our environment and be a positive influence to those around us, we need to first look after ourselves and our own health and wellness. In other words, by looking after ourselves, we then have the strength to look after others and our wonderful Mother Earth!

~ Beverly Maloney-Fischback, CEO, Founder & Publisher,
Organic Spa Magazine, www.organicspamagazine.com

WHAT IS SOCIAL RESPONSIBILITY?

Social responsibility (SR) is an ethical ideology that states "organizations and individuals have an obligation to benefit society at large. This responsibility can be passive, by not engaging in socially harmful acts, or active, by performing acts that advance social goals" (srsassociation.org 2012). **Corporate social responsibility (CSR)** is a principle that "businesses should actively contribute to the welfare of society, not only maximize profits. Most corporate annual reports will highlight what the company has done to further education, help minorities, give to social causes, and in general improve social conditions. The CSR concept is also used by investors in picking companies that are fair to their employees, do not pollute or build weapons, and make beneficial products" (answers.com 2012).

The *International Organization for Standardization (ISO)* is developing an international standard to provide guidelines for adopting and disseminating social responsibility: ISO 26000 – Social Responsibility (iso.org 2012).

> Promoting a holistic lifestyle at work and in our personal lives is both necessary and inspirational in today's spa world. It is important to maintain your own physical, mental, and spiritual health and well-being.

ACT LOCALLY: THE COMMUNITY

Businesses offer jobs and provide a service in the local community. Beyond running the business, supporting charities is a positive addition to the community. Philanthropy is a big part of sharing a business's success. People also value integrity and authenticity now more than ever.

LOHAS consumers are educated on issues and will want to know what your spa is doing for the community. People who see you giving back to the community will want to support your business. Consumers are looking for companies with ethical social values. Fair trade goods and responsible practices are becoming more common and are used in marketing messages.

Charity events and donations to good causes are promoted regularly in the beauty industry (Figure 5-1). "Locks of Love" and the "Look good, feel better" program are two examples in the beauty industry. Educational scholarships, river cleanups, and Earth Day themes are models of giving back to the community.

Another way to participate in giving back to the community is through donating time or services. Hosting a large fundraising event will have a positive effect on your company's reputation and public relations. Not only does it help those in need, but builds camaraderie among the staff. Some salons are giving away free services to those who cannot afford them or as staff rewards and benefits. Promote your efforts with press releases and e–newsletters.

Figure 5-1: Charity events are beneficial for business.

> "We didn't all come over on the same ship, but we're all in the same boat."
> ~ Bernard M. Baruch

Honoring Sustainable Cultures

Most destination spas are known for honoring and celebrating their local culture. It is natural to blend services, interior design, food, product choices, and other aspects into the "sense of place." From the Southwest to tropical locations, spas can showcase their local heritage, history and customs. Connecting with the local community helps keep tradition alive and is also great for marketing and branding a spa's unique image.

TAKING CARE OF THE STAFF

Taking care of the staff is vital to the success of the service and client–based business. In a salon, clients are loyal to their favorite hairdresser, manicurist, and esthetician. If the staff is not happy, no one is happy. Many larger tourist destination spas do not always rely on locals or regular clients, but quality employees still make or break the business. Your team is your most valuable asset (Figure 5-2). Be genuine and generous with the staff and the rewards will be plentiful. The profit of paying bonuses on retail sales far outweighs the cost. Leaders who truly care about their coworkers and mission are more successful and respected.

> Social responsibility investing (SRI) and angel investors who support social equity efforts are two examples of socially responsible business efforts.

Many employees care about being appreciated and valued beyond just a paycheck. A positive atmosphere builds loyalty. Supporting the staff through benefits and wellness programs is part of social equity. Providing a healthy environment, indoor air quality, and safety measures also takes care of the staff and clients. See Chapter 16 for more information on staff and team building.

Creating a Socially Responsible Culture in an Organization

Teaching social responsibility (SR) can be part of the training for new directors, employees, or cosmetology and massage students.

Figure 5-2: People are your most valuable asset.

Points to cover in teaching Social Responsibility:

- **Ethics:** Is it ethical to ignore impacts on others or the environment?
- **Respect:** SR shows respect for people, planet, and profit.
- **Actions:** Our actions affect fellow students, clients, and the community.
- **Relationships:** SR is a reciprocal relationship that benefits everyone.
- **Considerations:** Think beyond individual needs. Consider others in your decisions.
- **Culture:** We are all part of a group and culture of the spa team.
- **Together:** We are not isolated—we are all in this together (team, company, planet).
- **Purpose:** What is our common purpose?
- **Practices:** What are examples of SR in the facility?

Sharing the CSR message

If you have a CSR policy, publish it on your website. Your clients will be even more pleased to associate themselves with your sustainable brand. A good CSR plan will help businesses set and achieve sustainable goals. Good sustainability claims are about being honest and not about being perfect.

Think Globally: Society

Society and the planet are interdependent. The effects from local actions flow out into the world beyond our city. This is the piece of the social equity philosophy that is not as obvious. Jobs, consumption, health issues, the environment, and natural resources affect society worldwide. From living wages to global policies, businesses and manufacturing impact social equity. The more sustainably we conduct business, the more society benefits (Figure 5-3).

Figure 5-3: Society benefits from sustainable practices.

CHAPTER 5: Social Equity Means Everyone Benefits   47

SPA SPOTLIGHT

COMPLEXIONS SPA
A premier eco-friendly Gold LEED®- certified spa using century-old beauty rituals from around the world.

Contact: Denise Dubois, Owner and President (2012)

Complexions Spa For Beauty & Wellness

221 Wolf Rd., Albany NY

www.complexions.com

Facility size: 10,750 sq. ft.

Number of employees: More than 50

Number of treatment rooms: 15, plus 5 manicure, 5 pedicure, 8 hair styling stations, 2 barber chairs, 2 med spa rooms and 1 make-up room.

Established in: 1987

Facility Description
The spa is Gold LEED-certified for new construction, with the US Green Building Council.

Denise Dubois decided back in 2007 that the expansion into a new facility would take the environment's wellness into account and help to ensure that Complexions had an eco-friendly carbon footprint while converting a former fabric store. In 2008, an expanded 8450-square-foot new facility was built.

When they had the opportunity to expand into this new facility, it was an opportune time to build it "green." This enhanced and strengthened their commitment of offering wellness services to their guests in a facility that supports their green philosophy.

In 2012, a 2300-square-foot addition was added for a larger hair salon, another treatment room, additional changing room, a make-up bridal suite, and an event room. Additionally, we will have 2 more check-out stations and an outdoor relaxation garden.

Green Design Overview
- Complexions Spa is powered by wind and water sources in the Adirondacks.
- The facility is made of recyclable, renewable, and sustainable materials including low-VOC paint and wallpaper, cork flooring, recycled steel and tile flooring, recycled pre-consumer carpet, and energy-efficient appliances.
- Complexions Spa, registered with the US Green Building Council, was the first Gold LEED-certified spa for new construction in the country in 2009. Leadership in Energy and Environmental Design (LEED) is a building rating system developed by the US Green Building Council.
- Denise Dubois and her family did much of the work during the LEED certification process while adhering to a small budget. They researched the LEED standards and then physically did much of the work themselves, including sorting the construction waste into separate dumpsters for salvaging. Seventy-five percent of construction waste was diverted from landfills.

SPA GOALS AND VISION

What is your green business mission statement?
To offer our guests quality care through our services that have healing and healthy benefits all in an environment that supports our green mission.

What is your spa image?
A strong emphasis on health benefits, wellness and de-stressing—making it more of a necessity.

What are your sustainability goals?
Sustainability means using resources that are not depleting or permanently damaging, therefore our goal as a business is to continue to find ways that augment our green efforts daily.

What is important to you regarding sustainability?
That we offer services using products and materials that support sustainability. We also look to partner with companies that share our sustainable philosophies in their production/manufacturing practices.

What business practices or areas would you like to make more sustainable?
We continue to look for retail items that are more earth-friendly. Every day we are pleased that more and more products become available.

What are the challenges in being green?
Some of the challenges continue to be finding quality lighting fixtures, parts, and other needed materials that holdup to quality standards and support their claims.

Is the staff interested in greening the facility?
Yes; it is a corporate philosophy and all embrace it.

What business practices do you think your clients want to see with regard to sustainability?
Our clients are especially interested in the products we use and sell. They appreciate our green construction efforts that have helped create an environment that is healthy for them to come to.

Have you seen any positive effects from green practices you have implemented?
One of the positive outcomes of our green practices is how it has enlightened/highlighted the awareness of sustainable practices amongst not only our staff members, but some of our clients as well.

Additionally, we are consistently attracting new employees and clients because we are a green facility. When clients have the choice between two facilities we find that they are opting for the green spa! It has become our unique selling point.

What positive benefits do you offer your staff? (health, wellness, incentives)
The work environment is safe and healthier for our team members. They also receive special pricing for our services and products.

Do you promote your green practices?
Yes, at just about every turn we promote green practices. On Earth Day every year we celebrate by giving our clients tree saplings (this year will make for 400 saplings that we have given away in total!).

Do you have any words of wisdom for those spas that are going green?
Going green has been a bit of a challenge because of the quality of some of the materials available. A word to the wise: do your research and work with reputable companies that guarantee their products.

SPA ELEMENTS
The Menu
- Therapies from all over the world, combined with the finest botanical extracts from plants, herbs, and algae. Treatments are designed to deeply rejuvenate, relax and condition your body through traditional and century-old rituals.
- Our water system utilizes oxygenated water (water is infused with elevated oxygen levels by 350%) that further enhances the healthy aspect of our services by destroying bacteria, reducing inflammation, invigorating fatigued muscles, and more.

Esthetics
- An organic facial therapy incorporates a rare blend of organic Thai botanicals, along with a Royal Thai Facial Massage.
- The facility also houses a medi-spa where clients can receive medi-spa services such as laser hair reduction, microdermabrasion, chemical peels, acne care, cellulite reduction, IPL photo–rejuvenation, E-Matrix Sublative Rejuvenation for skin tightening and resurfacing.
- Esthetic services also include lymph drainage and gentlemen's facials as well.

Body
- Body wraps and polishes.
- VelaShape II combines four different technologies (radio frequency, infrared light, vacuum, and tissue manipulation) to reduce the volume and appearance of unwanted fat tissue and cellulite.
- Massage, Hydrotherapy Massage, and Balneo Therapy.

Wellness For Hands and Feet
- In Sebastian Kneipp's teachings, hands and feet need great care. Therefore most of our Mani–Kur and Pedi–Kur treatments are done using Kneipp (Kah–nipe) therapy to recondition utilizing the supportive, curative effects of herbs. "Kur" is German for a course of curative treatments.

Makeup
- Airbrush and mineral make-up application.

Hair Removal
- Laser, waxing, Epilfree.

Products
- We choose companies that have green manufacturing practices and that use environmentally friendly packaging. We also look for companies who use natural or organic ingredients.
- Inspired by Thai healing and beauty rituals, the Ytsara organic skin care line and spa programs offer a global and unique approach to age–old Asian holistic practices for use in the modern spa. Ytsara's herbs, roots, flowers and fruits are either cultivated on their organic farm in Thailand, or hand–picked in the forest, taking care to preserve the environment.

- We have our own eco-friendly label for all face and body products.
- *Face:* Ytsara, PCA Skin, SkinCeuticals.
- *Body:* Ytsara, Kneipp.
- *Hair:* Bumble & bumble, Rene Furterer, Surface.
- *Hands and Feet:* Kneipp, Ytsara.
- *Makeup:* Complexions' own eco-friendly label.
- *Hair Removal:* Candela Gentle LASE laser hair reduction.

Supplies
- We use recycled paper supplies, and all our cleaning supplies and laundry detergents are eco-friendly.

Energy
- Due to the spa's substantial energy reductions, New York State Energy Research Development Authority (NYSERDA) awarded Complexions with a bronze plaque and $31,000 in grant funding, as well as a Loan Fund which reduced their overall building loan by four interest points saving thousands of dollars in interest.
- Complexions Spa was one of 13 recipients of the Energy STAR's Small Business Award in 2008. The program recognizes businesses that implement policies and operations that result in drastic reductions in energy use and negative environmental impact.
- Complexions complements its sustainable building practices by purchasing all of its energy based on its generation by renewable resources such as wind and hydro.
- The spa estimates to save more than $10,600 annually in utility bills with its energy-efficient measures. The greenhouse gas savings is estimated at 56 tons annually, the equivalent of the CO_2 emissions from the electricity use of nearly seven homes for one year.

Building
- Construction exterior is brick.

Windows
- High-efficiency, double-pane, low-e, argon-filled windows were used in a sunroom addition added to the original building.
- The windows have a lower solar heat gain factor and low thermal transmittance.

HVAC System
- High-efficiency, roof-top HVAC units with a cooling energy efficiency rating of 12.5, and an annual fuel utilization efficiency of 82%, were installed. The equipment is Energy STAR qualified.
- The restrooms, locker rooms, and hair salon at the spa require specific amounts of air to be exhausted and replaced with fresh outdoor air, as required by local and state codes.
- The spa has added an energy recovery ventilator to recapture the energy of the exhaust air. This helps reduce the amount of energy needed to heat or cool the outdoor air to the desired space conditions.

Appliances
- New Energy STAR and energy-efficient appliances including two refrigerators, washers, dryers, domestic hot water heaters, and computers.

Type of Lighting
- Lighting fixtures are mostly LED and then fluorescent.
- Energy demand is reduced by installing high-efficiency lighting and lighting controls. The lighting design has reduced energy usage to 0.2 watts per square foot, plus many of the work rooms have light sensors to save more energy.

Water
- The spa reduced water use with low-flow toilets and faucets.
- Additionally, landscape design with drought resistant plants which require minimal watering were installed.

Green Materials
- The facility uses recyclable, renewable, and sustainable materials including low-VOC paint and wallpaper, cork flooring, recycled tire tiles, recycled steel, and energy efficient appliances.
- All wood used in cabinetry came from forests certified through Forest Stewardship Council (FSC), a non-profit organization devoted to encouraging the responsible management of the world's forests.

Indoor Environmental Quality (IEQ)
- All paints, wallpaper, and adhesives had to have low-VOC.

Purchasing
- All cleaning supplies, laundry detergents, and paper supplies come from eco-friendly sources.
- All of our printed materials are done on recycled paper.
- We do not use disposable cups, rather, we use glass and wash them using an eco-friendly dishwashing liquid.

Waste Reduction
- During construction, Complexions diverted 75% of construction waste from going to landfills.
- We used recycled material, including recycled steel, cork flooring, carpet, and flooring tiles made out of recycled tires; ceiling tiles and doors all contain recycled material.

Landscaping, Exteriors
- Landscape is designed with drought resistant plants.

Transportation
- VIP parking is available for guests who drive a hybrid car, and parking spaces are available for bicycles.

Marketing
- Staff members are updated during regular team meetings, and clients often read the literature we have on our walls. Additionally, we have much information on our website the general public can read about.

Education
- Guests are provided with "Getting Green" fact sheets and are encouraged to be more earth-friendly with discounts on retail products when they buy a Complexions reusable organic shopping bag.

An Introduction to Green Spa Practices

INTRODUCTION

Beauty services, products, supplies, operations, utilities, green building, and facility management are all components of a green facility. Let's look more closely at spa practices such as the treatment menu, resource savings, and waste management. Later chapters include detailed examples, potential savings, and the challenges and opportunities of these sustainable practices.

Buying healthier products and fewer disposable supplies are ways to green up the facility. When purchasing items for the facility, consider what could save natural resources. Additional aspects of the spa business to consider include food and beverage services, transportation, and the fitness center.

Words of Wisdom

On an average day, you are exposed to hundreds of untested chemicals–from the additives in your food to endocrine disruptors in your cosmetics and personal care products, to things you come in contact with like your mattress or household cleaning products. These chemicals create a "body burden" and may exacerbate allergies and asthma and lead to other serious health conditions. When you reduce your exposure to this daily assault, you in turn reduce your disease risk. A green spa is the perfect place to start your journey to stay healthy in a toxic world!

~ Beth Greer, Author of Super Natural Home, Environmental Health Consultant, www.BethGreer.com

THE TREATMENT MENU

When designing a treatment menu, consider the equipment, products, and supplies that will be needed (Figure 6-1). These all contribute to the overhead and cost of providing services. For example, a complicated treatment such as a body mask that takes excessive water for rinsing could use less water by changing to a product that is easier to rinse off. Using locally-sourced natural products such as local clay or herbs are also popular treatment choices. Services are discussed in Chapter 7.

Figure 6-1: The menu design reflects the green treatment choices.

CHOOSING GREEN PRODUCTS

Ecolabeling and product choices are major topics in the industry (Figure 6-2). Research the ingredients and packaging when choosing retail and back bar products. Many clients want organic healthy products in recycled packaging. Replacing plastic containers with recycled content packaging is a positive step in the packaging industry. Some buyers now want to know how responsibly products are manufactured and how toxic the chemicals are in producing our goods.

TREATMENT ROOMS

Choosing equipment, supplies, and other needs for the treatment rooms makes an impact on the business. Purchasing equipment that lasts will save money and time in the long run (Figure 6-3). A good magnifying light or steamer may last ten years, where an inexpensive one may only last two years. Using more durable equipment makes the services more reliable. Quality linens also improve the client experience and quality of the service. Water conservation is another important practice that can be implemented in the facility by using low-flow fixtures and instant hot water taps.

Figure 6-2: Product choices are primary topics in the industry.

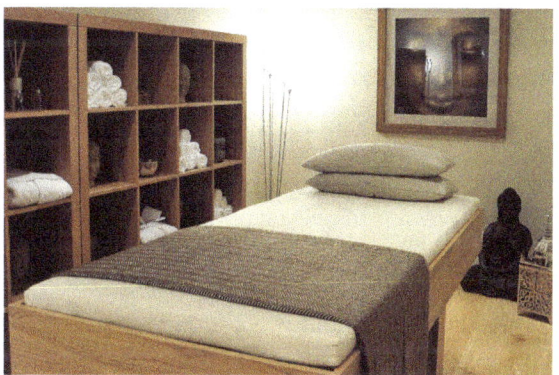

Figure 6-3: Purchasing durable equipment and supplies saves money and time.

CONSCIOUS PURCHASING

When purchasing materials, service, and office supplies, try to buy "green" and minimize packaging. Look for recycled paper, products, and containers. Print marketing materials on recycled paper and do more Internet marketing to save on printing as many expensive brochures. Use purchasing criteria that specify green materials for items such as paint and interiors. Conscious purchasing also reduces waste and recycling needs (Figure 6-4).

Using Fewer Supplies

With strict client safety and cleanliness standards, it is challenging to get away from using single-use, disposable supplies. It is essential to adhere to laws and regulations. Check local regulations for rules on using single-use items, such as drinking glasses, for clients in the facility. Due to hygiene standards, washable drinking glasses are not legal in some regions where regulatory boards require single-use throw away client cups in facilities. Of course, only disinfected or clean items are used for clients, but changes can be made to save on throw away supplies.

Choosing washable alternatives for single-use items such as 4x4 esthetic wipes spares you from throwing away thousands of cotton pads and other items. This also saves money and time spent on purchasing in the long run. Washable microfiber esthetic wipes are great choices to replace cotton wipes or sponges. Another way to save resources and money is to use towels instead of single-use, throw away paper items. Using smaller towels and fewer towels saves water and time spent doing laundry.

Other ways to save are to be conscious of products and supplies. Try to use less without sacrificing the quality of the service. Does the client need to put on a gown or can she just slip under the sheet?

Give clients the option. Additionally, spatulas and other items can be disinfected instead of thrown away. What could your staff do to work more efficiently and save resources?

Waste Reduction

The Three R's of waste reduction are *Reduce, Reuse, and Recycle.* **Precycling** by buying less is the first step in reducing waste. This helps save money and storage space. Be creative with displays and use what you have on hand or buy items you can reuse. Reducing plastic material and switching to glass is another easy way to help green up the facility. Glass can be recycled much easier than plastic. Another way to reduce waste and waste hauling bills is to use compost from food and beverage services in outdoor landscaping maintenance.

What is your spa footprint?
What resources do you use?

THE GREEN FACILITY

In a facility, energy conservation is the primary focus to save money. Heating and cooling a building is expensive. Reducing energy use by monitoring the temperature, using efficient light fixtures, and turning off power strips that are not in use can save thousands of dollars per year in a typical facility.

Figure 6-4: Conscious purchasing reduces waste and recycling needs.

Additionally, water is an important and increasingly scarce resource. Using conservation methods both indoors and outdoors in landscaping can also save hundreds to thousands of dollars per year in one facility. Low-flow fixtures with aerators are inexpensive ways to conserve water.

Another component of a green building is healthy indoor environmental quality. Using green materials such as non-toxic paint has many benefits. The green choices for furniture and interiors are definitely expanding. Good ventilation and use of non-toxic products without harmful chemicals are essential to the occupants' health. Indoor environmental quality includes comfortable room temperatures, acoustics, visual aesthetics, and scents. It is interesting to note that these healthy practices all relate to the elements that spas offer as part of the client's relaxing experience.

When greening the facility, include the stations, client lounge, changing rooms, front desk, reception, office, retail area, staff break room, and bathrooms. Start with small steps and goals to make your facility more sustainable. Share your progress with coworkers and clients. The greening process can also serve as a great team builder and an educational, promotional tool.

The Green Spa Network uses the following categories to rate a facility's green practices:

- Leadership
- Employee experience
- Guest experience
- Treatment protocols
- Retail products
- Linens and textiles
- Food and beverage
- Community connection
- Waste
- Water use
- Lighting
- Sanitation
- Equipment
- Laundry
- Energy
- New facilities/Extensive remodel energy use
- Pool operations

(Courtesy of the Green Spa Network)

SPA SPOTLIGHT

CRYSTAL SPA
Sustainably operating the resort from the standpoint of energy, environment, and economy is at the very heart of Crystal's business philosophy.

Contact: Brian Lawson, Director of Public Relations (2012)

Crystal Mountain Resort and Spa
12500 Crystal Mountain Dr.,
Thompsonville, Michigan

www.crystalmountain.com

Facility size: 18,500 sq. ft. (Spa: 11,000 sq. ft.; Fitness Center and Pool: 7,500 sq. ft.)

Number of employees: 27

Number of treatment rooms: 12

Established in: 2009

Facility Description

Crystal Spa is the Midwest's only Silver LEED-certified spa. The spa features 12 treatment rooms, including a couples retreat room and Vichy shower, meditation lounge, relaxation garden with hot tub, men's and women's locker rooms each with a eucalyptus infused steam room and infrared sauna, and a manicure and pedicure salon. Housed within the same building is the Peak Fitness Center with the latest cardio and strength training equipment, indoor pool with lap lanes, hot tub, locker rooms and indoor and outdoor motion studios for fitness classes and programs.

SPA GOALS AND VISION

What is your green business mission statement?

Preserving and protecting the breathtaking natural setting that surrounds and enhances Crystal Mountain has long been part of the resort's core principles. Utilizing and seeking out new ways to sustainably operate the resort from the standpoint of energy, environment, and economy, is at the very heart of our business philosophy.

What is your spa image?
Crystal Spa draws inspiration from the natural beauty and talented local artists to create a relaxing, rejuvenating environment that is authentic to northern Michigan. A healthy lifestyle community, Crystal Mountain's fitness programs, Peak Performance menu, and an endless list of outdoor activities from skiing to golf to mountain biking are an integral part of an experience that provides renewal and balance.

What business practices or areas would you like to make more sustainable?
The mission of our Green Team is to seek ways to operate more sustainably in every area of the resort. Waste reduction, energy efficiency and conservation, preservation of natural resources, and day-to-day operations (recycling, zero-waste events, buying local food) are all areas that we focus on and measure. *The proliferation of sustainability initiatives is critical to prosperity* so leading by example, offering counsel and collaborating with others is extremely important as well.

What are the challenges in being green?
There are the inherent challenges of the business. Operating and maintaining a resort requires the use of energy so one challenge is to determine how to best reduce our footprint while continuing to meet customer expectations and remain fiscally sound. When sustainability and environmental stewardship are part of your approach, the challenges are not really different from those in running any business.

Have you seen any positive effects from green practices you have implemented?
The LEED design of the spa requires 28% less energy than that of a baseline building, which will save us money over time. By retrofitting every lodging unit with compact fluorescent lighting, it will save the resort approximately $500,000 over the life of the bulbs. Being strategic in maintenance of our golf courses (use of inputs, mowing versus leaving areas natural) saves money and reduces environmental impacts. These are just a few examples. Our approach to sustainability and environmental stewardship has also earned us a number of compliments from guests and recognition from a number of organizations.

What positive benefits do you offer your staff?
All staff have unlimited access to the Peak Fitness Center, indoor pool, and fitness programs. We offer a Peak Performance Challenge to all employs to accomplish at their own pace. You earn points by participating in a number of healthy activities and receive an award when reaching each of three thresholds. It is a fun way to encourage employees to be healthy and experience the many opportunities at the resort.

Do you promote your green practices?
Mountain Life magazine, distributed semi-annually to 50,000+ (each issue), features a green page covering different environmental initiatives at the resort and suggestions on how to live more sustainably at home. We also have a letter within our directory explaining our philosophy on protecting the environment and living sustainably. We host events like *Taste the Local Difference*'s Summer Celebration and the Conference on Michigan's Future: Economy, Energy, and Environment that are open to the public. These are just a few examples.

SPA ELEMENTS

The Menu
- Organic and natural product lines are used.

Products
- Inventory measures are in place and continually updated and improved to incorporate control measures to reduce waste and excess shipping.
- *Face:* Naturopathica (certified natural and organic), Skin Authority.

- *Body:* Naturopathica product line and Pure-ssage.
- Pure-ssage massage oil, cream, and lotions are 99.4% pure, economical, unscented, and free of nut oils and parabens.
- *Nails:* Spa Ritual line and Eco-fin.
- SpaRitual offers a vegan, paraben-free, multipurpose system of spa treatments for body, hand, and foot rituals. All of our nail care products are vegan and free of DBP, toluene and formaldehyde.
- Eco-fin is a natural, petroleum-free alternative to paraffin made with a rich blend of palm, soy, jojoba, and organic coconut oils, plus shea butter, vitamin E, and essential oils.
- *Makeup:* Jane Iredale.

Retail
- All of the above lines are retailed, and our signature product line includes an organic bar soap, Crystal Spa Lavender Mint Body Bar, which is made in Michigan, custom for Crystal Spa.
- Refill program for Crystal Spa signature product line: bring back container to refill for only $6 (shampoo, conditioner, body wash, and lotion).

Supplies
- *Linens:* Comphy Co.
- *Single-use items* (cotton, plastic): Minimize usage of items.
- *Cleaning:* EcoLogic cleaning products.
  The product line, services, and resources are focused on being environmentally preferable.
- *Facility supplies:* Bulk amenity program.

Client Lounge
- We serve local, organic Light of Day tea grown organically and biodynamically under the guidelines of the National Organic Program, and Demeter Biodynamic.
- *Changing rooms:* Bulk amenities, paperless, non-disposables.
- *Bathrooms:* Bulk amenities.

Building
- Completed in January 2009, the facility is Silver LEED-certified so it is designed to maximize energy efficiency and minimize impact on the environment.

Energy
- We purchase wind energy credits equal to the carbon footprint of the facility.
- The heating system is a *pump and dump* heat pump system with the dump water feeding irrigation and snow-making equipment. LEED innovation points were generated from the use of the dumped heat pump water. When heat is extracted from the heat pump loop, the cooler dumped water is then used to make snow more efficiently than the warmer groundwater normally used.

- HVAC controls are master controlled to set back when unoccupied and only come up to operating temperature when the building is open. Space thermostats have limited controllability so spaces cannot be overheated or under-cooled to the point of wasting energy.
- All systems are measured for energy consumption.

Type of Lighting
- The use of natural lighting was considered and integrated into the building design.
- T-8 and T-5 fluorescent bulbs, or LED; all lighting is master controlled for building occupancy, as well as utilizing localized motion sensors and timers for operation efficiency.

Water
- Low water consumption auto faucets, auto flush valves, low-flow showerheads and waterless urinals are used.
- Landscaping is designed with native plant life to reduce irrigation water consumption.

Green Materials
- 30% of building materials met LEED local materials requirements.

Indoor Environmental Quality (IEQ)
- This facility meets ASHRAE ventilation requirements for acceptable indoor air quality.
- All adhesives, sealants, paints, and floor covering met LEED low emitting materials guidelines.

Purchasing
- EcoSoft 100% recycled facial tissue; bathroom tissue is made from 90% to 100% recycled fiber and a minimum of 75% post-consumer content; paper towels are Green Seal Certified.

Waste Reduction
- A Waste Stream Reduction program has been created at the resort to recycle or compost as much material as possible resort-wide.

Landscaping, Exteriors
- Native plant life was used in landscaping around the spa in order to conserve as much water as possible.

Transportation
- Crystal Mountain was the first resort in Michigan to install Electric Vehicle Charging Stations (2). They are free of charge (pun intended) to resort guests.

Food Service
- Crystal Mountain is the title sponsor of *Taste the Local Difference*, a program from the Michigan Land Use Institute that promotes local food and farmers.
- We use as much locally grown food as possible in our restaurants and host the Michigan Beer and Brat Festival and Taste of Michigan events each summer, which feature only Michigan-made and grown food, beer, and wine.

Marketing
- Our semi-annual lifestyle magazine, *Mountain Life*, includes at least one page focused on green initiatives at the resort or ways in which guests can be more environmentally friendly. We frequently share our green initiatives and philosophy with media.
- Environmental stewardship is a frequent topic during our all-employee meeting each December. A portion of our website is dedicated to environmental stewardship.

People
- Even prior to state mandates we were a no-smoking property.
- All staff have unlimited access to the Peak Fitness Center and Indoor Pool and reduced rates for fitness programming.
- Tips on being environmentally friendly are frequently included in our employee newsletter, the *Communique*.
- During an all-employee meeting a few years ago, each attendee (300+) received a compact fluorescent light bulb.

Education
- We have a Green Team composed of members from each department at the resort.
- *Lunch and Learn* meetings as well as presentations during our employee meeting each year educate our staff on environmental stewardship and the importance of these measures.
- In 2009 and 2010, Crystal Mountain hosted the conference on *Michigan's Future: Economy, Energy, and Environment*.
- Crystal Mountain CEO Jim MacInnes frequently writes op-ed pieces for local papers on energy and environment as well as giving presentations on the local and state level.

CHAPTER 7

The Service Menu and Beyond

INTRODUCTION

Service menus are filled with unique custom services for each spa. Using natural and organic products for services is the easiest way to add green touches to your menu. This is good for business and attractive to clients. Promoting wellness services or treatments based on local culture is another way to green up the menu and stay current with spa trends. To be competitive, offer simple, well-priced products and services. The service menu design is important because it conveys your image. Your clients want more of a distinctive experience, so enhance the menu and train technicians and staff to offer exceptional quality services. Many trade journals and organizations discuss menu design concepts and ideas. A checklist for service menu planning is also included in Chapter 17.

WORDS OF WISDOM

When incorporating natural products and treatments into your seasonal menu, simply choose bulk unscented base ingredients that you can continue to use when the seasons change. Use smaller size ingredients to give your product bases a seasonal twist. For example, White/Kaolin Clay can be used to create a mask over any part of the body. This clay is available as a powder and has a long shelf life when kept dry. By mixing with other active powders or essential oils, you can create seasonal menus and customize treatments without any waste.

~ Mariah Culbertson, Universal Companies,
www.universalcompanies.com

What services and products do you offer?
Evaluate and adjust your menu every year.
What is your price point? What amenities are offered
with your services?

STIMULATING THE FIVE SENSES

The beauty and spa world is all about the five senses. Touch, smell, sight, hearing, and taste buds are all stimulated in an ultimate client experience. Creating the mood and the experience during the service will depend on the menu design as well as the atmosphere. The attention to details in the building design, décor, staff attentiveness, scents/aromatherapy, music and waterfalls, and additional touches such as tea or fruit all influence the atmosphere. Are you creating an atmosphere of health and wellness or a salon full of fun and excitement? The atmosphere reflects what you are offering and this also relates to indoor environmental quality.

HOLISTIC HEALTH AND BEAUTY SERVICES

Health and wellness focused services are very popular. These services lean toward the green aspects of supporting the client's well being. Many facilities offer wellness seminars and services such as ayurvedic treatments. This not only cares for clients, but also captures attention and brings in additional business. Clients want real therapeutic benefits from their services beyond the beauty aspects. For example, detoxification and specialty foot treatments are two services that address this need. Wellness services promote a healthy lifestyle.

HIGHLIGHTING LOCAL CULTURE

A sense of place speaks to people. Using local treatments focused on the place, or geographic location, is a popular practice. By promoting the local flavor, the region is highlighted and respected. For example, in the Southwest, the Indian spiritual culture and plant ingredients are used in a number of spas. In Hawaii, the Island culture and tropical plants are used in designing treatments.

Figure 7-1: Honoring local culture distinguishes the unique features of your spa.

Using local ingredients such as clays and herbs found in different regions supports the local economy. Going local also cuts down on shipping costs and fuel. Additionally, buying from local vendors keeps more dollars circulating back into the community. Honoring the local culture and tradition creates interest and distinguishes the unique features of your spa (Figure 7-1).

PLANNING THE SERVICE MENU

The menu includes services, pricing, products, and treatment packages. The first consideration in menu planning is client demographics. The theme or image of the salon/spa also guides the menu design. The product lines that are used help determine the treatments. Nearly every spa has signature treatments. A simple menu helps clients decide on treatments without having to make too many choices.

Streamlined treatment options also save on training and product costs. The best menus have simple core services that incorporate additional seasonal express treatments and promotions. Various services are included in this section to provide a template, but this is designed to let your creativity flow by leaving the specific menu ideas up to you and your team. See Chapter 21 for marketing ideas.

To green up your menu, analyze your product lines and supplies used for treatments. Using natural and organic products has been the biggest green change used in spas and salons. Focus on health and wellness services. Add express treatments that do not use as many resources or amenities. This cuts down on supply use and helps make spa services more affordable for clients. A menu design checklist is included in the planning chapters and online resources.

Menu Design Tips

- What is your image and theme?
- Keep it simple.
- Offer well-priced products and services.
- Address demographics.
- Design with product line protocols.
- Consider product use and resources (energy, water, disposable supplies).
- Add mini treatments.
- Use monthly or seasonal promotions.
- Determine packages: half-day packages, full-day packages, themes.
- Evaluate and change it up once a year.
- Convey a green lifestyle.
- Add local features.
- Promote your green features.
- Include educational programs.
- Use programming and events that are engaging and interactive with the community.

Communicate your green practices and mission statement in the menu.

Are you a member of a green association? Have you won awards? Highlight the green features of the menu, such as local products. What makes you unique and sets you apart from others? Many clients look for these features when choosing where to go for services. Include green practices, certification logos, and memberships in the menu and on the website (Figure 7-2).

What are your green menu design features?

- Locally focused treatments:
- Health and wellness services:
- Express treatments:
- Packages:
- Organic products:
- Sustainable values and statement:
- Printed on…. ("30% recycled content paper with soy ink"?)
- Member of the….(note "Green Business Organizations"…)

Menu Printing Costs

Using recycled paper, less paper, and eco-friendly ink for printing all are greener practices that save money by reducing printing costs. Professional marketing materials are necessary, but how can we reduce the paper use? Half sheets rather than full sheets can be used for many things we print. Many companies use sustainably harvested paper and note that on their brochures. If each brochure costs $1.00, then e-mailing or having them online saves printing costs, paper, and postage. That can add up to a savings of thousands of sheets of paper per year. The additional income can be spent on creating a job and paying someone for Internet marketing or social media promotions. Having that dedicated marketing person can expand the business by giving more attention to growing the business.

Figure 7-2 : Menu Design.

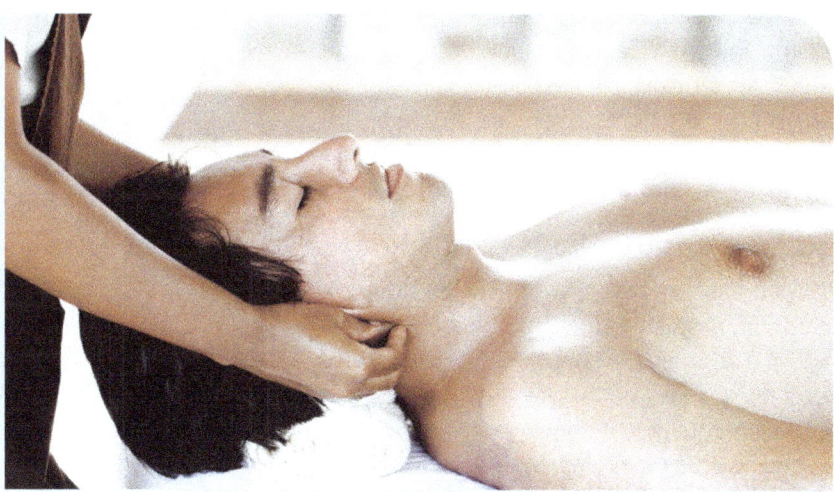

The Five Senses
Touch, smell, sight, hearing, and taste buds are all pleasantly stimulated in an ultimate client experience.

Another suggestion is to use whiteboards for specials that change often. Have ready-to-use templates for new menu options and shelf talkers. Just change out the specials by inserting changes on the signs to keep the large sign cost down. One new green practice can easily lead to another one. What creative ideas do you have to keep costs down on marketing materials?

What services and features would you like to add to your menu?

FOOD SERVICE

Many resorts and hotel spas have built-in food options from their restaurants. Serving organic, local, healthy food is popular for spa packages, which is an added benefit for clients. Juice and tea bars are other popular additions to spas and fitness centers. Use durable or recyclable containers (instead of disposables) to save money and resources. On-site gardens and composting are becoming more standard practices. There are many benefits to having an on-site fresh food source and using the waste for composting. These are smart practices that save money and time.

FITNESS AND GYMS

Large resorts and other facilities include fitness centers and classes along with their spa offerings (Figure 7-3). Along with the client amenities and pool areas, gyms are available to guests. Day passes are great options for those who want to spend a day relaxing at the spa. Expanded fitness programs and even green gyms are becoming *en vogue*. Outdoor programs and walking maps are available at some resort properties, such as Hyatt. Another example is Westin Hotels, who offer a wellness program for guests.

Other green practices include towel and water bottle conservation in the gym. Saline pools are becoming a popular alternative to cut down on chlorine use. Green building materials and energy efficient equipment are becoming more standard for fitness centers. Some gyms have even installed stationary bikes that create electricity by riding them. More innovative fitness ideas will likely appear on the horizon.

SPA INDUSTRY SERVICES AND STATISTICS

It is helpful to compare your business model to others to determine how your business is doing in the industry. Keeping up on client preferences and expectations is also important. In order to gauge where the industry is going, it is useful to have a picture of the different services and facilities out there.

The following ISPA statistics give an overview of the industry. Facilities include relaxation areas, locker rooms, fitness areas, consultation areas, and wet rooms. There are an average of six treatment rooms and ten hair stations per US spa (ispa.com 2012).

The ISPA 2011 US Spa Industry Study

The spa industry categories used in this study are club, day, destination, medical, mineral springs, and the resort/hotel spas. A large majority of spas (85%) indicated that they use one or more environmentally sustainable practices (2010). Recycling is the most common sustainable practice currently used (71%), followed by packaging made from recycled materials and offering organic products, both at 47%.

Figure 7-3: Fitness centers.

The percentage of environmentally sustainable practices that are used in facilities:

- Recycling: 71% of facilities
- Provide packaging made from recycled materials: 47%
- Offer USDA-certified organic products: 47%
- Use low-flow faucet aerators: 28%
- Used eco-friendly building materials: 21%
- LEED certification: 6%
- None of the above: 15%

The Main Treatment Revenue Categories in Spas

The main treatment revenue categories in spas comprise massage and bodywork, skin care, hair, and nails. The average treatment numbers varied by spa type. Across the industry, massage and bodywork treatments accounted for 33% of all spa revenue; skin care treatments, 25%; hair department, 12%; and nail department, 8%. Wellness programs, alternative treatments, and medical services continue to expand. With a 33% revenue share, the total value of massage and bodywork treatments is estimated at $4.3 billion, followed by skin care treatments at $3.2 billion. The combined revenue from hair and nail treatments is $2.6 billion.

[**The average retail purchase per guest was $43 in 2010.**]

Composition of Retail Revenue

Retail accounts for 11% of total spa revenues, ranging from 10% for resort/hotel spas to 14% for medical spas. The sale of skin care products accounts for the majority (57%) of retail spending by spa visitors. Hair care products account for 18% of retail revenue. As a source of revenue, hair products are most prominent in the day spa sector (21% of retail). Cosmetics account for 9% of retail sales and nail care is 4%.

Enhancing the Spa Menu

One of the ways in which spas have managed the effects of the recessed economy has been to re-engineer the menu. Almost all spas have taken one or more steps in that direction. A majority of spas have introduced shorter express treatments (30 minutes or less), offering a less expensive option that also allows busy clients to enjoy the spa experience.

(Statistics courtesy of ISPA 2011)

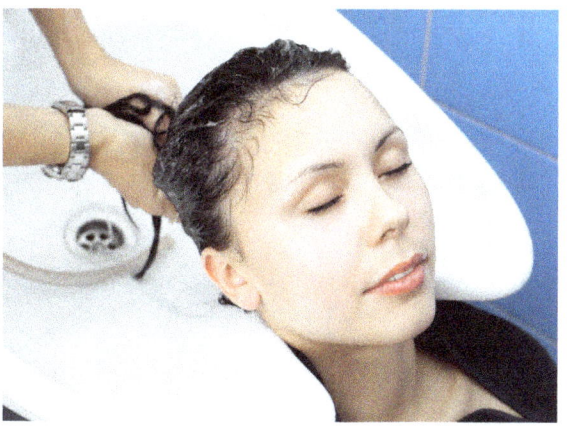

SPA SPOTLIGHT

ELAIA SPA, HYATT AT OLIVE 8
The first LEED-certified hotel in Seattle and the first for Hyatt in North America.

Contact: Leah Krieger, Spa Director (2012)

Hyatt Olive 8/Elaia Spa
1635 8th Avenue, Seattle, Washington

www.elaiaspa.com

Facility size: 15,000 sq. ft.

Number of employees: 20+

Number of treatment rooms: Twelve treatment rooms, including a couple's suite with an over-sized Japanese soaking tub, and four manicure and pedicure stations.

Established in: 2009

Facility Description
This spacious LEED facility includes separate men's and women's locker rooms each featuring a steam room, dry sauna, showers, a vanity area, and lounge seating. There is a 65' saline lap pool with underwater music. Alongside our co-ed pool is a Jacuzzi overlooking Olive Way. Our large relaxation lounge includes teas, hazelnuts, and chocolate. Lunch can be ordered from the hotel's *Urbane* restaurant.

SPA GOALS AND VISION

Elaia is the Greek word for Olive, a symbol of peace, wisdom, and resilience—all important principles of the Green Movement.

What is your green business mission statement?
The ethics of Elaia are on the first page of the brochure and include the market fresh concept, LEED, and being respectful to the Earth. The spa is dedicated to using as many locally produced ingredients as possible. By employing eco-friendly practices and utilizing environmentally-minded procedures, Elaia upholds the ideal that to be truly respectful to the human body, we must also be respectful to the Earth. We are truly passionate about our work and our community. We are present, connected, and engaged with every guest. We recognize and anticipate the desired results each guest wishes to accomplish and are committed to exceeding their expectations. We will continue to research the best possible practices and products. We will identify organizations and research new practices that enable us to contribute however we can to our community.

What is important to you regarding sustainability?

Combining a luxury experience with a natural element. Keeping our promise to our guests that they will receive the best possible treatment with gentle, organic products. All elements are important: from the paper we use to the recycle containers in all public areas to the behind-the-operation systems we have in place. Products can absorb into the bloodstream so it is important to educate people that organic products are healthy and are effective in treating skin.

What are the challenges in being green?

There are many wonderful products we would love to incorporate in our menu, but we are limited to natural/organic. The continual search for the luxury natural line is the main challenge.

Have you seen any positive effects from green practices you have implemented?

Yes! It really is easier than you think. Our concept and mission statement attract sustainable-minded guests, as well as gives us an opportunity to educate those who are not. We have seen great effects all around. Sixty to 74% of guests are local. The green, organic element is the reason—we stay true to the organic concept.

SPA ELEMENTS

Service Menu
- Offers "market fresh" seasonal treatments; holistic massages with aromatherapy.
- Menu is printed on recycled paper.

Retail and Service Products
- All products are natural and organic.
- Looking for local product line vendors; use organic olive oil from Portland.
- Luzern, Eminence, USPA, and Spa Ritual are used.

Packaging
- All of our vendors use recycled and recyclable materials.

Supplies
- We try to buy supplies with recycled content.
- Corn derived cups are used in the fitness center and locker rooms.

Facility
- Saline lap pool and Jacuzzi.
- Non-lead-based paint throughout hotel and spa.

Energy
- LEED-certified building has many energy efficient features; LED lights throughout the facility.

Water
- We do not have bottled water. We use Natura water, a filtered water we provide in the lounge, and there are water stations throughout the facility.

IAQ/IEQ
- Paint: low-VOC.

Green Materials
- LEED-specified green materials.

Cleaning Supplies
- As green as possible, but they need to be hospital grade (legal, EPA registered).

Purchasing
- Recycled paper and double-sided printing is standard practice.
- Flash drives with spa information are given out instead of press kits.

Waste Management
- The employee café composts.
- The entire hotel (guests too!) discards more recyclable material than waste, which is significant.

Recycling
- Everywhere. Everything we can. It is a way of life. Recycling bins are located throughout the building.
- During construction, 94% of the construction waste was recycled.

Landscaping and Outdoors
- There is a green roof and herbs are grown on the roof for the restaurant.

Transportation
- Located in downtown Seattle, most of our staff either rides the bus or walks to work.

Staff
- As an associate of Hyatt Olive 8, you are expected to be sustainable and support our concept while at work. Usually, that bleeds into the rest of your home life too!

Clients and Community
- Seattle is a wonderful population of educated, sustainable-minded people. They keep us on our toes…and appreciate our dedication as a truly organic spa.
- The green features are listed on the website.

CHAPTER 8

Defining Green Products

INTRODUCTION

Choosing retail and back bar products for services is one of the most important business decisions in a spa/salon. Using natural and organic products has perhaps been the biggest green change for spas. Many clients expect to see green products on the shelves so it is important to carry a more natural, organic line. This increases a spa's market share. The variety of natural product lines has grown substantially, so it is one area where it is easier to go green. Quality and cost are always considerations in purchasing and choosing products.

If your spa has an organic line, are you automatically considered green? There is much more to being eco-conscious than just carrying healthy organic products. This is the most direct way to show your conscious business side to the public, but other responsible practices in the facility are necessary to avoid Greenwashing.

With never-ending ingredient choices and numerous certifications to cover, the product section is divided into three chapters. Comparing marketing claims in ingredient declarations takes time and effort. Personal care certifications and standards include ANSI 305, Natrue, and USDA NOP. See Chapter 9 for a review of product certifications and standards. Chapter 10 has guidelines on choosing specific products and ingredients.

WORDS OF WISDOM

We believe that the last thing a guest should worry about while relaxing at a spa is whether the products being used in the spa services might be hazardous to their health. The lotions, oils, and skin care products used at some spas may contain potentially harmful chemicals, some of which are believed to cause cancer, reproductive, or neurological problems. At Spa Habitat, we research every ingredient in every product we use or sell to ensure that it's safe and beneficial, and that the companies we work with use organic and eco-friendly business practices.

~ Greg Bohn, CEO, Spa Habitat – Organic Spa and Apothecary (with 4 organic spa locations in the Dallas, Texas area), www.spahabitat.com

WHAT MAKES A PRODUCT GREEN?

What a product does not contain is just as important as what it does contain. A *green* product is generally described as "free from harmful ingredients" such as petroleum-derived, suspect ingredients. Cleaner product formulations contain fewer synthetic chemicals. Natural and organic products are both considered green, but there is a difference.

Research the ingredients and packaging when choosing retail and back bar products. Many clients want organic healthy products in recycled packaging. Containers and packaging are additional green factors. Green chemistry, harvesting, and manufacturing practices are also considerations in choosing products.

Figure 8-1: Third party certification helps authenticate products.

The supplier's practices affect how sustainable the brand or product line is. Ethical practices and fair trade issues are other factors to think about. No animal testing is important to many consumers, but that does not make a product green. Brands are expected to be authentic and transparent. Certification and evidence-based testing are two of the requirements for green products.

A third-party certification stating the product is natural or organic helps authenticate it (Figure 8-1). Additionally, a product's *ecological footprint* includes transportation miles, carbon outputs, and social impacts. The *life cycle analysis* of goods and services we sell can also be measured. It is confusing to both consumers and business owners to wade through the product choices, so look for certifications and read the labels.

Watch out for vague words such as eco-friendly and natural. It is unfortunate that false claims have given natural, organic products a bad name and created skepticism, as consumers do not know who to believe. See Chapter 21 for more discussion on Greenwashing.

Buying sustainability? An oxymoron?

Ideally, the future will offer even more choices in healthier and greener products. Nevertheless, sustainability can be contradictory to buying and shopping. Reducing purchasing is contrary to the current economic model, but if selling is concentrated on necessary and sustainable goods and services, there is still a healthy market there. A good point is that we cannot shop our way to sustainability.

Healthy Ingredients

Healthy ingredients or products could be described as chemically clean or "to do no harm" (Figure 8-2). Skin is the largest organ of the body and absorbs products, ingredients, and drugs, so it makes sense that what we put on the skin can affect our body and health. There is much controversy over ingredients and mystery chemicals used in thousands of products. Women use an average of 12 personal care products per day (safecosmetics.org 2011). A lifetime of exposure adds up to a **toxic burden**, a build-up of synthetic chemicals in the body.

Figure 8-2: Healthy ingredients or products are described as chemically clean or "to do no harm."

Scientific research is showing that certain chemicals are not as safe as we once thought. Toxicity levels measured in the body reveal carcinogens and hormone disruptors caused by what we ingest and what we are exposed to. Government regulations in the US have been lacking when it comes to personal care products. The FDA does not test or analyze personal care ingredients.

There is debate on whether synthesized lab products are green or natural. Do they have to come straight from nature? Products formulated without harmful ingredients or preservatives could be considered healthy. Another consideration is the nutritional aspect of products.

NATURAL VERSUS SYNTHETIC INGREDIENTS

Green formulations do not contain questionable synthetic chemicals, but not all are natural. What are natural ingredients? *Natural ingredients* are derived directly from nature, not synthesized in a lab. Plants and herbs provide an abundance of naturally beneficial ingredients. These are mixed and formulated into products, but they retain their natural properties. A combination of both natural and synthetic ingredients is a common chemical formulation for skin care products.

Natural products directly from nature can have powerful skin benefits; however, some of the most effective cosmetic ingredients are not derived from plants. Natural and synthetic ingredients can both have drawbacks. Certain synthetic ingredients are effective cell renewal stimulants; however, it should be remembered that some synthetic ingredients may be considered unhealthy and do not harness the real essence or purity of herbs or oils.

Even some natural ingredients (extracts and essential oils) may not be as effective because they are extracted or preserved with questionable chemical compounds (such as butylene glycol or parabens, respectively). Some third-party certifications allow the use of *"nature-identical"* preservatives. These are synthetic yet "safe" because they are identical to their natural counterparts but have more stability.

What is natural? **Natural** ingredients are derived directly from nature, not synthesized in the lab.

What is organic? **Organic** ingredients are grown without the use of pesticides or harmful chemicals.

Some ingredients used in skin care products—including fragrances, essential oils, and preservatives—may cause adverse skin reactions. Fragrances and some preservatives are among the most common allergens. Natural ingredients may cause allergies in people who are sensitive, while synthetic versions of the same ingredients may not. Being aware of a client's allergies and the ingredients being used in treatments is very important to avoid problems or reactions.

The quality and the sources of ingredients are both important factors to consider when choosing products. Many manufacturers are combining natural ingredients and chemical synthetic ingredients to obtain the best of both worlds. Clients will prefer one philosophy over the other and will be attracted to either natural or more clinical treatments. Knowing the benefits of both types of treatments is important for those selling products.

It is estimated that everyone uses approximately ten personal care products in the morning. How many do you use?

ORGANIC INGREDIENTS

Organic ingredients are grown without the use of pesticides or chemicals. Ideally, they are harvested and manufactured in a more natural way. Unfortunately there is no organic labeling standard for cosmetics in the United States at this time, but it is in the works and the standards are continually evolving. The USDA does certify manufacturing facilities.

It is difficult to formulate products without preservatives and other functional ingredients to stabilize a product. Additionally, most products are 60 to 90 percent water, so the product may be labeled organic by the water alone. Marketing statements do not always tell the whole story. False claims are common in the billion-dollar skin care industry.

> www.safecosmetics.org
> lists the top harmful ingredients in products.

Green chemistry is becoming more common with manufacturers who are improving their processing to reduce their environmental footprint. Products are considered more sustainable because of the ingredients used, the manufacturing processes, or for the resources that are conserved.

Scientific research is expanding the knowledge of how chemicals and ingredients affect our health. New organic product lines are flourishing as consumer demand increases. Technological advances have also made it easier to blend effective skin care products from organic and natural sources.

TOXINS AND CHEMICALS

"There are over 85,000 synthetic chemicals in the US. Over 80% of these chemicals are not tested." Just because they are allowed on the market is not proof that they are all safe and nontoxic. In the US many chemicals are safe or innocent unless proven otherwise (ewg.org 2011).

The market is shifting to using safer alternatives to personal care products regardless of the lack in regulations. The natural and organic market is booming because demand is fueling the need for companies to adapt. A good point to consider is to compare the cost of more expensive, healthier products against the potential cost of health issues from exposure to unhealthy products. Is it worth the extra money to buy a healthier product?

> Chemicals hiding in "fragrances" are unknown.

The Environmental Working Group (EWG) is a valuable research organization that also has an extensive, helpful cosmetic safety database: Skin Deep. Some professionals note that some of the ingredient ratings on various websites may not be entirely accurate due to studies that do not address skin care directly, or from data gaps, so it is advisable to use more than one source when doing research.

Chemical Exposure

Statistics on cancer and illnesses from chemicals and environmental exposure are sometimes difficult to substantiate. Toxins are found in our consumables, food, air, and water. Not only does this affect our health, it has financial implications in the form of health care costs and environmental damage.

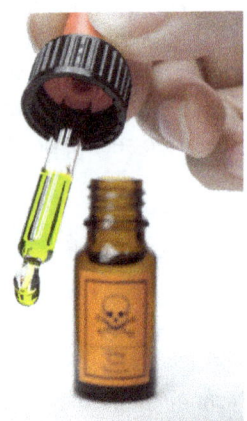

Effects from chemicals depend on the dosage amount and length of exposure. An average of 200 toxic chemicals are found in the body (Figure 8-3). According to EWG, "Babies are born with up to 300 chemicals detected in their bodies. Parabens and phthalates are found in babies and teens" (2011). This evidence suggests the need for stronger federal regulations on chemicals in products, food, plastics, and other goods.

Another point in favor of using fewer chemicals and drugs is that "what goes into the body gets flushed out through the sewer and wastewater treatments and eventually into the water supply. This discharge goes into streams and oceans, and is reclaimed for drinking water. These chemicals and drugs cannot be filtered out and end up in our food and our bodies. Proper disposal of unused drugs helps keep some of them out of the water. Birth control pills and hormones are just a few examples of what we may unknowingly be ingesting through the water supply" (ewg.org 2011).

Figure 8-3: An average of 200 toxic chemicals are found in the body.

Toxic Chemicals in Our Personal Care Products

The Environmental Working Group's (EWG) research states that "22 percent of all personal care products, including those made for children, may contain the cancer-causing contaminant 1,4-dioxane. More than half of all sunscreens contain oxybenzone, a potential hormone disruptor. Other studies have raised serious concerns about lead in lipsticks, secret chemicals in fragrance, and artificial preservatives in products" (2011).

The Campaign for Safe Cosmetics partner, EWG, analyzed cosmetics and personal care ingredients against databases of hazardous chemicals and found that "more than 1 in 5 personal care products contain chemicals linked to cancer. Eighty percent contain ingredients that commonly contain hazardous impurities and 56 percent contain penetration enhancers that help deliver ingredients deeper into the skin. An average consumer may use 25 different cosmetic and personal care products each day, according to industry estimates. This can add up to more than 200 different chemicals applied daily. Legally, the term cosmetic refers to any products you apply that are not drugs. Shampoo, conditioner, deodorant, soap, sunscreen, lip balm, and hand lotion are all cosmetics. Yet almost 90% of the 10,500 ingredients used in our personal care products have never been evaluated for safety in the US" (safecosmetics.org 2011).

> There are over 85,000 synthetic chemicals in the US. Over 80% of these chemicals are not tested (ewg.org 2011).

Changing the existing manufacturing mindset and infrastructure seems just about impossible in avoiding all of these chemicals. As noted by EWG, "you may be giving your clients a free gift of a complimentary dose of toxic chemicals with some products." For instance, nail products contain harsh chemicals such as toluene, dibutyl phthalate, formaldehyde, solvents, and acrylic polymers. Another valid point from consumer advocates is *pinkwashing*: selling products that may be unhealthy to support cancer awareness and research. Make sure your "pink" retail items are healthy. The burden of environmentally induced cancer and illnesses should not be underestimated (ewg.org 2011).

> The *Story of Cosmetics* video advocates healthy product ingredients and is available on www.storyofstuff.com.

Controversial Ingredients

Controversial ingredients used in products include sodium lauryl sulfate, parabens and other preservatives, synthetic color agents, nanoparticles, and phthalates (plasticizers). Accutane and hydroquinone are also controversial. Scientific research and testing continues to determine potential side effects from using certain chemicals. Some concerns are valid, while others are not yet proven. There are many rumors and incorrect information on the Internet. Professionals and consumers need to research and verify facts from reliable sources to determine what the real concerns are.

Phthalates

Phthalates are "a family of industrial chemicals used as plasticizers, additives in cosmetics, fragrances, toys, automotive products, PVC products, and many other items….Recent studies of adults and children in the US have found widespread exposure to phthalates. Phthalates are found in our blood and in breast milk" (ewg.org 2011).

Phthalate Facts:

- A 2003 EU directive banned phthalates in cosmetics sold in Europe.
- Commonly used phthalates in cosmetics are DEP, DBP, and DEHP.
- Nail polishes frequently contain phthalates (usually DBP) to make them non-chip.
- Fragrances often contain DEP. Phthalates are rarely identified in ingredient lists as they are often listed under the catch-all of fragrances.
- Phthalates are endocrine disruptor chemicals (epa.gov 2012).
- Phthalates can impair reproduction and development, alter liver and kidney function, damage the heart and lungs, and affect blood clotting (chemicalbodyburden.org 2012).

Chemicals to avoid include:

- BHT & BHA
- Benzalkonium chloride
- Butylene glycol
- Cetrimonium chloride
- Cocoamidopropyl betaine
- Diazolidinyl urea, Imidazolidinyl urea
- Diethanolamine (DEA), Triethanolamine (TEA), Monoethanolamine (MEA)
- EDTAs (ethylene diamine tetraacetic acid, terasodium EDTA, disodium EDTA)
- Formaldehyde
- Hydroquinone
- DMDM hydantoin
- Lead acetate
- Nanoparticles
- Nonylphenols
- Oxybenzone
- Parabens (methyl, propyl, butyl, and ethyl)
- Petrolatum, petrochemicals
- P-phenylenediamine (PPD)
- Polyethylene glycol (PEG)
- Phthalates
- PVP/VA copolymer
- Quaternium-15
- Silicone derivatives
- Sodium lauryl/laureth sulfate
- Stearalkonium Chloride
- Synthetic colors
- Synthetic fragrances
- Talc
- Toluene
- Triclosan

(Courtesy of EWG 2011)

GREEN CHEMISTRY

The challenges of formulating certified ingredients include the effectiveness and stability of the ingredients. Cost is another issue. The options are limited when using natural fragrances, emulsifiers, and surfactants, but the number of sustainable raw materials is growing. Formulators have access to a wider selection of natural, organic, and fair trade ingredients (Figure 8-4).

Raw material suppliers and certification bodies have guides to assist formulators with ingredient selection and use. Formulation issues in adhering to natural and organic cosmetic standards include prohibited ingredients and chemical

Figure 8-4: Currently, there is a wider selection of natural and organic ingredients available.

processes (organicmonitor.com 2010). Certification is expensive and the process is complex.

GROWING AND HARVESTING INGREDIENTS

Part of being natural and organic is how ingredients are grown. Chemically free from pesticides is the first consideration. *Biodynamically grown* is the highest level of organic due to the soil purity. This integrated and holistic approach uses compost, plants, and animals to nourish the land and maintain a healthy ecology (biodynamics.com 2012). Harvesting methods also need to preserve the purity of the ingredients.

Another point to consider is that the use of sustainable materials can have other consequences. For example, "some natural cosmetic ingredients and bio-plastics such as *Polylactic Acid (PLA)* are made from food crops....Growing and harvesting crops to make beauty products can contribute to food scarcity issues and food cost inflation" (organicmonitor.com 2010). Other issues noted are that GMOs (genetically modified organisms) could be used, and that composting facilities for some materials could be a challenge. PLA is a #7 plastic, so it cannot always be recycled with other plastics.

MANUFACTURING AND SOURCING

The manufacturing process starts with buying and extracting raw materials. Manufacturing, transporting, and shipping uses energy, water, and other resources. Spas can partner with suppliers who are conscious of the effects of resource use and try to minimize these effects. Cleaner manufacturing processes and fair trade sourcing are part of sustainable practices.

Fair Trade

Fair trade is about social equity and paying people a decent wage for products we purchase (Figure 8-5). Some workers in underdeveloped, poor countries are not paid a living wage and fair trade goods address this issue. Ingredients grown and harvested by people who are paid a decent wage are labeled fair trade. This industry is growing with expanded fair trade certification standards.

PACKAGING

There are efforts to reduce packaging and make products in greener wrappings (Figure 8-6). Packaging for products wastes tons of resources. Trying to open packages sealed in plastic is frustrating and makes one wonder why it is so wastefully packaged and so difficult to unwrap. For salons/spas, reducing samples and single use sizes saves resources and costs. Ask suppliers and manufacturers to use greener packaging and shipping methods.

Figure 8-5: Fair trade is about social equity and paying people a decent wage.

Wildcrafting is a tradition of "collecting plant materials in their natural habitat for food, medicine, and craft. People harvest such things as moss, ginseng and other medicinals, natural dyes, mushrooms, wild roses, and berries" (wildcrafting.com 2012). Ingredients for an assortment of organic personal care products are wildcrafted.

Figure 8-6: There are efforts to reduce packaging and make products in greener wrappings.

Packaging companies are providing lighter weight options made of recyclable materials, PCR plastics, glass, biopolymers, and bamboo. One example of reducing packaging is that companies "have saved tons of paper by simply printing instructions on the inside of packaging instead of leaflets. One company, Lush, sells 55% of its products with no packaging at all. Aveda uses PET (polyethylene terephthalate) bottles made of 100% Post-Consumer Regrind (PCR) content" (organicmonitor.com 2010).

> **Truth and integrity:**
> Remember, transparency and authenticity are key points in keeping it real.

VENDOR RELATIONSHIPS

Building a relationship with vendors/suppliers who use sustainable practices is an important part of purchasing (Figure 8-7). Many companies are now requesting their suppliers to use certain practices, such as recycled packaging and shipping containers. Questions to ask vendors are included in Chapter 10.

Replacing plastic with glass or recycled-content packaging is a positive step in the industry. Some buyers now want to know how responsibly products are manufactured and how toxic the chemicals are in producing our goods. In addition to the product's contents, vendor operations and certifications are being assessed and documented. Remember, transparency and authenticity are key points.

Figure 8-7: Building a relationship with vendors/suppliers who use sustainable practices is an important part of purchasing.

Vendors may not meet all the requirements or have answers to all the questions, but knowing the answers to share with your clients shows you have done your homework and research. It is perfectly acceptable to say I don't know but I will find out. Distributors can answer customers' questions and help research green products.

SPA SPOTLIGHT

GLEN IVY HOT SPRINGS
Green is a way of life at Glen Ivy: Sustaining the land and a promoting a natural lifestyle for generations.

Name: Jim Root, CEO/President (2012)

Glen Ivy Hot Springs
25000 Glen Ivy Road, Corona, CA 92883

www.glenivy.com

Property size: 82 acres

Number of employees: 450

Guests: The Hot Springs (plus the day spa in another location) saw 240K guests in 2011.

Number of treatment rooms: 77 at Glen Ivy Hot Springs

Established: Commercially established in 1860; historical operation is 152 years old, current operation is 35 years old. "Elevating life experience since 1860."

Property Description
17-plus acres with natural hot springs as part of an 82-acre parcel.

 ## SPA GOALS AND VISION

What is your green business mission statement?
Our philosophy is practical sustainability. What we do today affects where we are tomorrow. It's a path and needs to be attainable. Money dilutes the conversation. Spas have lost their authenticity. Organizations should embrace more thoughtful leadership responsibility. It's a responsibility to nurture and give a sense of welcoming to all people. Authenticity is the most important aspect of the spa. The magic is based on people. Sustainability goes far beyond measures. It's about people, culture, and connection. The company's mission statement is to inspire memorable, meaningful, and enjoyable experiences in everyone, every day. We are educating a lifestyle.

What is your spa image?
Stewards of the land and hot springs: "Nature's day spa." As stewards of the land, it grows and evolves over time. Our image transitions with change and clientele from the magic feeling from the experiences. It's not about image, but where we will be in the future. Health, fitness, and well-being is part of a lifestyle to take home with you. Glen Ivy is a place to come home to.

> "Sustainability is a lifestyle, not a strategy."
> ~ Jim Root, CEO,
> Glen Ivy Hot Springs

There is a spiritual facet to a spa lifestyle: A sense of community, a connection with nature, exercise, sharing of good food, the healing power of touch, a sense of spiritual renewal, and an expansion of knowledge all encompass the ideal spa lifestyle. Discovery and trying new things with a feeling of emotional safety and security where one can let their veil down is part of what the spa offers. A spa "buffet" or spectrum of lifestyle choices is available, holding new opportunities in each visit. Part of the spa stewardship is embracing the three R's of the spa: renew, refresh, and rejoice.

What are your sustainability goals?
Initiating more alternative energy sources; for example, solar power installation on covered parking lots. However, cost is always a consideration. Other goals are to eliminate invasive plant species and ecological restoration; to use greywater for irrigation and find new ways to reuse water; and improve water conservation efforts—comprehensive analysis of water usage and conservation possibilities.

What is important to you regarding sustainability?
The spa lifestyle itself has to be sustainable to be carried through consistently; it's not just a personal endeavor but proves that we're all connected to each other, to nature. It's our responsibility to seek ways to support those connections for future generations. The education component of spa as a lifestyle is something we support and nurture in our daily operations, communications and programs—not just for our employees and guests, but also the larger community.

What business practices or areas would you like to make more sustainable?
Glen Ivy's history is deeply rooted in the importance of a sacred location at the base of the Santa Ana Mountains, which is one of the last intact coastal ecosystems in Southern California. Before the spa became a commercial operation, Native Americans gathered here, as a place of peace, healing, and refuge. Understanding the importance of this special place inspires our stewardship of the land, carrying on the tradition.

As water has been the very unique resource drawing people here, our focus is to continually finding new ways to improve water conservation, such as greywater for irrigation and using drought tolerant plants. Any surface water drainage is channeled to a series of catch basins and wetlands where it is naturally filtered and allowed to recharge the groundwater basin/aquifer.

What are the challenges in being green?
Cost efficiency with limited resources.

Is the staff interested in greening the facility?
S.E.E.D. is Glen Ivy's employee volunteer group committed to Sustaining Earth's Environment Daily, the energy behind many of Glen Ivy's green initiatives. The container recycling program is all staff volunteers. Money from these efforts is pooled to provide a company-wide sustainability fair to further promote eco-efforts to all employees.

What business practices do you think your clients want to see with regard to sustainability?
Carrying reusable tumblers throughout the day for beverages, recycling, and reusing of brochures throughout the spa, and opting for online information versus printed and mailed collateral. Additionally, guests appreciate that our cuisine is made with local, seasonal produce, supporting local farmers and communities and reducing transportation costs. Composting practices reduce food waste and support horticulture and garden efforts.

Because Glen Ivy is about more than just the business of being a spa, but concentrated on promoting an integrated, healthy spa lifestyle, our guests understand the positive benefits of our actions, strengthening guest loyalty and engagement. Our ongoing guest programming provides an educational component where participants can learn more about sustainable practices and connect with nature through classes and activities like Container Gardening, Water Wise Gardening, Farm-to-Table Cooking Classes, and the Botanical Garden Tour.

Have you seen any positive effects from green practices you have implemented?

Even though the sustainable practices are not promoted loudly, the recommitment to values and priorities of sustainable practices is felt. The spa measures on a global scale, not by specific returns on investments. If it's the right thing to do, they do it without focusing on specific paybacks. The benefits come through the increased guest satisfaction and visits. The Hot Springs sees 850 guests per day. An interesting point is that the seasons bring different guests who expect different experiences. Managing the guest experience can be challenging and the spa is flexible in showing different facets that attract different guests. Some are celebrating life, while others are getting away from it all.

The spa has seen an increase in guests from 140K in 2007 to over 193K in 2010 that we can attribute to these values and a sustainable business. In 2011 and beyond, a purposeful initiative to reduce imprints and provide personalized connections and strengthen authentic experiences has led us to explore options with optimal occupancy, which balances business needs and responsible stewardship.

What positive benefits do you offer your staff? (health, wellness, incentives)

Full benefits and use of the premises including all program activities (yoga, tai chi, stretch, hooping, and aqua aerobics). We have healthcare benefits and a wellness rewards program. A company culture that promotes learning, growing, exploring, and community.

For example, the Landscaping and Sustainability Team cares for 13 chickens near their office, which employees are free to visit—quick walks to see the chickens promote the opportunity for employees to step away from their desks, get out of the office, and really connect with nature. The eggs produced are free and available for any employee to take home. The chickens are put to work, too; "chicken tractors" are sometimes used over a small plot of land to keep chickens in the area—turning the soil with their feet, eating weeds and fertilizing the area for future planting. Working gardens around the property provide other education and exploration opportunities for guests and employees alike. The harvests of these gardens are shared with employees and guests.

How do you promote your green practices?

Website, blogs, marketing messaging.

 SPA ELEMENTS

The Menu

- The menu is not specifically green, but the whole practice is looked at sustainably, including natural products, local printing services, and the environment.
- The revised menu in 2011 is reflective of this process with considerable edits to reduce the size of the menu and using a local printing company.

Products

- Body Bliss—providing organic, ethically wildcrafted or ecologically sensible essential oils and extracts for body treatments and massage therapy.
- Primavera—a natural, organic skin care with a vision and operation based on the integrity of sustainable practices and natural resources.

Packaging
- We look for less packaging, vendors of like-minded practices.

Energy
- Timers, audits, and CFLs are used.
- Building a small straw bale structure in late 2012.
- All new decking is made from recycled plastic.
- Wood is all certified non-old growth.

Water
- The water management practices are all about reinvigorating the land and habitat renewal. Water is recycled from the springs.
- Greywater is used for the habitat and irrigation.
- A series of reclamation ponds supports wildlife such as deer and many other animals.
- All water comes from on-site wells that Glen Ivy manages.
- Fresh well water is altered only to meet standards of health and safety.
- Glen Ivy well water is used throughout the spa and in the adjacent community.

Green Materials
- It's a historic facility, but any renovations use green materials for paint, carpet, air quality, etc.

Indoor Environmental Quality (IEQ)
- Cleaning supplies are biodegradable; products are mandated in the cleaning company's contract.

Purchasing
- We look for like-minded vendors who are making efforts and it's important to build a good relationship with them.
- Use consolidated vendors to reduce carbon emissions from delivery trucks.

Waste Reduction
- All typical recyclables are sorted and recycled.
- Eliminated Styrofoam and plastic utensils and cups as much as possible.
- Paperless paychecks and other company-wide initiatives to show that each person can make a huge difference in adding up the efforts. Not only time and materials saved on printing and distributing, but less paper waste and consumption.
- Composting: the compost is used in the gardens and landscaping.

Landscaping, Exteriors
- The spa has a Director of Landscaping and Sustainability.
- Drought tolerant and native species used in landscape design polishes the transition between the spa grounds and the natural surrounding landscapes.

- **Plants:** Native species; many plants are grown on-site.
- **Water:** Greywater, xeriscaping.
- **Chemicals:** Organic.
- **Compost:** Compost all of our green waste—tree trimmings, grass clippings used in planter beds.
- **Worm farm:** 10,000–12,000 worms that eat scraps from the café, providing nutrient-rich soil combined with compost from green waste and chicken manure for vegetable gardening soil.

Wildlife
- 150+ bird species, habitat.
- 13 heirloom chickens and about to grow to include goats and turkeys.
- Shared environment with animals—including mountain lions, bobcats, raccoons, skunks, possums, coyotes, snakes, and lizards.

Transportation
- Priority parking spots for carpoolers; supports California carpool transport initiatives.

Food Service and Gardens
- Glen Ivy Organic Farm is a certified organic farm on the edge of the spa.
- Organic avocado and orange grove; organic vegetable gardens.
- An effort put toward using and preserving rare and unique species of plants from around the world.

Marketing
- Mainly it's about the mission and lifestyle. Social media is used to create a sense of community and values.

People
- The use of the facility benefits the staff.
- There are staff trash pickups, a green festival with presentations for employees, and a sustainability page is from employee ideas.
- There is a non-smoking policy for the whole spa property.
- The Employee Services, Development, and Opportunity Department is not the typical human resources department.
- Community: support about 400 different organizations from youth to education charities. Access to Glen Ivy is part of the donations.
- Carpooling is a corporate initiative.

Education
- One of the many programs offered is "How to be Indigenous for a Day." This includes working with clay and learning about the plants and sustenance used by Native Americans. Tours include the Botanical Gardens of Glen Ivy, showing both tropical and arid environments found on the land. Class topics have included Container Gardening, Water Wise Gardening, Wilderness and Wildfire.
- A bird guide is available to guests interested in education on wildlife and the spa is located in an *ecotone* (adjacent ecosystems). There is a full program of classes, workshops and retreats.

CHAPTER 9

Product Standards and Regulations

INTRODUCTION

Product certifications for natural and organic products are constantly emerging and changing. While well-regarded organizations are implementing new standards, companies and marketers are coming up with their own standards and certifications. Jumping on the green bandwagon is common practice and product Greenwashing will always occur. Hopefully, consumers will take a closer look at these claims, but it is hard to separate facts from fiction.

The main personal care product certifications are discussed here, but it is a maze and a moving target. There are various international labeling and third-party certifications for organic products. Other types of ecolabels and certifications are included in Chapter 11, Purchasing and Green Materials. Green products and choices are discussed in Chapters 8 and 10.

WORDS OF WISDOM

As the demand for natural and organic products grew, so did the number of brands, manufacturers, and suppliers, which led to an increasingly complex, less accountable marketplace. Today, ingredients are sourced from multiple manufacturers, in multiple countries with multiple standards, making a third-party regulatory standard body essential. Third-party certification standards level the playing field by ensuring products are what they say they are, and that the language communicating claims is clear, consistent, and correct.

~ Mark Wuttke, Principal, Wuttke Group,
www.wuttkegroup.com

NATURAL AND ORGANIC STANDARDS

The terms *natural* and *organic* are often used in referring to skin product ingredients, but some say these terms have no singular or regulated definition. The FDA regulates US food labels and certifications, but skin care labels are not yet regulated for these terms. Other descriptive terms applied to products are discussed in the Greenwashing section of Chapter 21, Marketing Green.

"Several brands are already using the words *organic* and *natural* in their company name and in their marketing to imply to consumers that they are organic and natural, when actually they may be Greenwashing" (greenspanetwork.org 2010). So how do we verify the green aspects of the products we sell? Third-party independent certification is the most acceptable way to validate claims. The number of natural and organic cosmetic standards and certifications is growing regionally and globally, but many countries do not have specific regulations. This leads to divided standards, rather than one global or national standard. Consumers, businesses, manufacturers, and ingredient companies are all trying to wade through the maze of differences between these standards. Some standards are technical and difficult to attain, while others are perhaps too easy to obtain.

It can be a complicated and expensive process to obtain one of the more stringent certifications. Small companies are not able to compete if they cannot afford the rigorous testing of strict organic certification guidelines even though their products may be organic. So don't rule out small product lines without certificates or accept large companies' claims specifically based on their own dubious certifications.

Companies that supply certified ingredients, as well as formulators and manufacturers of products, can each become certified. Standards are based on the formulation and ingredient requirements. Certain preservative systems and prohibited ingredient lists are part of certification requirements. Additionally, processing, growing, and harvesting are all specified in many of the guidelines. The standards are being continually assessed. Certification agencies are fighting for territory in Europe and North America. This increasing proliferation in the number of seals and logos causes confusion in assessing certified products. Certification standards need to be transparent and traceable.

> Ingredient lists on personal care products must include specific terminology to describe the contents, which is the *INCI (International Nomenclature of Cosmetic Ingredients)* standard.

Federal product regulations are needed for consumers' health and safety. Unfortunately, cosmetics are not regulated in the US. Consumer rights groups are pushing the FDA and EPA for increased standards. There is a movement pushing to regulate the thousands of chemicals in the US. In this country, ingredients are innocent until proven guilty. Only 20% of chemicals out of thousands have been researched in the US. Conversely, in some countries in Europe, ingredients are guilty until proven innocent. The European Union has stated that chemicals do not belong in cosmetics and has banned over 1100 chemicals (ec.europa.eu 2012). In contrast, the FDA has only banned 11 chemicals in cosmetics as of 2010 (safecosmetics.org 2012).

> Using a *precautionary principle* is a good method to determine if a product is harmful. This means that "if an action has a suspected risk of causing harm to the public or to the environment, in the absence of scientific consensus that the action is harmful, the burden of proof that it is not harmful falls on those taking the action." (wikipedia.com 2012) Being cautious and avoiding a substance, rather than waiting 20 years to see if a chemical causes health problems, is perhaps a safer approach.

Health and Beauty Product Standards include the following:

- **ANSI 305** (American National Standards Institute): ansi.org
- **BDIH**: kontrollierte-naturkosmetik.de/
- **CosmeBio**: cosmebio.org
- **COSMOS**: cosmos-standard.org
- **EcoCert**: ecocert.com
- **EcoControl**: eco-control.com
- **Green Seal**: greenseal.org.
- **ICEA**: icea.info
- **Natrue**: natrue.eu
- **NPA** (The Natural Products Association): npainfo.org
- **NSF** (National Sanitation Foundation): nsf.org
- **OASIS** (Organic and Sustainability Industry Standards): oasisseal.org
- **Oregon Tilth**: tilth.org
- **Soil Association**: soilassociation.org
- **USDA NOP** (Natural Organic Program): usda.gov

CERTIFICATIONS AND ECOLABELS

Several European bodies have certification options that specialize in skin and body care product standards. French-based *EcoCert* and UK-based *Soil Association* have organic certification. German-based *BDIH* has natural certification and *Natrue* has organic certification. *EcoControl* is a certification for brands that want to set their own standards. According to Mark Wuttke, brands are trying to differentiate themselves in the highly competitive and crowded marketplace (2011) (Figure 9-1).

Figure 9-1: Brands are trying to differentiate themselves in the highly competitive marketplace.

In an effort to standardize natural and organic, the five leading European certification groups BDIH, Soil Association, EcoCert, CosmeBio, and ICEA are coming together under *COSMOS*, hoping to create a unified European standard (cosmos-standard.org 2012). Standards are mainly adopted on a national basis. In Europe, the Soil Association standard is common in the UK, ICEA in Italy, Cosmebio in France, and BDIH in Germany. EcoCert originated in France and is becoming one of the main standards globally (organicmonitor.com 2011).

US standards include *USDA, ANSI 305* and *Oregon Tilth*. As of 2012, *Natrue* and *NSF ANSI* are expected to merge in North America. The *NPA* (Natural Products Association) for natural products is also a major standard in the US. *Whole Foods* new guidelines for personal care products impacted the industry in 2010 with stricter requirements, prompting companies to pursue additional certification.

The nonprofit organization *Green Seal Inc.* has created "GS-50, reportedly the first US certification standard for cosmetic and personal care products that covers the whole product life cycle" (greenseal.org 2011). The not-for-profit organizations have higher standards than the for-profit organizations. It is also good to be aware that some product lines have certification for some of their products, but not others. Some certifications consider water as part of their specified natural or organic content, where others, such as Natrue, do not calculate water as a percentage of their natural ingredients. Including water as part of the natural or organic content skews the actual percentage amounts.

The standards can be complex, but it is helpful to be familiar with the different standards and the criteria used to determine a natural or organic product. It is predicted that in the future, all consumer brands and products will have an associated sustainability value and a set of standards. Find additional information on standard specifications and useful lists of ingredients on the various certification websites.

> An *ecological product* is generally made from plant material, excluding organic chemical derivatives. It is manufactured so as not to be harmful to the environment or its users" (ecocert.com 2012).

> *REACH* is the "European Community Regulation on chemicals and their safe use. It deals with the Registration, Evaluation, Authorisation and Restriction of Chemical substances." REACH has a database of safe and unsafe ingredients. According to the standards, ingredients must be removed, diluted, or proven safe (ec.europa.eu. 2012).

National Organic Program (NOP)

The National Organic Program is designed for organic agricultural food products. NOP's "applicability to non-food products" such as skin care is still very limited. As of 2012, the USDA program has been working to adopt ANSI standards.

Quality Assurance International (QAI)

Quality Assurance International (QAI) is a "USDA-accredited certifying agency (ACA), approved to provide organic certification in accordance with the USDA's National Organic Program." QAI also certifies the NSF/ANSI 305 standard for personal care products that contain organic ingredients, a standard considered a best practice by the Organic Trade Association (qai-inc.com 2012).

Oregon Tilth (OTCO)

Oregon Tilth Certified Organic (OTCO) certifies for a number of standards, including the USDA national organic program, NSF/ANSI 305, and the Global Organic Textile Standard (GOTS). See tilth.org (2012).

Natural and organic cosmetic standards are featured at the Sustainable Cosmetics Summits hosted by Organic Monitor. Check out sustainablecosmeticssummit.com.

SPA SPOTLIGHT

NATURAL BODY SPA AND SHOP
A multi-award-winning day spa with 16 locations throughout the Southeast and Midwest.

Contact: Cici Coffee, CEO (2012)
Natural Body
1145 Zonolite RD. Suite 9 Atlanta, Ga
www.naturalbody.com
Facility size: 16 locations
Number of employees: 400
Number of treatment rooms: 195
Established in: 1989

Facility Description
Natural Body holds the first LEED Platinum Day Spa, first Platinum Nail Bars and one of the first of 3 freestanding Platinum retail stores in the country. The Atlanta location in Brookhaven features both a full-service Natural Body Spa and Shop as well as the company's newest concept, 10TEN Nail Bar. Built in 2008, the spa has been awarded Platinum-certification under the US Green Building Council's LEED (Leadership in Energy and Environmental Design) program. This is the first spa in the country constructed and designed in accordance with the highest level of LEED specifications.

Natural Body Spa and Shop is a full-service green day spa and is dedicated to environmental stewardship in each spa location and in business and spa practices. Spa services include massage, facials, body therapies, and signature spa packages for both women and men. Locations carry aromatherapy, skin, hair, and body care products, and home spa products.

SPA GOALS AND VISION

What is your green business mission statement?
Natural Body is dedicated to environmental stewardship. This is always a key component in the planning, building, design, and daily operations of each Natural Body Spa and Shop, as the company focuses on reducing the environmental impact of its operations while educating both its employees and guests.

What is your spa image?
We provide a nurturing and educational environment offering holistic spa services and products.

What are your sustainability goals?
Reducing our impact on the earth is always at the forefront of our thoughts when designing a new spa location.

What is important to you regarding sustainability?
That we challenge ourselves to be disciplined about decisions and make choices that will last.

What business practices or areas would you like to make more sustainable?
The health of our employees.

What are the challenges in being green?
Getting 100 percent of our staff and those who service our company to buy into the cause.

Is the staff interested in greening the facility?
Most of them appreciate the company philosophy.

What business practices do you think your clients want to see with regard to sustainability?
That they don't need to read labels or vet a company and that we do it for them.

Have you seen any positive effects from green practices you have implemented?
The most exciting was lowering our energy bills during the recession because of LEED construction and energy audits.

What positive benefits do you offer your staff? (health, wellness, incentives)
Medical, wellness days, company gatherings, and competitive wages.

Do you promote your green practices?
Only more recently. After running our business by treading lightly on the environment for 23 years we thought it was old news.

SPA ELEMENTS

The Menu
- We focus on organic certifications for most of the back bar products.
- Our menu is printed with soy-based ink and FSC paper; most paper collateral includes post-consumer content.
- We have designed the majority of our services to be performed with proper ergonomics for our staff, reasonable water use, safe air quality, and non-toxic materials.

Products
- We carry 3 major skin care lines: Primavera, Jurlique, and Naturopathica (a botanical-based natural line from the US).
- We also carry Aveda, Jane Iredale, and many Fair Trade and locally made lines of retail products. The Blending Bar features essential oils to custom blend for the ultimate aromatherapy experience.

Supplies
- Our suppliers are required to answer a questionnaire before we purchase from them.

Treatment Supplies
- Linens are chosen for longevity and quick-drying properties.
- Single-use items (cotton, plastic): the goal is to use biodegradable when possible.
- Glass and plastic are recycled.
- *Cleaning:* only safe products, even with the janitorial services.
- Facility supplies are all decided with sustainability in mind.

Facility
- Regional building materials were incorporated into the design of the location, including service room floors crafted of 50% post-industrial materials as well as flooring created from wood reclaimed from a 100-year-old Georgia barn.
- As with all other Natural Body spa locations, recycling is used to remove all recyclable occupant materials.

Energy
- Electrical power will be offset using hydropower credits, a renewable power source.
- Energy-efficient heating and air systems; temperature controls: 7 zones for varying needs and control.
- Ventilation system: High MERV (minimum efficiency reporting values) rated filters with fresh air exchange and heat exchange.

Appliances
- Energy Star appliances such as washer/dryers and refrigerators.

Type of lighting
- Energy-efficient lighting utilizing LED or compact fluorescent light bulbs.

Water
- Low-flow toilets, faucets and showerheads.
- Signature 10TEN alabaster foot basins, which use half the amount of water as standard industry basins.
- Tankless water heaters.
- Non-toxic cleaning supplies and low-impact laundry detergent.

Green Materials and Indoor Environmental Quality (IEQ)
- We utilize sustainable building materials whenever possible.
- Recycled rubber floors in therapy rooms; low-VOC paint; sustainable cabinetry and shelving (bamboo choice has minimal VOC).

Purchasing
- Every decision is made in an effort to reduce, reuse, and rethink.

Waste Reduction
- Recycled paper and soy ink for all collateral materials; recycling programs in all stores.

- The spa newsletter, letterhead, menus, and other collateral are printed with soy ink on recycled paper.
- We contract with outside sources to recycle when landlord does not offer on-site recycling and have been very successful in getting full cooperation with nearby tenants to join us in their own recycling efforts.
- On our last build-out we were recognized for recycling 98% of our construction waste.

Transportation
- The Brookhaven center is in a high-density, mixed-use development, chosen specifically for its proximity to a wide variety of resources such as mass transit, shopping amenities, and green space.

Marketing: Yes, we market our green features.

People
- Employee donation program for Earth Share—won "Rookie of the Year" in Atlanta for high employee participation in 2006.

Education
- A founding member of the Green Spa Network.
- Education has always been our mission.

> ### Brookhaven Post-Occupancy Savings
> The Brookhaven location has just paid off the LEED certification cost of going Platinum in its 24th month of operations through energy savings. We save 13 cents per square foot compared to one of our older stores, which amounts to $751.66 dollars a month. When you multiply that by 24 months, at $18,039.84 you fully cover the cost of the LED's, more fresh air, and a seven-zoned HVAC system (extra zones only).
>
> The massage therapists and estheticians have control of the temperature, nail techs and retail specialists all have their own temperature within reason, and Natural Body doesn't have these wide swings in temperature depending on who is in the driver's seat.
>
> The last and most important note shared by Natural Body is the happiness indicator reported from the last post-occupant survey to their team. The results indicated that the staff was much happier in the Brookhaven space because of the natural lighting, fresh air, and low/no VOC's. They reported fewer sick days and overall better health.

CHAPTER 10

Choosing Products and Ingredients for the Spa

INTRODUCTION

What specific ingredients do you look for in natural or organic products? Now that green products and certifications have been introduced in previous chapters, this section focuses on product choices and ingredients. Products are organized by categories: hair, nails, skin, body, and makeup/cosmetics. You can also evaluate other retail items for green factors. Avoiding certain chemicals and using healthy ingredients are the main goals in choosing products. Natural, organic products support the spa patrons' focus on a healthier lifestyle.

Organic Monitor research reports that the market for natural and organic personal care products sales in North American exceeded US $5 billion in 2010. The market share of natural and organic products is forecast to be over 10% of personal care product sales in the coming years. Distribution of over 600 different brands is expanding in drugstores and other large retailers (organicmonitor.com 2011).

According to statistics, many consumers agree it is difficult to differentiate between brands that are organic and those that are not. One idea to help avoid confusion is to label cosmetics in a manner similar to food. A "Nutritional Facts" label would help consumers find healthy, ethically grown, chemically clean brands (greenspanetwork.org 2011). For example, the *Timberland* brand instituted something similar for their products. It is important to be as clear as possible on the product features and brands you sell. Third party certification and labeling helps distinguish brands. Simple, clear labeling on packaging is recommended for retail products.

WORDS OF WISDOM

To do any business well, the primary objective must be to make things better–better for people, better for the environment, just find a better way. If you are not sure if you can make things better, then tread lightly, making as little impact as possible.

~ Marianne Griffeth, President and chief chemist at
Prima Fleur Botanicals, www.primafleur.com

CHOOSING GREEN PRODUCTS AND INGREDIENTS

Deciding what product lines to use and retail can be one of the biggest business decisions a spa owner or director can make. The product line and retail sales affect the success of the business. If the staff likes the product and uses it at home, it will be preferred in treatments. It will also be easier to promote and sell.

Product choices are part of your business branding and image (Figure 10-1). These will blend in with the theme of your spa/salon and partly determine your service protocols. Conduct a marketing analysis

Figure 10-1: Product choices are part of your business branding and image.

that includes demographics, local competitors, and price points to help determine which products and retail items to carry. If you already have your product lines in house, evaluate potential authentic green selling points and marketing avenues for your current lines.

Changing brands/lines is expensive and time consuming, but if a line is not selling, you will want to transition over to a new one. If you want to add a green product, make sure it is something your client base wants and that the technicians who work with the product will like it. For marketing, emphasize the healthy features to build interest in the new products. Another consideration is if the manufacturer is going to be around in ten years, or if it is trendy and too new to forecast its longevity.

How green are your products?

Product Criteria

What criteria are important to you in choosing products? Of course, the performance and desired results for any product are crucial. In addition to the basic factors such as ingredients and cost, add green aspects to the list of your considerations.

Ingredient and product technology is an area demanding continual attention and review, but it is also one of the most interesting aspects of the industry. There are countless personal care ingredients and hundreds of product lines. Researching the different product options will help spa directors and technicians become familiar with these choices.

When choosing a skin care or other type of product line, consider the following points:
- What are the green features and ingredients?
- Are the ingredients high quality and beneficial?
- Does the line have performance ingredients and achieve results?
- Are the products versatile—that is, effective for all skin or hair types?
- Is the wholesale cost and the retail pricing affordable?
- Is the product name recognizable and reputable? Many clients choose a product based on its name and how it is marketed.
- Another option is choosing a product for exclusivity or uniqueness. Is private label a good choice?
- Do local competitors carry the same line? Do you want something different?
- How are the products packaged?
- What preservatives or fragrances are used?
- What can clients in your area afford?
- What support can you anticipate from the company or supplier? The costs of samples and brochures, return policies, and marketing promotions affect your business.
- What educational opportunities and training are provided by the supplier? These can help you become more knowledgeable and successful.

(Lotz 2012)

Product Prices and Costs

Pricing and costs of products are considerations for both you and your client. Product costs can be high, so choose wisely. Let your client know why green professional products available only from spas and salons cost more than those they can purchase over the counter. When comparing prices, evaluate the quality of the ingredients and the concentration of performance ingredients (Figure 10-2). Comparing skin care lines helps determine what your clientele prefer and can afford (Lotz 2012).

Figure 10-2: When comparing prices, evaluate the quality of the ingredients in the products.

Products and Retailing

A good way to determine product cost is to break down the costs into daily or weekly amounts. This gives salons and clients a better idea of how affordable the product is and how much they are spending on the recommended products. For skin care, this is usually not more than a cup of coffee per day. This is a very good price for maintaining beautiful skin.

How much would it cost for your product line? For example, add the product costs and figure out the total cost per day for three products (at $50.00 each). Use the cost divided by how long the product lasts (6 months), then divide the total product cost ($150) by the number of days ($150 divided by 180 days). This is only 83 cents per day! Another good point is that, just like exercise and dental care, skin needs daily care to maintain it. You can adapt this selling point to hair products and other retail items (Lotz 2012).

GREEN CRITERIA FOR PRODUCTS

In addition to the general considerations, the following criteria help to analyze products and vendors. Suppliers will also benefit from evaluating their own products and having the answers to these questions.

Questions to ask suppliers:
- May I have a complete ingredient list for each product? (active and inactive ingredients)
- What are the preservatives?
- Where does your company source raw materials and ingredients?
- Does your company offer fair trade products?
- Does your company have third-party certification? If so, is it for all products or just a few?
- What are your operations and green practices?
- What types of packaging does your company use?
- Do you have information on your manufacturing processes?

If you wanted to take it one step further, additional questions could be:
- What is your company's ecological footprint?
- Does your company use carbon offsetting?
- Does your company have a corporate social responsibility program?
- Does your company support or give a percentage of revenue and/or profit to charities?

Table 10-1: Make a copy of the chart, or create your own and fill in the blanks while researching different products.

TABLE 10-1 CHART FOR COMPARING AND RATING PRODUCTS						
Product Line/ Manufacturer	**Face** (see example below)	**Body**	**Hair**	**Hands/ Feet/Nails**	**Makeup**	**Waxing**
Green Features	Yes					
Main Ingredients: Natural, Organic	Yes					
Cost; Affordability	Average, $50					
Quality	Good					
Chemistry; Manufacturing	No Info					
Sourcing; Raw Materials; Fair Trade	Organic					
Operations & LCA	CSR, tbd					
Green Packaging	Recycled Content					
Certification	EcoCert					
Marketing, Support, Education	Some					
Green Rating*	9					

* **Rating Scales:**
  A: Use 1–5: 1 = not green; 2 = minimal green; 3 = light green; 4 = medium green, 5 = dark green.
  B: Use 1–5: Rate 1 if it meets one of the green criteria; Rate 5 if it meets 5 of the criteria.
  C: Alternatively, use your own customized rating system such as excellent, good, fair, or poor; or check yes or no. Expand the table to make specific notes for each category.

Top 10 Greenwashing Words

1. *Made with…*—could mean made with as little as 1% or 1 drop.
2. *Organic*—many brands say organic but contain few or no organic ingredients.
3. *Natural*—can give the illusion the product is "of nature" when it's not.
4. *Certified Green*—by whom?
5. *Free of…*—it may claim to have no parabens but substitutes phenoxethanol.
6. *Derived from*—some byproducts require use of carcinogenic chemicals for extraction.
7. *Nontoxic*—by which standards?
8. *Allergy-Friendly Fragrance, Fragrance-Free*—may still contain artificial coloring or fragrances used to cover up the chemical smell of other ingredients.
9. *Dermatologist Tested, Sensitivity Tested, Hypoallergenic*—by whom?
10. *Environmentally Friendly, Eco-safe*—these phrases are too vague to be meaningful to consumers.

(Beth Greer, 2011, Author of Super Natural Home)

PERSONAL CARE INGREDIENTS

Ingredients are derived from a variety of sources including herbs, oils, plants, and synthetic ingredients. There are thousands of personal care ingredients to choose from. Performance ingredients and functional ingredients are combined chemically in many different formulations.

Skin care ingredients are one of the most interesting and complex areas of the beauty industry (Figure 10-3). Products have many benefits and can make a significant difference in the skin's health and appearance. From anti-aging to acne, ingredients define the product effectiveness.

Tables 10-2 through 10-5 include specific ingredients found in products. Chemist Marianne Griffeth of Prima Fleur reviewed and contributed to the tables. Figures 10-4 and 10-5 explain *ethoxylated compounds* and *ethanolamines*.

Figure 10-3: Ingredients are one of the most interesting and complex areas of the beauty industry.

Skin Care Product Categories

Consider client needs when selecting treatments and home-care products.

TABLE 10-2 SKIN CARE PRODUCT INGREDIENTS		
Skin Care Products	**Preferred Natural / Organic Ingredients**	**Main Synthetic Ingredients To Avoid or Examine/Research**
Cleansers	sodium lauroyl glutamate, sodium cocoyl glutamate, coco glucoside, Sapindus mukurossi fruit extract, sodium lauryl glucoside, sodium cocoyl glucoside	sodium lauryl sulfate, ammonium lauryl sulfate, ethoxylated compounds, cocamidopropyl betaine, lauramidopropyl betaine, ethanolamines and their compounds
Toners/Fresheners	hydrosols (floral waters), herbal extracts in water or glycerin, natural emulsifiers and botanicals	SD alcohol that is not organic, glycols, silicone derivatives, synthetic colorants, synthetic fragrances
Exfoliants	enzymes from pomegranate, apple, pumpkin; sugar, salt, natural AHA (apple, lemon, maple sugar) and BHA (willowbark, aspen bark, lactic acid) extracts, jojoba beads, bamboo silica, botanical powders	natural exfoliants too harsh for the face (e.g., walnut shells, apricot kernels, sea salt) in facial products, synthetic beads (usually listed as polyethylene or polyethylene microbeads), synthetic glycolic acid
Masks	vegetable gels with botanical extracts, hydrosols in clays, or botanical powders	irradiated clays, propylene glycol, butylene glycol, synthetic colorants, synthetic fragrances, formaldehyde donor preservatives, xenoestrogen preservatives
Hydrators and Moisturizers	sodium hyaluronate, Opuntia ficus-indica extract, Pyrus malus (apple) fruit extract, glycerin, plant oils, squalane, jojoba; see antioxidants and lipids	propylene glycol, butylene glycol, isoparaffins, mineral oil, formaldehyde donor preservatives, xenoestrogen preservatives
Serums and Ampoules	natural vegetable oils or water-based botanical extracts such as hydrosols with natural actives in tested, clinically-proven active percentages; see performance ingredients	glycol-based systems with synthetically-derived actives, formaldehyde donor preservatives, xenoestrogen preservatives
Sunscreens	minerals, titanium dioxide, zinc oxide	chemical sunscreens in synthetic bases (e.g., oxybenzone, PABA), nanoparticles
Eye Creams	Crithmum maritimum, hexapeptide 11, Polygonum fagopyrum seed extract, hydrosols, non-ethoxylated emulsifying waxes; see performance ingredients	glycols, petrochemically-processed emulsifiers (e.g., carbomer, triethanolamine), formaldehyde donor preservatives, xenoestrogen preservatives, silicone derivatives, ethoxylated compounds, mineral oil, isoparaffin, iodopropynyl butylcarbamate
Lip Conditioners	shea butter (butyrospermum parkii), olive butter, beeswax (cera alba)	artificial colors, petrolatum, microcrystalline wax, cyclomethicone, oxybenzone

TABLE 10-3 PERFORMANCE INGREDIENTS

Performance Ingredients	Preferred Natural / Organic Ingredients	Main Ingredients To Avoid or Examine
Botanicals	authentic; harvesting in habitat that does not degrade environment, or imbalance ecosystem; naturally processed and in natural carrier media: glycerin, water, vegetable oil. Extracts naturally preserved: high % glycerin, ferment filtrate extracts, sodium benzoate	GMO botanicals, botanicals extracted in glycols, preserved with parabens, phenoxyethanol, other synthetic preservatives
Peptides	hexapeptide 11	synthetics
Antioxidants	olive leaf extract, Pinus pinaster bark extract, white and green tea extracts, rosemary CO_2 extract, super oxide dismutase, ascorbic acid polypeptide (vitamin C), tocopherol (vitamin E), beta carotene (vitamin A)	BHA, BHT, synthetic vitamins
Lipids	Shea butter, kendi oil, plant oils, squalane, jojoba	synthetics
Brighteners	Ascophyllum nodosum extract, bearberry extract, Glycyrrhiza glabra (licorice) root extract, Pancratium maritimum (white lily/sea daffodil) extract, Undaria pinnatifida extract, Dictyopteris membranacea (sea fern/Parfum d'Antee) extract, stonecrop	hydroquinone, kojic acid, chemical treatments that cause harmful inflammation
Enzymes	botanical sources: pomegranate, apple, pumpkin	synthetics
Chemical Exfoliants	naturally derived AHA's and BHA's, vitamin A (retinol)	synthetics
Sunscreens	zinc or titanium dioxide	nanoparticles (i.e., fullerenes, buckyballs), oxybenzone, PABA, retinol palmitate, formaldehyde donor preservatives, xenoestrogen preservatives, iodopropynyl butylcarbamate

TABLE 10-4 FUNCTIONAL INGREDIENTS		
Type of Functional Ingredients	**Preferred Natural or Organic Ingredients**	**Main Ingredients To Avoid or Examine**
Emollients	plant oils, jojoba, almond, sunflower, sesame, coconut, shea butter, cocoa butter, beeswax, squalane	PEG compounds, isoparaffin, silicone derivatives, isopropyl alcohol, mineral oil
Emulsifiers	lecithin, borax/beeswax, acacia gum, plant waxes (e.g., jojoba, carnauba), xanthan gum	carbomer, PEG-100 stearate, sodium lauryl sulfate, polysorbates, triethanolamine, TEA's
Fragrances	essential oils, cold pressed citrus oil, CO_2 botanical extracts	synthetic fragrances—you do not know what you are getting: phthalates, synthetic musks, ethylene oxide, parfum, BHA
Oils	expeller expressed or cold pressed vegetable oils, non-GMO, certified organic such as sunflower, apricot, borage, evening primrose, heliocarrot, sesame, hazelnut, carrot seed, rosehip seed, safflower, sweet almond, kendi/kukui, marula, argan, coconut, Calophyllum inophyllum/tamanu, natural essential oils	solvent extracted oils, mineral oil, GMOs
Preservatives	essential oils, plant-based alcohols, salt, herbal extracts, ascorbic acid, benzyl alcohol, benzoic acid, sorbic acid, potassium sorbate, sodium benzoate, Naticide, dehydroacetic acid, sorbitol, Neopein, Biopein, salicylic acid	parabens, imidazolidinyl urea, diazolidinyl urea, Bronopol, BHA, BHT, DMDM hydantoin, SD alcohol, hexachlorophene, methylisothiazolinone, methylchloroisothiazolinone, Germall, iodopropynyl butylcarbamate
Color Agents	annatto, beets, turmeric, carrot, saffron, alkanet, chlorophyll, minerals	D&C dyes, FD&C dyes, aluminum lakes, ultramarines
Solvents	water, ethyl alcohol, plant glycerin, vegetable oil, carbon dioxide	petrochemical solvents, ethyl acetate, butylene glycol, propylene glycol
Surfactants	castile soap, yucca extract, soapwort, soap bark extract, coconut oil derivatives	ethanolamines, ethoxylated compounds, sodium lauryl sulfate, ammonium lauryl sulfate, Quats, petrochemicals
Thickeners	xanthan gum, guar gum, clay minerals, locust bean gum, acacia gum	carbomer, cocamide DEA/MEA, methacrylate copolymers, emulsifying wax NF, isoparaffin
Buffers	sodium bicarbonate, sodium borate (borax)	ethanolamines
Delivery Systems	naturally derived	synthetics

TABLE 10-5 OTHER PERSONAL CARE PRODUCTS

Other Products	Preferred Natural or Organic Ingredients	Main Ingredients To Avoid or Examine
Oils	argan, sweet almond, soy, jojoba (though technically it's a wax), sesame	mineral oil, ethoxylated compounds
Hair Care: Shampoo	vegetable proteins and amino acids, natural humectants like cactus, honey, plant extracts, aloe vera	silicone derivatives, ethanolamines, ethoxylated compounds, xenoestrogen preservatives, diethyl phthalate (DEP), sodium lauryl sulfate, ammonium lauryl sulfate, artificial dyes, polyethylene, iodopropynyl butylcarbamate, methylisothiazolinone, methylchloroisothiazolinone, formaldehyde donor preservatives
Conditioner	vegetable oils, plant extracts for scalp condition, inulin, betaine, honey	Quats are not naturally processed but provide desirable slip, keep to a minimum in products if at all; see other categories
Styling Products	natural gels from corn, vegetable waxes, natural vegetable oils and butters	hair straighteners: formaldehyde; isobutane, iodopropynyl butylcarbamate, formaldehyde donor preservatives, xenoestrogen preservatives, methylisothiazolinone, methylchloroisothiazolinone
Hair Color	natural colors (e.g., henna)	lead acetate, toluene, para-phenylenediamine (PPD), Resorcinol, 1-naphthol
Makeup, Cosmetics	natural pigments and minerals, Naticide	lead, metals, petrolatum, talc, BHA
Nail Products	See similar products	phthalates, toluene, dibutyl phthalate (DBP), formaldehyde, solvents, acrylic polymers
Body Products, Lotions	See similar products	triclosan, ethoxylated compounds, formaldehyde donor preservatives, xenoestrogen preservatives, petrolatum, methylisothiazolinone, methylchloroisothiazolinone, iodopropynyl butylcarbamate
Soap	ethanol, ethyl alcohol, saponified plant oils, essential oils, natural colors	triclocarbon, triclosan, sodium tallowate, artificial dyes, synthetic fragrance

Disclaimer: Please note these tables are only a partial listing of what is available and are by no means complete. There will always be debates over synthetics versus natural ingredients and it is up to the individual to make the decision on acceptable chemical formulations.

Note: Part of this chapter has been adapted from the author's work in chapters from Milady Standard Esthetics Fundamentals, 11th ed. textbook (Gerson, Lotz 2012).

Xenoestrogen ("xeno" is Greek for "foreign") preservatives mimic estrogen and increase cell division, which contributes to the risk of breast cancer (canceractive.com 2012). The following preservatives fall into this category: Alkyl hydroxyl benzoates (methyl-, ethyl-, propyl-, butylparaben), BHA (butylated hydroxyanisole), and BHT (butylated hydroxytoluene).

Formaldehyde donor preservatives in the presence of water, have the potential to release formaldehyde, a carcinogenic preservative used in embalming fluid. These can cause contact dermatitis and sensitivity. Ingredients include DMDM hydantoin, diazolidinyl urea, imidazolidinyl urea, Germall 115, Quaternium-15, and Bronopol. Paraben-free products may contain these alternatives. Extensive research shows these ingredients are carcinogenic (ewg.org 2012).

Natural pigments and minerals occur in nature and are recognized as being safe. Some of these include, but are not limited to, the following: mica, gold, potassium carbonate, calcium carbonate, bismuth oxychloride, aluminum oxide, titanium dioxide, zinc oxide, and silica.

CHAPTER 10: Choosing Products and Ingredients for the Spa 99

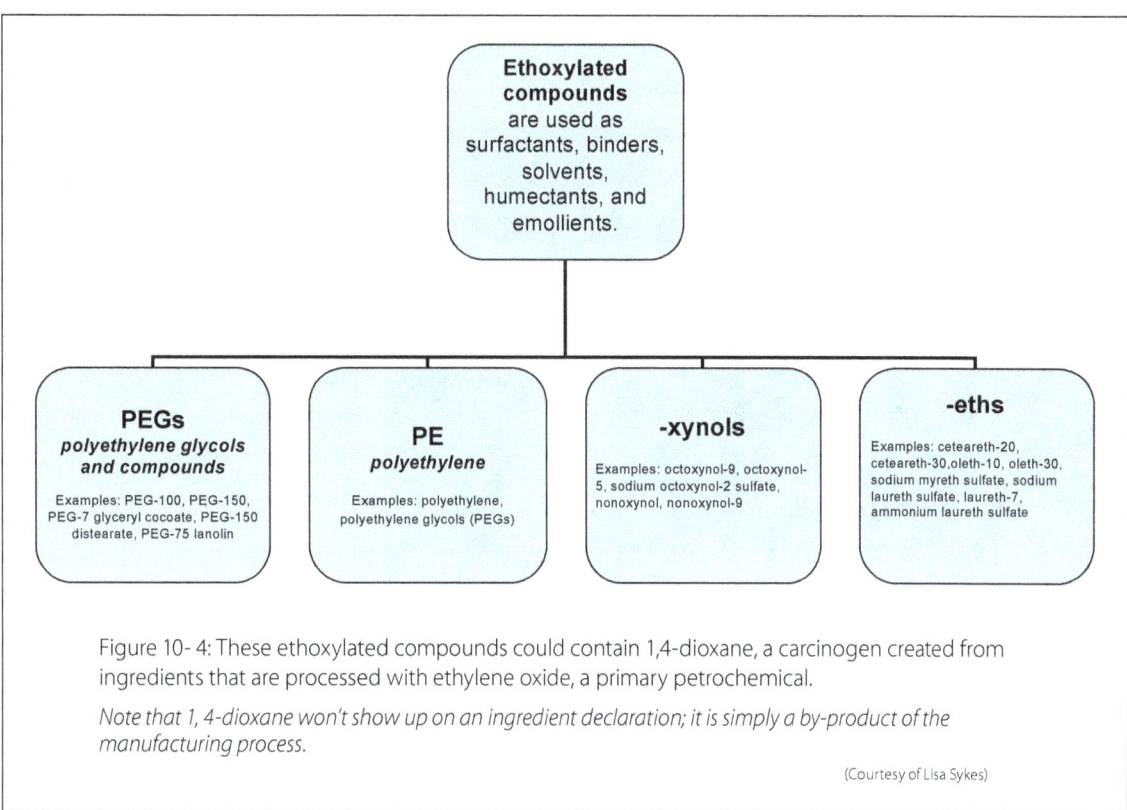

Figure 10-4: These ethoxylated compounds could contain 1,4-dioxane, a carcinogen created from ingredients that are processed with ethylene oxide, a primary petrochemical.

Note that 1, 4-dioxane won't show up on an ingredient declaration; it is simply a by-product of the manufacturing process.

(Courtesy of Lisa Sykes)

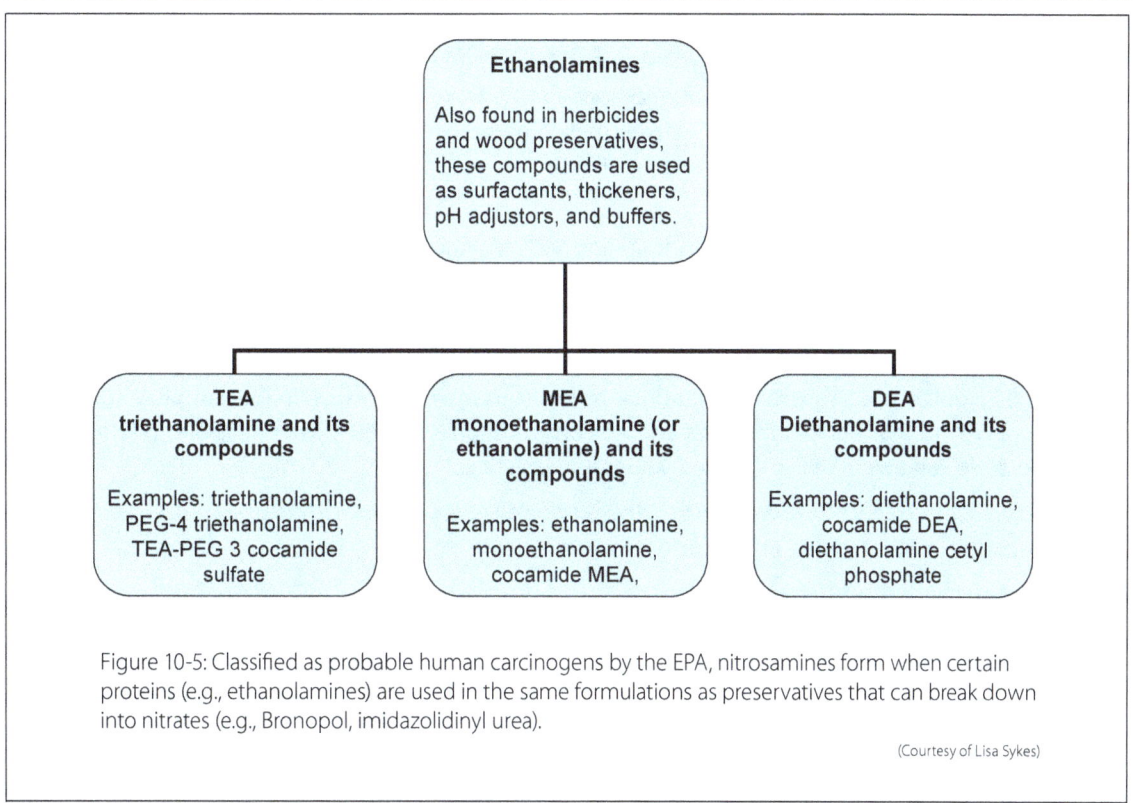

Figure 10-5: Classified as probable human carcinogens by the EPA, nitrosamines form when certain proteins (e.g., ethanolamines) are used in the same formulations as preservatives that can break down into nitrates (e.g., Bronopol, imidazolidinyl urea).

(Courtesy of Lisa Sykes)

SPA SPOTLIGHT

NATUROPATHICA HOLISTIC HEALTH

Contact: Susan Wells, Director (2012)

Naturopathica Holistic Health
74 Montauk Highway
East Hampton, NY 11937

www.naturopathica.com

Facility size: 5000 sq. ft.

Number of employees: 24

Number of treatment rooms: 12

Established in: 1995

Facility Description

Day spa/wellness boutique.

 ## SPA GOALS AND VISION

What is your green business mission statement?

Social and Environmental Responsibility Statement: Social and environmental responsibility permeates everything we do—from how we run our company to how we impact the communities where we do business. We believe small steps can collectively make a difference. At Naturopathica, we are taking action and are committed to sustainable business practices.

What is your spa image?

We are a Healing Arts Center dedicated to facilitating and inspiring healthy lifestyles with innovative natural products and wellness education.

What is important to you regarding sustainability?

While we may not have the ability to be sustainable in all areas of our operation, we believe that every step makes a difference. We strive to continue to lower usage of non-sustainable supplies, paper, and packaging. We monitor our electric, heat and AC consumption and adjust when feasible. In addition, we seek wholesale vendors with like-minded values and practices.

What business practices or areas would you like to make more sustainable?

Proper recycling is not possible in our current location.

What are the challenges in being green?

Our greatest challenge derives from our location. The spa is located in a facility where recycling is not possible. We strive to take our own measures to recycle within the company. In addition, we are limited in our options regarding laundry service, which does not allow us to control usage, detergents, etc.

Is the staff interested in greening the facility?
Yes, to a limited degree.

What business practices do you think your clients want to see with regard to sustainability?
Minimal use of paper products, recycling.

Have you seen any positive effects from green practices you have implemented? (economic, environmental, social equity impacts)
The positive effects primarily stem from our use of environmentally friendly paper goods, fewer non-recyclable supplies are being disposed of.

What positive benefits do you offer your staff? (health, wellness, incentives)
We offer monthly open forum gatherings that give staff a chance to learn more about holistic wellness; in addition, we offer occasional complimentary movement classes.

Do you promote your green practices?
We promote our Social and Environmental Responsibility Statement on most literature within the spa.

SPA ELEMENTS

The Menu
All of our treatments, esthetics, and massage use a majority of Ecocert certified products.

Products
- Regarding backbar, we continually analyze and adjust usage.

Our Products:
- Are certified by Ecocert as natural and organic when raw materials can be sustainably harvested and supplies are available at reasonable quantities and pricing.
- Contain no petroleum based ingredients, harsh surfactants, or paraben preservatives.
- Are sourced by sustainably harvested ingredients.
- Use minimal outer packaging with recycled paper content.
- Our tubes are made from 100% post-consumer HDPE milk bottles and PE plastic.
- Our custom bottles are made from 100% post-consumer PET plastic .
- All other packaging is made from PET plastic or glass.

Supplies
- Our cleaning supplies, paper goods, and cups are all purchased from vendors committed to sustainable practices.

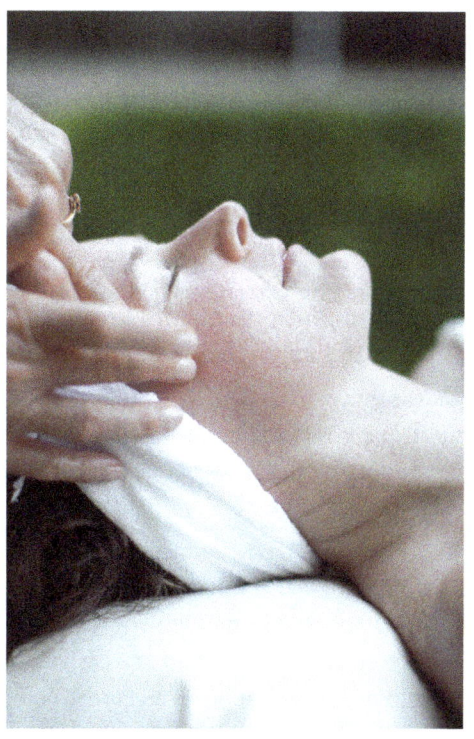

Energy
- We are enrolled in our region's Green Choice Utility Program to offset 100% of our electricity usage at our corporate headquarters, spa, and warehouse.
- We use energy efficient lighting.
- We have a boiler system; usage is tracked.

Water
- Because we do not offer wet treatments, we do not use a high volume of water.

Indoor Environmental Quality (IEQ)
- We use therapeutic-grade essential oil air fresheners and diffusers in our treatment rooms and retail area rather than synthetic-based sprays.

Purchasing
- Product packaging is eco-friendly.
- Supplies: All supplies purchased for office, spa, and packaging use are from recycled content and/or are compostable. Our menus and gift cards are printed on FSC certified paper.
- Cups: Our cups are made from PLA and meet ASTM standards for compostability.
- Vendors: The vendors we source for our retail area must be practicing sustainability methods in their own operation.
- Treatment equipment: Our treatment tables are from a vendor committed to sustainability practices; highlights of their process include an FSC-certified manufacturing facility, biodegradable upholstery, and a plant-a-tree program for every table they produce.

Waste Reduction
- We reuse and recycle all viable shipping and packaging materials received by our warehouse.

Marketing
- We place informational material strategically in the spa to educate clients about our standards and practices.

People and Staff
- Our Social and Environmental Responsibility Team meets regularly to discuss ways to improve our environmental impact.
- We foster a work environment that encourages all employees to perform to their fullest potential.
- Each employee is entitled to a cash incentive toward the purchase of a hybrid vehicle.
- Employees participate in an Earth Share workplace giving campaign.
- All full-time employees are entitled to paid time off to volunteer with a charity of their choice.

Our Community
- We donate to non-profit organizations related to environmental and women's health issues such as

American Botanical Counsel, Natural Resources Defense Council, The Nature Conservancy, and Pollinator Partnership for the sustainability of honey bees, and Stop Global Warming.
- Approved member organization of Co-op America and the Economic Action for a Just Planet.
- We strive to utilize vendors with like-minded values and practices.

Education
- Founding member of the Green Spa Network.
- Member of the Sustainable Packaging Coalition.
- Member of Campaign for Safe Cosmetics since 2004.
- Member of the Coalition for Consumer Information on Cosmetics, an organization against animal testing.

CHAPTER 11

Purchasing and Green Materials

INTRODUCTION

Weaving through every part of the discussion about purchasing choices are green materials. Material components are used in every product we buy, from clothing to building materials. The number of "ecolabels" is constantly expanding and there is plenty of Greenwashing going on with labeling. Choosing and evaluating materials and consumer goods can be complicated.

This chapter overlaps with other sections, as it has to do with indoor air quality, waste, and everything we buy. Fortunately, green purchasing for spas is not as extensive as what is covered here, but it is good to be familiar with the concepts and what suppliers can analyze before consumer goods go to market. Supplies and interiors are the main categories discussed here. Products, resource use, and green building are covered in separate chapters. Planning checklists for choosing materials are listed in Chapter 17 and in the online resources.

WORDS OF WISDOM

Training the conscious mind to be actively green is to be true to it in all phases of our personal and professional lives. The green spa is not hard to convert to, as Mother Nature reminds us each day. In the spa, it's easier than any other beauty industry department, because it can truly be a benefit to health and wellness without chemicals–from daily maintenance to all our professional and retail products!

~ Bonnie Canavino, Red Cherry Group,
redcherrygroup.com, theamritorganic.com

WHAT IS A GREEN MATERIAL?

Sustainable or green materials are ideally renewable, recyclable, and healthy (Figure 11-1). These criteria do not always go together. Some materials may be healthy, but not recyclable. Others conserve resources. A truly sustainable material is healthy for people and the environment, as well as being renewable and affordable.

When it comes to personal care products or other products we use, our personal health is the main concern. What are the ingredients? Are they full of toxic chemicals? In comparing products we buy, we can weigh the environmental effects from making the products. The life cycle analysis (LCA) is one method used for this (see Chapter 2).

Another factor is the cost of goods or materials. Is it affordable and sustainable? How long will it last? Will we have to buy another one next year—is it designed for break down? Consumer goods are not made like they used to be. For example, washers from a major appliance manufacturer used to last 20 years. Now it seems they need to be repaired or replaced much sooner.

WHAT CRITERIA MAKE A MATERIAL GREEN?

The criteria for green products are that they are made from environmentally friendly materials, lack detrimental materials, have a reduced environmental impact, reduced operational impacts, and healthy indoor environmental quality. Materials science is extensive and can evaluate the materials and their components for various factors.

Materials selection takes into account the material performance, service life, cost, and aesthetics (Figure 11-2). Added factors to consider are toxicity, resource efficiency, durability, and quality. The virgin material quantity, embodied energy in the entire LCA, operational resource requirements, maintenance needs, and manufacturer policies/practices can also be assessed. Other considerations are packaging, transportation, installation, maintenance, life expectancy, emissions, resource conservation, and end of life: is it cradle to cradle or cradle to grave? Green materials selection is discussed in numerous green building journals and taught in the Sustainable Building Advisor Institute curriculum, but these concepts are not limited to building materials.

Figure 11-1 Sustainable or green materials are ideally renewable, recyclable, and healthy.

Sustainable materials meet the following criteria:

- Organic or natural ingredients: saves chemicals used and processing.
- Life cycle assessment and embodied energy assessment (throughout the entire life of a product): saves initial resources and makes recycling easier.
- Quality performance and a long service life: items last longer, reduced operational and maintenance costs, less replacement needs.
- Durability of items, better quality: saves money and resources.
- Cost and affordability: saves purchasing costs.
- Low toxicity: reduces wasted time dealing with health issues, liability, and chemical handling requirements (healthier staff and clients, higher productivity).
- Resource efficiency: saves energy, water, virgin materials, and processing.
- Sustainable manufacturing and supplier company policies: reduces resource use and makes purchasing easier (positive environmental and social choices).
- Recyclable materials and packaging: materials can be reused again, extending their lifespan.
- Made of recycled content: uses resources efficiently.
- Locally made items: reduces shipping and packaging waste, supports the community.
- Reduced carbon footprint: reduces pollution and potential climate change effects.

Purchasing categories in the salon/spa:
- Products and retail items.
- Facility and service supplies: office, clients, amenities, cleaning, laundry, linens, paper, and printing.
- Interiors: furniture, décor, textiles.
- Equipment: services, treatment rooms, offices, fitness center.
- Building and building materials.
- Food and beverages.
- Outdoors and landscaping.

Main questions to ask when making purchasing decisions:
- What is it made from?
- Is it healthy?
- Does it save resources?
- Is it recyclable?

Eco Innovations
New products and services are coming on the market as the need for new eco products, packaging, and manufacturing continue to evolve. Consumer goods such as tennis shoes, carpets, and furniture are just a few examples where innovations have led to improved technology using LCA concepts in design.

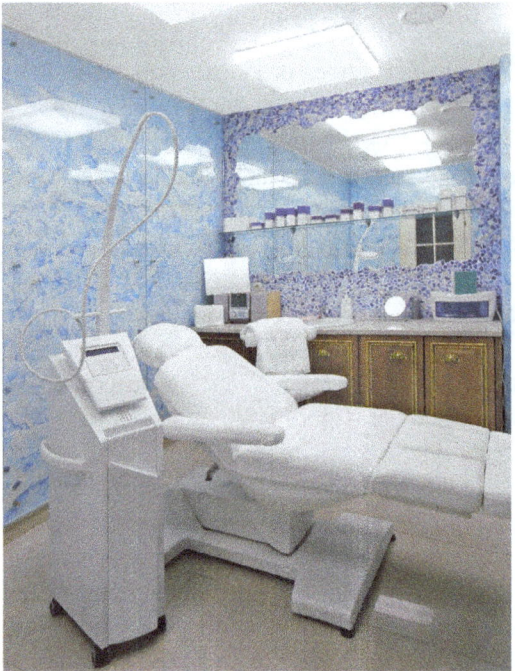

Figure 11-2: Materials selection takes into account many factors.

Bamboo is wonderful for certain products, but needs to be harvested correctly. Some bamboo products, such as clothing, may not be as sustainable or as durable as advertised.

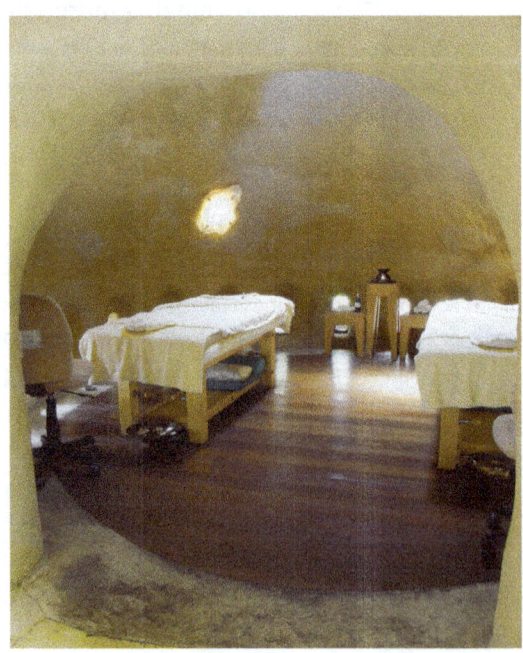

Spotlight on Sustainable Spa Textiles

How do spa owners navigate choices and stay true to their values? Most people have never asked, "What are the sheets, towels, blankets, and robes used on my body actually made of?" If the answer is cotton, does that mean that these textiles are "natural"—as a spa might imply?

Let's pull the curtain back on cotton textiles, one of the spa industry's biggest purchases. If you consider that the cotton, unless "certified organic," is grown with GMO (genetically-modified) seeds and sprayed with heavy doses of toxic pesticides, insecticides, herbicides, and artificial fertilizers, and likely dyed with harmful chemicals, one would realize that conventional cotton textiles are hardly pure, natural, or healthy in tandem with a typical spa mantra. In fact, less than 3% of the world's agriculture is cotton, but over 25% of the most damaging insecticides and 10% of the most carcinogenic pesticides are used on conventional cotton. Then there's the unsustainable labor and social compliance issues in the manufacturing of cotton textiles.

The use of organic cotton textiles is a choice that exemplifies true wellness. Grown and sewn without GMO seeds and chemicals such as pesticides, organic cotton is categorically better for our bodies, human health, farmer welfare, the planet, and future generations. And to be certain that organic textiles are certified from farm to finished product, the GOTS (Global Organic Textile Standard) seal can assure authenticity, including the requirement of low-impact dyes, which have less than a 5% runoff and are free of toxic heavy metals, formaldehyde and chlorine bleaches. In addition to chemical reduction, GOTS and Oeko-tex, another textile certification, also address waste, water, and energy savings in textiles.

Recognizing that our skin is the largest organ in our bodies and our primary organ for absorption, spa textiles should not only look and feel good physically, but should be as pure and sensuous as a spa environment itself. Health and vitality are not just about what we put into our bodies, but what we put onto our bodies as well.

This may lead some of you to say, "It's a good thing, then, that my favorite spa uses bamboo textiles." Not exactly. Bamboo, while it's a poster child of the renewable resource set and makes a fine material for flooring and furniture, it epitomizes the word Greenwashing. So much so, that the Federal Trade Commission (FTC) has dubbed it illegal to market bamboo textiles as eco-friendly. What most people don't realize is that during the manufacturing of bamboo into a textile, extraordinary amounts of dangerous chemicals are used to break down the bamboo fibers, ultimately emitting high doses of toxic waste and pollution, and leaving only a bamboo resin in the end.

So what is a truly sustainable alternative to bamboo, which can add a smooth silky luster, as well as durability to a cotton textile? One of the most innovative new fabrics on the market is ECOlyptus™. This fiber is derived from the cellulose extracted from renewable eucalyptus wood pulp, grown on managed tree farms and on non-arable land not suitable for food crops. With minimal water and energy use, and broken down using a recycled non-toxic solvent, ECOlyptus™ is manufactured in a closed-loop system, whereby waste become by-products for other industries. Three times stronger than cotton, chemical-free, and wrinkle-resistant, ECOlyptus is also highly absorbent and biodegradable.

As spas nationwide reassess their purchasing decisions, ask for sustainable textiles such as organic cotton, ECOlyptus, Fair Trade Certified or even RPET, a fiber made from recycled plastic bottles. Portico at Hyatt and Under the Canopy at Ritz Carlton are just a few examples of initiatives that have begun to champion the crusade of spa style and sustainability. Instrumental in defining the Global Organic Textile Standard (GOTS) and the first US Fair Trade Textile Certification, Marci Zaroff coined the term and pioneered the market for ECOfashion® and is a partner of the Portico Brand Group, including brands she founded—Under the Canopy and FASE (Fashion • Art • Soul • Earth). Her website is marcizaroff.com.

(Courtesy of Marci Zaroff 2012)

Some Facts on Textiles

- Conventional cotton is one of the most heavily sprayed industries in the world, making it a leading cause of air and water pollution.
- It takes 700 gallons of fresh water to make one cotton t-shirt.
- In 2009, the world used 3 trillion gallons of fresh water to produce 60 billion kilograms of fabric.
- The average US citizen throws away 68 pounds of clothing every year.
- 1 trillion kilowatt hours are used every year by the global textile industry, or 10% of total global carbon impact.
- According to the World Bank, 20% of industrial fresh water pollution comes from textile treatment and dyeing.
- Recycled polyester, recycled cotton, TENCEL® (lyocell), hemp, and linen are all considered sustainable fibers.

(Source: Textile Exchange Market Report, 2011, textileexchange.org)

ECOLABELS EVERYWHERE

Who would have thought there would be so many ecolabels coming on the scene? It is amazing that there are over 400 ecolabels and counting (Figure 11-3). These include regional, state, and global standards. The Ecolabel Index website lists all ecolabels in North America. Labels abound for every industry, including building, personal care, food, electronics, packaging, hotels, and travel (ecolabelindex.com 2012).

Does a product save resources, energy, or address climate change? There are categories for every product characteristic and attribute. Unfortunately, some labels ignore detrimental features and capitalize on only one feature. This is misleading for consumers. It is important to research these labels if you want to avoid Greenwashing and make sure you are being truly dark green. Below is a select list of the more common ecolabels you may come across. Some of these personal care and building standards are found in the corresponding chapters.

Figure 11-3: There are over 400 ecolabels.

Table 11-1: The following are examples of some of the standards and labels for consumer goods. Most are registered trademarks.

TABLE 11-1 ECOLABELS BY CATEGORY			
Personal Care Products	**General Business**	**Building**	**Food**
ANSI 305	CarbonFree® Certified	Built Green	Certified Naturally Grown
BDIH	Cradle to Cradle Certification	CRI Green Label & Green Label Plus	Non-GMO
CosmeBio	EcoLogic	Earth Advantage	USDA Organic
Cosmos	Fair Trade	Energy Star	
EcoCert	Green America	Green Guard	
Green Seal	Green Globes	Green Seal	
ICEA	Green Seal	Forest Stewardship Council	
Natrue	Recycled Content	Sustainable Forestry Institute	
NPA	SCS Certified Biodegradable	WaterSense	
NSF	Sustainable Tourism Eco-Certification Program	LEED	
Oregon Tilth	TerraCycle	NAHB Green	
Soil Association	The National Green Pages™	NPA Natural Standard	
USDA NOP		NFS/ANSI	

SPA SPOTLIGHT

OSMOSIS DAY SPA SANCTUARY
To create a healing sanctuary providing nurturing services in resonance with nature.

Contact: Lauren Santibañez, Service Provider Manager and Green Team Catalyst (2012)

Osmosis Day Spa Sanctuary
209 Bohemian Hwy, Freestone CA

www.osmosis.com

Facility size: 4200 sq. ft.

Number of employees: 90

Number of treatment rooms: 16

Established in: 1985

Facility Description

Osmosis is a Japanese-style retreat on 5 acres in a scenic valley of west Sonoma County. Facilities include the main building with 7 massage rooms, 3 facial rooms, the Cedar Enzyme Baths, and boutique. There are 5 gardens on the property, including an award-winning Japanese meditation garden, and 4 outdoor massage pagodas.

SPA GOALS AND VISION

What is your green business mission statement?

To create a healing sanctuary providing nurturing services in resonance with nature.

What is your spa image?

An eco-friendly healing and vitality center with an Asian esthetic focusing on meditation gardens, the Cedar Enzyme Bath, and holistic wellness.

What are your sustainability goals?

Osmosis endeavors to be as "green" as we possibly can, from daily operations to treatments offered and benefits for employees. We have specific sustainability goals but we try to hold ourselves to the best environmental practices for a business. Among our sustainability goals is creating a chemical-free environment (including treatment products, cleaning products, paint and décor, etc), reducing waste, reducing consumption (utilities), and enhancing the body-nature connection with our guests.

What is important to you regarding sustainability?

Community involvement is also an essential component of what it means to be a green business because improving community is a key link to improving sustainable lifestyles. As a founding member of the Green Spa Network, Osmosis strives to set a positive example for our local community and other spas around the nation. We were the first spa to use the GNS Sustainability Assessment Tool to assess and monitor progress.

What business practices or areas would you like to make more sustainable?
One main area is the goal of "zero waste"—something we can constantly strive for but will be very difficult to ultimately achieve.

What are the challenges in being green?
Sometimes there are more upfront costs with sustainable options. Reducing utilities while keeping the environment comfortable (i.e. temperature control in treatment rooms) is a challenge. Also, maintaining green standards even in tough times due to the economy.

Is the staff interested in greening the facility?
Overall, yes—many of our employees were attracted to Osmosis because of our green reputation. Almost all of our employees really appreciate we are an eco-friendly business, and about a third of them are actively interested in making Osmosis and their personal lives more environmentally friendly.

What business practices do you think your clients want to see with regard to sustainability?
Sometimes I think our clients don't realize how thorough our efforts actually are to be environmentally friendly. Some of the more obvious things (like recycling, energy conservation, and eco-friendly products) tend to be what guests look for. We do have some guests who ask more in depth questions, like how we get materials for the Cedar Enzyme Bath and if our gardens are composed of native species.

Have you seen any positive effects from green practices you have implemented?
There have been many. Some positive effects include reduced utility bills, increased clientele from the LOHAS market, healthier work environment, employee participation, employee pride in the cutting garden, and lots of positive feedback from guests who appreciate an environmentally friendly experience.

What positive benefits do you offer your staff?
Discounts on treatments and products (including wellness products and services like the detox cleanse, supplements, enzymes), a free treatment program, opportunity to use facilities for trading with each other, health insurance for full-time employees, commission and booking incentives for concierges.

In 2012, we just announced VitalOz, our new employee wellness program. As a work in progress in its first year, we will explore areas (based on employee interest) to expand the benefits and offerings for our employees (like healthy foods available for snacking and access to yoga and wellness classes). There will also be four Quarterly Teams, which will focus on a shared wellness goal and support each other in achieving that goal. The first QT will focus on nutrition with a dozen participants who will receive Transformation Enzymes supplements and nutrition counseling with a certified nutritionist, all free as part of the program.

Do you promote your green practices? What promotional methods do you use for this?
We are rather vocal about our green practices and Osmosis is proud to be an award-winning green spa. We have a dedicated Green page on our website, and our eco standards are usually mentioned on printed marketing materials, such as the brochure.

We support and participate in events like Freestone Fermentation Festival and Peak Hike with Breast Cancer Fund. The month of April is entirely dedicated to promoting our sustainable efforts with specials to encourage guest participation (like a discount for those who ride their bike or drive an alternate fuel vehicle to Osmosis).

🌿 SPA ELEMENTS

The Menu

- ***Esthetics:*** Very high standards for products (see below), "organic facials" often used in brochures and marketing.
- ***Body:*** We use chemical-free products and only offer modalities that do not require large amounts of electric equipment (i.e. hot stone massage).
- ***Hair removal:*** Facial waxing is offered and we only use chemical-free products.
- ***Other:*** Our signature treatment, the Cedar Enzyme Bath, is a high-heat therapeutic treatment that only uses enzymes and natural fermentation as the heat source. In general, our menu and brochures are from Greenerprinter.com and printed on recycled paper with soy inks. Some smaller print projects are from a local company (also on recycled paper).

Products

Face

- Osmosis has very high standards for all products used, but this is especially seen with our skin care products. Our products were chosen for having very clean (chemical-free) ingredients, environmental practices in the companies, while still being effective and results-oriented skin care products. We also do not carry products with animal derived ingredients or that use animal testing.
- Brands: Phyt's, Naturopathica, Chado-En, Tecniche, Glisodin.
- Phyt's, our primary skin care line, is a French company with the highest level of organic certification available (COSMEBIO) for every single one of their products. COSMEBIO standards also apply to manufacturing, packing, and business practices, not just ingredients.

Body

- Massage oils and lotions are organic, vegan, and of course chemical-free. We proudly supply our massage therapists with pure, organic, expeller pressed coconut oil, which is melted in a crock-pot as needed.

Makeup

- We only retail a small selection from Phyt's, including mineral foundations, lip colors, eyeliner and mascara (organic, chemical-free, no animal testing, etc).

Hair removal

- Our waxing products contain no artificial fragrances, dyes, or chemicals. We use cornstarch instead of baby powder to prep the skin and a product made from orange peel oil to clean equipment.

Retail

- Most products in our retail boutique fall under one or more of the following categories: locally made, organic, sustainable, fair trade, or made from recycled materials.

- All products are checked for ingredients to maintain our chemical-free standard. We do not carry products with animal derived ingredients or that use animal testing.
- We often try to source products from local companies, although we import a few specialty items, like our Japanese robes, because they are part of the Osmosis experience.

Supplies

Linens
- Comphy brand sheets for facials and massage are made of synthetic materials designed to release oils, launder easily, dry in less time, and are recyclable at the end of their life.

Single-use items (cotton, plastic)
- Aestheticians try to minimize use of disposables (e.g. cotton rounds) by eliminating unnecessary waste, such as using tanning goggles that can be disinfected to protect eyes under the magnifying light.
- Supplies are purchased from a local company (SpaEquip in Sonoma) or a larger, national company that supports green initiatives (Universal Companies supports the Green Spa Network).

Paper
- Toilet paper, paper towels, and facial tissues are made of recycled content and do not use bleaching agents.
- Office paper is made of recycled content and reused internally before we recycle it.

Cleaning
- Strictly chemical-free cleaning supplies used throughout the spa.
- Non-toxic disinfectants and sanitizers for aestheticians and massage therapists.
- No bleach; vodka is used in showers for mold control.

Facility supplies
- Consolidated orders/deliveries from UNFI include paper products, foods, some cleaning supplies, etc., to minimize transportation and fuel.
- Décor throughout the spa, including lobby and treatment rooms, has no-VOC paints, locally made furniture crafted from indigenous materials like driftwood, and flooring is modular carpet, cork, or Marmoleum (eco-friendly linoleum).

Energy

- Thermal solar panels for the hot water heater, installed in 2011, noticeably reduced our gas consumption.
- Electric (PGE) is tracked from monthly bills into a spreadsheet to identify and investigate any spikes in usage.

Building
- Year built: 1970s; minor remodeling projects throughout the years.
- Standard wood siding construction.
- R-value: Attic is R-50. Doors and doorways were upgraded to improve insulation and most windows in the spa are double-paned.
- Weatherization performed in different areas over the years; biannually or as needed.
- Energy audits quarterly.

HVAC system
- Temperature controls are regulated to minimize electricity usage depending on season and climate.

- Ventilation system: fresh air filters; air is circulated continuously.

Appliances
- Laundry: We use an offsite service that maintains our standards of using non-toxic cleaning products.
- Energy Star appliances.
- Installed a small quiet dishwasher so we could use ceramic cups and eliminate paper cups.

Equipment
- Cedar Enzyme Bath is created with natural fermentation from over 600 Japanese enzymes with cedar and rice bran to create an all-natural source of heat (no electricity used or hot water added to tubs).
- Enzyme Tubs use blasters, which circulate hot water (from solar panels) through copper tubing underneath the metal shell of the tub to boost heat during the cold season.

Hot water heating
- Solar panels on the roof are used to heat several hot water tanks, which are insulated for maximum efficiency.

Type of lighting
- Fixtures: fluorescent, conventional and LED; Bulbs are mostly CFL or LED, some halogen.
- Lighting controls include dimmers, and occupant sensors in tea kitchens.

Water
- Signage throughout the spa encourages guests to conserve water.
- Landscape uses drip irrigation to minimize evaporation.
- We pioneered an exciting water conservation project—the first county-approved greywater system to be installed in a non-vineyard. This process took many months to plan and get all permits approved.
- We installed a wetland near the rear of the property to act as an all-natural (and quite effective) biological filter to recycle waste water and reuse it for irrigation. Our plumbing was updated to circulate all greywater (from sinks and showers) through the wetland. The water output from the wetland has been tested and deemed safe to use for irrigation. In addition, we planted the wetland with native species that also attract birds and wildlife.

Quality/Filtration
- All tap water in the spa originates from the city of Freestone and is run through an advanced filtration system using patented technology from Japan to improve taste, oxygenate, and remove all chlorine.
- Greywater is run through a wetland with sand and biological filtration to be used for landscape irrigation.

Fixtures
- Low-flow fixtures and aerators on almost all sinks; low-flow and/or dual flush toilets.
- Showers are not currently low flow (less than 2.5 gpm) because it is challenging to find a hand-held shower head with low flow that is made of durable materials.

Landscaping
- Drip irrigation uses water from the well and recycled water from the greywater system.

Green Materials
- The staff break room is located in an old train car originally left on the property.
- Cleaning products are non-toxic.
- Recycled furniture.
- Life cycle analysis has been noted on a few things including cedar for enzyme bath and linens.
- Consolidated orders of office supplies from Staples, which offers competitive pricing on recycled-content supplies like paper goods.
- Main component of the Cedar Enzyme Bath is Port Orford Cedar. A company collects fallen trees to make arrows out of the wood and we purchase their byproduct (leftover wood) and finely mill it to create our soft, fluffy bath material.
- The used Enzyme Bath material is available for the public to purchase and makes an excellent ground cover in gardens.
- No-VOC paint.
- Cork flooring in facial rooms, tea kitchens, and 1 massage room.
- Carpeting in other areas of the spa is modular so we can replace small sections as needed to extend the lifetime of the carpet overall.
- Some pagodas were made out of recycled redwood from the bridge that previously crossed Salmon Creek in front of the spa. The deck in our Meditation Garden is made out of local reclaimed redwood.

Indoor Environmental Quality (IEQ)
- Ventilation fans in each treatment room.
- Fresh air from operable window in each treatment room and in offices.
- No chemicals are used.
- HVAC system circulates fresh air almost constantly.
- Several years ago, we installed a prototype system that uses temperature sensors throughout the spa and computer software to regulate AC and heat for optimal temperature with minimal energy use.

Purchasing
- Paper cups were eliminated when we added the dishwasher and ceramic cups.
- All paper contains recycled content.
- Boxes and packaging are reused from our orders to ship out products to clients.
- Suppliers are requested and encouraged to minimize packaging and/or use recyclable packaging like paper instead of Styrofoam peanuts.
- We collect the Styrofoam peanuts and donate to a local shipping company that reuses them.

Waste Reduction
- Sorting is practiced throughout the spa and offices: waste, recycling, and compost.
- Reduce: eliminated paper cups, minimize printing, print double-sided, reuse paper for scraps then recycle, we remove our name from junk mail lists, and minimize catalog and magazine mailings.
- Reuse: old printed paper is used for notes, employee break room has clothing free trade, reuse packaging and boxes.

- Recycle: everything possible, packing peanuts taken to collection center, some garden scraps and paper materials are composted onsite while some is sent to municipal compost collection.

Landscaping, Exteriors
- Drip irrigation.
- Greywater system is used for some of our irrigation.
- Japanese-themed gardens with many native species minimize water demand.
- A full-time Master Gardener oversees the landscaping.
- Chemicals are never used!
- We compost on-site (with worms) and have local municipal composting.
- Recycled enzyme bath material is used as mulch, composted, and recycled at county facilities.

Food Service
- Boxed lunches available for purchase (and included with packages) are now done through a partnership with Ceres Community Project, a local non-profit that gives teens the opportunity to cook with whole, nourishing foods to create beautiful and healthy meals, often donated to people in need.
- Snacks for purchase and complimentary lobby snacks are made with organic ingredients.

Marketing
- Our green features are pivotal to the promotion of our business.
- All staff is educated on our environmental efforts when they are hired at Osmosis, and kept aware of updates as they happen.
- Our sustainability factor is beneficial to our marketing efforts and is included in most of our collateral and campaigns.

People
- Most of our sustainable efforts directly benefit employees by providing a safe, non-toxic work environment, in addition to new programs like VitalOz, which will promote health and wellness in our internal community.

Education
- A lot of internal communication is sent via email instead of print; signs are posted in key areas for each department.
- Live trainings are organized on days when many people are already here and carpooling is encouraged.
- Web trainings like webinars have recently been used to share information in circumstances when not everyone can travel to attend a specific training off-site.

CHAPTER 12

Waste Reduction and Purchasing

INTRODUCTION

Purchasing is where it all starts—buying what we need to run a business. Purchasing has a huge impact on all facets of sustainability. Evaluating criteria for green purchasing can take time and determination. The main things to look for regarding waste reduction are the recycled content of products and how easy they can be recycled. While the criteria listed here can be complicated, even small steps are a good start to conscientious purchasing.

This chapter reiterates some of the concepts in Chapter 11, purchasing and green materials, as waste reduction is part of your purchasing decisions. As with the other green topics, the purchasing benefits, practices, and concepts are included here. Education and awareness lead to solutions. For further information on purchasing, refer to the planning and checklists sections. Use the worksheets to track your waste reduction.

WORDS OF WISDOM

We can't recycle our way out of the situation we have created, but plastic collection recycling events remind us how much plastic surrounds us in our daily lives. When we save our plastics for a year and watch the mound grow, it can inspire us to modify our buying habits. Consumers can speak by choosing to purchase durable products rather than disposable (single use), poorly made products, or ones housed in plastic. Let your retailers and manufacturers know how you feel about having to deal with the (plastic) by-product from buying their products.

~ Risa Buck, Waste Zero Specialist, Recology Ashland
Sanitary Service, RecologyAshlandSanitaryService.com

GREEN PURCHASING GUIDELINES

Consider the life cycle assessment when purchasing items. When purchasing supplies, look for recycled paper, products, and containers. Reducing plastic material and switching to glass is another easy way to help green up the facility. Glass is 100% recyclable and can be recycled much easier than plastic. Non-disposable items save money and reduce waste. As noted in Chapter 11, use the sustainable materials criteria for purchasing (Figure 12-1).

The mantra reduce, reuse, recycle is now common knowledge. *Precycling* is trying not to buy items in the first place that generate waste. Buying less is the first step in reducing waste. This also helps save money and time in dealing with the garbage or recycling bins. *Repurposing* is extending the life by reusing for something else instead of throwing it away. For example, sheets and towels can go to a homeless or animal shelter to be reused. Old towels can be used as cleaning rags. Seasonal display items can be adapted creatively and used more than once.

Reimagine Our Buying Habits

The Four R's of waste reduction are Reject, Reduce, Reuse, and Recycle.

- Reject buying certain things in the first place.
- Reduce consumption and only buy what we need.
- Reuse and repurpose what we have.
- Recycle and repair what we can.

Figure 12-1: Use the sustainable materials criteria for purchasing and waste reduction.

The Benefits of Waste Reduction

Saving money by more conscious purchasing is good for business. Saving natural resources and reducing externalized costs to the environment and landfills are less obvious benefits, but have a huge impact. Every little bit adds up if you think of the billions of people purchasing and using resources.

Purchasing greener products in the spa reduces supply costs, packaging and plastics, product and shipping costs, and waste disposal costs. Green purchasing also reduces manufacturing impacts, chemicals, and toxins. Buying less helps reduce clutter in the workplace and frees up storage space.

> **Main considerations when making purchasing decisions for waste reduction:**
> - What is it made from?
> - Is the material made from recyclable or renewable materials?
> - Does it save resources?
> - Is it durable and will it last?
> - Is it recyclable or compostable?
> - Is it reusable (repurposing)?
> - Where is it made?
> - Has it been sustainably manufactured?
> - Is the packaging made with recycled content or made from recyclable material?
> - Is it made with a plastic or is it a throw away container?
> - Is it a single-use item?
> - Are there second-hand, recycled alternatives (such as furniture)?

Spa Purchasing Solutions

Here are some guidelines for purchasing and waste reduction:

- **Treatments:** Use reusable bowls and applicators, rather than throwing away so many disposables.
- **Service supplies:** Buy larger packages and fewer disposable items.
- **Retail and backbar products:** Buy items with less packaging and in bulk containers.
- **Office supplies:** Use refillable ink cartridges and pencils, use energy efficient lighting, and buy used items (desks, trays, containers). Buy quality chairs that last. Laptops use less energy and materials to produce than desktop computers.
- **Paper goods:** Buy paper with recycled content, reduce printing, print double-sided copies.
- **Bags, packaging and containers:** Buy reusable items made of recycled content and recyclable material, and avoid plastics. Reuse or recycle shipping materials and packaging. Avoid Styrofoam. Use cloth bags.
- **Equipment, appliances, electronics:** Buy durable, good quality that is made to last. Recycle or donate old equipment.
- **Laundry:** Try to reduce linen use; buy concentrated, green cleaning supplies.
- **Repair:** Sometimes it is less expensive and less wasteful to repair something than replace an item.
- **Recycle bins:** Use recycle bins for paper, glass, plastic, and comingle items.
  - Do not use bins that resemble trash cans, locate bins away from trash cans.
  - Use a separate container for each item collected to avoid confusion and contamination.
- **Reuse:** Give books and magazines to others or to the library. Donate used goods.
- **Recycle e-waste properly:** Batteries, ink cartridges, electronics, etc.
- **Hazardous waste:** Use proper disposal methods for chemicals, etc. Do not pour chemicals down drains.
- **Water bottles:** Avoid plastic, use quality stainless steel.
- **Food and beverage:** Consider packaging and avoid plastic containers, buy in bulk, avoid single-use items and take-out containers. Use reusable containers, cloth napkins, and real silverware. Compost food scraps for the garden.
- **Landscaping:** Design for easy care, reduce chemicals, use organic methods, and chip or compost green waste/yard debris.
- **Train staff:** Educate the staff on recycling and waste reduction.
- **Marketing:** Print minimal marketing materials and print on recycled paper. Do more Internet marketing and save by printing less expensive brochures.

> **Reduce your junk mail:** "StopJunkMail.org and CatalogChoice.org are two resources for getting your name off mailing lists" (ecologycenter.org 2012).

GREEN PACKAGING

There is a trend to green up packaging—the "face" of beauty products (Figure 12-2). "Consumers are looking for signs that they are making eco-responsible purchasing decisions, which includes packaging. In Mintel's 2011 *Green Living Report*, 66% of US survey respondents said packaging should have recycled content and that it influences their purchases; 44% said they purchase beauty products that use recycled paper" (oxygen.mintel.com 2011). Other research statistics show similar results. Green packaging claims made by companies have increased substantially.

Advancements in using eco-friendly materials range from "recyclables, bioplastics, biodegradables, and post-consumer regrind board stocks. These have all contributed to innovative packaging trends." The entire manufacturing process is becoming more efficient and green. While companies strive to emulate the large brand icons who have successfully implemented sustainable packaging, it is a very complex process. Some individuals and companies are asking manufacturers to make every part of the container green with "100% recycled paperboard, soy inks, biodegradable glue, and no metal or plastic at all on the package" (beautypackaging.com 2012).

Key trends involve reducing the total amount of materials in packaging and labeling, and developing materials from bio pathways (biodegradable materials made with biomass). Chemical substances such as PET (polyethylene terephthalate) are now coming from plant-based sources instead of petroleum-based sources. Life cycle assessment (LCA) has to be part of the equation as there are pros and cons to every material.

Other positive trends discussed in articles for glass manufacturers include weight reduction on glass packaging and glass recycling, which saves raw materials and energy. Glass is environmentally friendly, since it is 100% recyclable. Products made from recycled glass produce fewer emissions and embody the "cradle to cradle" approach (beautypackaging.com 2011). It is encouraging to see changes from manufacturers as businesses and consumers are more aware of the issues. It will be interesting to see what happens in the packaging world in the years to come.

Figure 12-2: There is a trend to green up packaging.

"Just because a product may come from a plant-based source, does not automatically make it sustainable" (oxygen.mintel.com 2011). Food and paper sourcing can lead to resource shortages.

What do your vendors offer in the way of green packaging, products, and supplies? How much waste do you recycle?

WASTE AND RECYCLING

"Reusing the stuff in our lives slows down the waste stream" (ecologycenter.org 2012). Waste reduction gurus say it is only waste if you treat it like it is. In other words, use the cradle to cradle model so everything is designed for reconstruction or reuse. According to the EPA, in 2010, "Americans produced about 250 million tons of municipal solid waste (MSW), or about 4 pounds of waste per person per day (Figure 12-3). Of this, the agency says 34.1% is recovered and recycled or composted, 11.7% is burned at combustion facilities, and the remaining 54.2% is disposed of in landfills" (epa.gov 2011).

Figure 12-3: Americans produced about 250 million tons of municipal solid waste (MSW) in 2010.

Recycling

Recycling is good for business and saves money, but where does that container go when we throw it in the garbage or recycle bin? Not everything that goes into the recycle bins gets recycled. If there is not a market for the collected recyclables, they may go to the landfill. Recycling only works if people buy recycled products, too (Figure 12-4).

Other resources can be recycled easier than plastic. Trees need to be sustainably harvested, but paper is commonly recycled. Glass can be recycled multiple times: it makes great recycled products and is even used for road beds in landfills. Metal supplies are limited and nonrenewable, so it is important to recycle aluminum and other metals. Yard debris and food scraps can be composted and thus reduce chemical use in gardening. "It takes energy to sort, clean, and convert cans, bottles, and paper to new recycled products, but much less energy than starting with virgin materials. Air and water pollution impacts are also reduced significantly by recycling" (ecologycenter.org 2012).

Plastic

Every day, mountains of used plastic consumer products and packaging head to landfills, wasting the materials and energy that created them. Reducing and reusing can divert millions of tons of garbage from landfills every year. "Plastic has economic, health, and environmental costs and benefits. While it is flexible and lightweight, it creates problems including consumption of resources, pollution, high energy use in manufacturing, accumulation of plastic in the environment, and polymers and additives in foods." Making products from recycled plastic uses 2/3 less energy than it takes to make virgin products. "As plastic producers increase production and reduce prices on virgin plastics, the markets for used plastic are diminishing. Processing used plastics often costs more than virgin plastic so PET recyclers cannot compete with the virgin resin market. PET is a type of number 1 plastic that is easier to recycle. Additionally, because of increased plastic use, glass container plants have been closing" (ecologycenter.org 2012).

[For an interesting video on buying and the Life Cycle Assessment check out thestoryofstuff.com.]

It takes more energy, resources, and transportation to manufacture, ship, and go out and buy disposable silverware, dishes, and napkins than it does to wash reusable ones (ecologycenter.org 2012).

Figure 12-4: Recycling only works if people buy recycled products.

How long does it take garbage to break down or decompose?

Plastics and aluminum cans take 500 years. Organic materials, cotton, rags, and paper take 6 months. (planetpals.com 2012)

The Great Garbage Patch

"In the ocean, plastic waste accumulates in swirling seas of debris....The largest of these garbage swills is known as the Pacific Gyre, or The Great Garbage Patch. It is roughly the size of Texas, containing approximately 3.5 million tons of trash. Bags, wrappers, toys, and bottles are only part of what can be found in this dangerous dump floating midway between Hawaii and San Francisco. The effects on sea life and fish are severe" (education.nationalgeographic.com 2012).

SPA SPOTLIGHT

SPA ANJALI
At the Westin Riverfront Resort and Spa at Beaver Creek Mountain

The spa's goal is to take care of people and the planet by reconnecting them to nature and providing an authentic wellness experience.

Contact Name: Gaye Steinke, General Manager (2012)

East West Resorts
126 Riverfront Lane, Avon, CO
www.spaanjali.com
Facility size: 23,000 sq. ft.
Number of employees: 100
Number of treatment rooms: 14
Established in: 2008

Facility Description

Located in Colorado's only LEED Silver-certified hotel, Mother Nature takes center stage in the design and treatment styles of the 23,000-square-foot, 14 treatment room Spa Anjali. Spa guests can take a dip in an outdoor saline lap pool, relax in any of the three infinity hot tubs, and receive complimentary access to the Athletic Club Fitness Center.

SPA GOALS AND VISION

What is your green business mission statement?

The Green Team's mission is to uphold the Westin Riverfront Resort and Spa's dedication to sustainability leadership in the Vail Valley through associate and guest education, community outreach, and continued commitment to our LEED Certification responsible practices.

What is your spa image?

Spa Anjali is committed to offering a spa experience that values both the health of our clients and the environment.

What are your sustainability goals?

The spa's goal is to take care of people and the planet by reconnecting them to nature and the elements: earth, fire, air, and water. This is achieved with product choices, elements on the décor, and views from the spa. Inside, guests will find rock and natural wood finishes and plenty of natural light. Outside, guests enjoy mountain views, witness sunsets, watch the river flow by, and inhale fresh alpine air.

What business practices or areas would you like to make more sustainable?

We are always looking for improvement in product packaging, procurement from local vendors, energy efficiency, and greywater reclamation.

What are the challenges in being green?
It sometimes is a bit more difficult to find the products desired, in the required quantities, but we've been very fortunate to have local vendors with a similar mindset who support our mission.

Is the staff interested in greening the facility?
The staff is highly engaged and supports the green efforts on a daily basis.

What positive benefits do you offer your staff?
Weekly complimentary yoga is offered and enjoyed by the housekeeping staff.

Employees are eligible to join the fitness club at a greatly reduced rate.

Complimentary chair massage is offered at employee health fairs, meetings, and celebrations.

Do you promote your green practices?
Yes, through a variety of ways.

SPA ELEMENTS

The Menu
- Meaning "divine offering" in Sanskrit, Spa Anjali offers three incredible mystical excursions and healing journeys to the Alps, Himalayas, or Rocky Mountains.
- A journey to the Alps introduces healing through aromatherapy and soothing water therapies.
- A traditional Riverstone Massage or a Red Clover and Honey Body Mask offers energetic healing properties of the Rocky Mountains.
- The Himalayan journey offers unique treatments based on Ayurveda, or the "science of life", that include Abhyanga Massage, Shirodara, and the Ayurvedic Facial.

Products
- We seek to only buy from companies that are environmentally and socially responsible as well as offer products that are free from harmful ingredients.
- All treatment products are 100% organic when possible and always without harmful or synthetic ingredients.
- Retail shops offer items that are sustainable, organic, or natural.
- *Face:* ISUN and Eminence.
- *Body:* Local handcrafted products from Buzz, as well as Pino and Tara.
- *Hair:* Davines.
- *Nails:* Spa Ritual.

Treatment Supplies
- Spa sheets and robes are made from organic bamboo fabric.
- Organic muslin and bamboo sheets are used for treatments (plastic body wraps avoided).
- Hydraulic cranks are used on treatments tables to save energy (instead of electrical cranks).

Building
- Built in 2008, the building is LEED Silver certified.
- Concrete slab/stucco/stone construction.

Energy
- Weatherization procedures have been performed.
- Energy audits are performed monthly and annually.

HVAC System
- The boiler system uses natural gas; temperature controls are regulated.
- Zoned HVAC.
- Use of glass for natural lighting and passive solar heating.
- Consumption is measured monthly and annually.

Appliances
- Energy STAR.

Type of Lighting
- High efficiency lighting.
- Occupancy sensors in spa rooms, guest rooms, and public spaces.

Water
- Ozone infusion in the laundry.
- Fixtures: sinks, faucets, and toilets are low flow.
- Outdoor saline pool and hot tub.

Green Materials
- The spa was built using eco-friendly interior finishes and materials including flooring made from sustainable bamboo.

Indoor Environmental Quality (IEQ)
- Environmentally-sensitive cleaning products are used in the spa and fitness center.

Purchasing
- Plastic water bottles are not used. Biodegradable cups made from corn are used throughout the spa and fitness center (will biodegrade at a local compost facility).
- Vendors are selected due to their sustainable business practices; local vendors are preferred.
- Recyclable and/or compostable containers are made with sustainable fibers.

Waste Reduction
- Recycling collection in all guestrooms and at all office locations. Central collection of recyclables on all guestroom floors. We co-mingle all plastic, paper, and metal into a single stream.

- Hotel guests may opt for our priority green check-in: arrive to your appointment in your Westin Heavenly robe and eliminate the need for an additional robe or locker.
- Our 55-gallon massage oil drums are reused to make outdoor BBQs.
- Dual-sided printing is mandated.
- Certified soy-based inks are used. Toner recycling program is in place.

Landscaping, Exteriors
- *Plants:* We utilize native vegetation as much as possible.
- *Water:* Irrigation is minimized through zoned and timed infrastructure, watering only when needed at optimal times of day.
- *Soil:* We utilize compost generated on-site for soil regeneration.
- *Chemicals:* Chemicals are only used if vital for the health of the plants, and then only those which are deemed environmentally safe are used.
- *Compost:* We compost organic waste on-site which is used in our herb/vegetable garden and other landscape areas on-site.

Transportation
- We offer incentives to associates who carpool and have preferred designated parking for carpool and electric vehicles.

Food Service
- 80% of all food items served in the resort are organic.

Marketing
- As a LEED Silver property, we ensure our green practices are a part of our marketing philosophy and are included in all meeting proposals.

Community
- Staff participates in semi-annual river, trail, and highway cleanup projects.

Education
- A portion of employee orientation is spent on the resort's sustainability philosophies and practices (1 hour).
- On-going communication from the resort's Green Team keeps new programs and current focuses in front of associates.
- The hotel hosts a community outreach program, the Eagle Valley Alliance, with quarterly meetings to help individuals and businesses employ green practices.

CHAPTER 13

Healthy Indoor Environmental Quality

INTRODUCTION

Indoor Environmental Quality (IEQ) is an extensive topic that goes beyond good air quality. Making spaces beautiful and pleasing addresses the mental and physical comfort of the occupants. This is the basis for indoor environmental quality and encompasses clean air, along with thermal, physical, visual, and acoustic comfort. Using green materials is part of ensuring healthy indoor air quality (IAQ). In a spa, these are important components for the guests, staff, and the atmosphere.

In salons, toxic chemicals from hair and nail products are prevalent. New healthier products address some of these issues. Ventilation in salons is very important to people's health. Many illnesses are unknowingly caused by bad air quality in homes and businesses. This is not surprising, as our indoor habitat is where most of us spend 90% of our time (epa.gov 2009). Chapters 23 and 24 have more information on IEQ and building.

WORDS OF WISDOM

The creation of a building is by no means a simple act. Thousands of decisions will go into that process and those decisions will be based on stated or unstated cultural values. A facility built with the intention of being the largest space for the least amount of money will look, feel, and act very different than one where the driving force of the design is "authenticity," the health of the occupant, and concern for our ecology. It costs a little more per square foot for a building that won't harm our health, and more again to build one that will deeply nurture us. When it comes to assessment of real estate there is a disproportionate emphasis on initial "cost per square foot" and this remains a stumbling block for building owners who would choose quality over quantity. Buildings are our greatest investment not just financially but in our health, the health of the environment, and in our children's future.

~ Paula Baker-Laporte, FAIA, Architect, Certified Building Biology Practitioner. Principle of Econest Architecture Inc, primary author of *Prescriptions for a Healthy House*, and co-author with Robert Laporte of *Econest– Creating Sustainable Sanctuaries of Clay, Straw, and Timber*. www.econest.com

DESIGN FOR HEALTH

Using nontoxic green materials and giving occupants personal control over lights, temperatures, noise, and air flow as much as possible is considered part of good design. Studies have shown that ventilation, daylight, and indoor pollutants all affect the performance of workers and students.

CHAPTER 13: Healthy Indoor Environmental Quality 127

Occupant productivity and health is affected by material choices and building design. If the staff are not comfortable, they cannot concentrate on their jobs. Working in a place that is beautiful and healthy leads to increased productivity and satisfaction. This leads to a more stable, sustainable, and profitable business.

Fans in treatment rooms and operable windows help control temperatures and air flow without relying on temperamental mechanical HVAC systems. This saves energy and staff frustration. Humidity and mold control is especially important in spas that have water treatments, steam rooms, and Jacuzzis. Scents and fumes are other facets of indoor air quality. Essential oils and candles affect air quality. People are sensitive to fragrances and certain fragrances can irritate allergies.

Non-toxic cleaning products are another major focus of spa/salon purchasing that affects IAQ. One thing we cannot get away from in the beauty industry is using disinfectants for proper decontamination procedures. Unfortunately, most green, non-toxic products are not strong enough to comply with regulations or protect client health. Make sure proper EPA registered products and procedures are used in cleaning and disinfecting the facility, equipment, and tools before supplementing them with healthier cleaning products.

Good IEQ = good work productivity and happy occupants.

Temperature Control

Heating and air conditioning is the hardest thing to balance in a building. Temperature control is not necessarily a green topic, but a consideration for occupant comfort and health. Making sure everyone is comfortable may take more heat, but could also mean using less air conditioning in certain climates.

Consider vents and HVAC locations when designing a building. Do not locate vents right over spa treatment tables, as the air can be too cold or interfere with product effectiveness. Thermal comfort among occupants is a constant challenge. Everyone has his or her own thermostat and preferences. Studies show that individual climate controls can reduce employee sick leave by over 30% and increase productivity (plants-in-buildings.com 2011).

Conscientious spa technicians know that client comfort comes before theirs and being overly warm is sometimes part of giving the service. In a spa, it is imperative that guests are comfortable and warm, as relaxation and products applied to skin tend to make one cooler. Have you ever had a service but were cold or uncomfortable the entire time, so it was not

Healthy IEQ components: Good air quality, thermal (temperatures and humidity), visual, physical, and acoustical (sound) comfort. Key space features to consider are visuals, daylight, fresh air, good lighting, thermal controls, and nature.

IEQ is related to the 5 senses: visual, auditory, olfactory/smell, taste, and tactile/touch.

Figure 13-1: Colors, lighting, and views all affect peoples' health and mood.

enjoyable? Having control over the temperature in a space is better for the occupants, but facilities have issues with this because it is hard to regulate individual spaces with large mechanical systems.

Visual Aesthetics

Colors, lighting, and views all affect people's health and mood (Figure 13-1). We need natural light as much as possible. A feeling of warmth and views of nature are two important aspects to indoor design. Use natural materials when designing for health. This can include having focal points outside windows and using natural elements in the décor.

We try to bring nature and beauty inside with us through decorating, plants, fountains, art, and other objects. Many facilities use beautiful murals when windows are not an option. Themes such as Zen or Native American will invoke a certain mood. Beauty and aesthetics are aspects of our buildings that are sometimes forgotten in standard design. The beauty field is all about aesthetics and that transcends into the facility atmosphere, so in spas it is especially important to have good design and use of space.

Figure 13-2: Color choices and lighting can stimulate retail sales.

Color Choices

Clearly, colors and décor affect moods. It is usually a subtle effect, but interior designers know the value of color. Wall colors, fabrics, and furniture all convey an atmosphere. Keep in mind that using low-VOC paint and natural fabrics and textiles are necessary for healthy IAQ. Color and lighting are also used to stimulate retail sales (Figure 13-2).

Lighting

Natural lighting, views, and mood lighting affect the ambience in a space. Setting the tone with lighting is considered one of the most important aspects of interior design (Figure 13-3). If there is a beautiful view, take advantage of it. Natural light from windows and skylights is free energy. There have been many studies on natural light and how lighting affects people's moods and happiness. Working in an office with no windows is not a good environment. Fixtures and lighting are discussed in the energy and green building chapters.

Color Therapy

Color is used in design, lighting, and treatments. Think about color choices before decorating.

- Red is stimulating and energizing.
- Green is balancing and soothing.
- Blue is calming and relaxing.
- Neutral, warm tones are relaxing.

Acoustical Elements

Noise control is an important feature of the spa atmosphere. Salons may be loud and exciting with blow dryers and conversations drowning out the music, but if spa services are offered, a quiet area is necessary. Background noise and humming from equipment can also be irritants.

Many day spas have trouble controlling noise levels, so designing soundproof treatment rooms located away from noisy areas is vital for the client

Figure 13-3: Lighting is considered one of the most important aspects of interior design.

experience. Floor-to-ceiling walls are necessary. Many facilities put in rooms that are not completely enclosed for facials and body services. This is not recommended. Why go to a noisy day spa for a massage when you can find a more relaxing one down the street? Soundproofing is worth the extra expense, as it will increase revenue.

The sound of water is a calming feature used in some facilities. The sounds of a creek running or ocean waves are some of the most relaxing sounds in nature (Figure 13-4). A small water fountain with a quiet pump can add to the aesthetics as no other feature can. Meditation areas usually have a water feature.

Figure 13-4: The sound of water movement is one of the most relaxing sounds in nature.

Music and noise are other aspects of the atmosphere that can make or break a service. Think about the client's experience, as staff music preferences are not always the best choice. If the client does not like the chanting music in a massage, or the loud rap music in a salon, they cannot enjoy their service and will probably not return. If the facility has the same automated music throughout, it should be consistent and very calming for the treatment rooms.

INDOOR AIR QUALITY (IAQ)

Every aspect of building design affects the environmental quality (Figure 13-5). Chemicals, particles, and microbes are all irritating pollutants typically found outside that can end up indoors. "Indoor environments are highly complex and building occupants may be exposed to a variety of contaminants from products, chemicals, cleaning products, carpets and furnishings, perfumes, smoke, machines, water-damaged building materials, microbial growth (fungal/mold and bacterial), insects, and outdoor pollutants" (cdc.gov 2012). Other factors such as indoor temperatures, relative humidity, and ventilation levels also affect individuals.

New inventions and technologies such as plastic and toxic binders have led us to sick buildings (sick building syndrome) and not so healthy products. Tight buildings (that do not "leak" air and heat) are great for saving energy, but without adequate ventilation are not good for indoor health. Another concern related to IAQ is how cancer and asthma have become so prevalent. In the bigger picture, manufacturing processes and other emissions in the atmosphere affect indoor and outdoor air quality. Externalizing the cost of pollution and toxins from chemicals and manufacturing is common, while regulations and voluntary practices seem to fluctuate.

Certification and selection standards are available to compare the IAQ for building materials. A valuable website is greenbuildingpages.com. Green Guard, GreenSeal, Pharos, LEED, LCA, GreenSpec, FSC, and many

Relative humidity levels at 60% or greater are conducive to mold growth (ashrae.org 2012). A humidity gauge is helpful to monitor levels.

Figure 13-5: Every aspect of building design affects the environmental quality.

other guidelines help consumers and the building industry wade through material choices. Specific resources for materials and IAQ are listed in the green building chapters and in the resources at the end of the book.

Carbon Dioxide (CO_2)

Monitoring carbon dioxide levels is one way to make sure the ventilation in tight buildings is adequate or optimal. Crowded rooms can have high levels of CO_2. Lack of ventilation leads to high CO_2 levels, which causes fatigue. CO_2, lead, asbestos, radon, mold, and other hidden materials can be detected through testing.

CHEMICALS AND TOXINS

Material choices can affect our health for many years. Paints, glues, finishes, and carpets have chemicals that will affect our lungs and skin over long periods of time. Moisture causes mold in different areas of buildings, mostly unseen, and can go undetected. The building envelope structure and components can also be a cause of poor IEQ.

When choosing materials, avoid VOCs, formaldehyde, and polyvinyl chloride (PVC). These are prevalent in materials and the main source of poor IAQ. Many people are allergic to mold, mites, and chemicals. Many health effects go unnoticed and no one knows how much our exposure from indoor pollutants has led to health problems. We have become acclimated to unhealthy chemicals and pollutants. For example, that new carpet or car smell is due to the off-gassing of VOCs.

Benzene, ethylene oxide, formaldehyde, and vinyl chloride are all known carcinogens used in many products and materials.

The World Health Organization (WHO) has "guidelines for the protection of public health from a number of chemicals commonly present in indoor air. The substances benzene, carbon monoxide, formaldehyde, naphthalene, nitrogen dioxide, polycyclic aromatic hydrocarbons (especially benzo[a]pyrene), radon, trichloroethylene and tetrachloroethylene have indoor sources, are known to be hazardous to health, and are often found indoors in concentrations of concern to health" (who.int 2010). The US Department of Health and Human Services report on carcinogens identifies agents, substances, mixtures, and exposure circumstances that are known or suspected to cause cancer in humans (osha.gov 2012).

Multiple Chemical Sensitivity (MCS) is a term for individuals who experience unusually severe and chronic sensitivity or allergy-like reactions to many different types of pollutants. These often include solvents, VOCs, perfumes, petrol, smoke, pollen, and other chemicals commonly found in indoor environments. MCS is challenging to diagnose and to determine the exact cause. Symptoms may include burning eyes, nausea, fatigue, migraines, vertigo, rhinitis, poor memory, sore throat, light and noise sensitivity, sinus problems, sleep problems, digestive pains, and muscle and joint pain (multiplechemicalsensitivity.org 2012).

In 2003, the Centers for Disease Control (CDC) released a national study on *body burdens* found in Americans. Findings indicated widespread, low-level contamination from chemicals known to cause health issues. Notably, chemicals that cause fetal developmental issues and neurological damage, such as phthalates and mercury, were highest in women and children. The study also noted that toxic chemicals that had previously raised concern, such as lead, DDT, and PBT, were down by half the amount from tests done a decade earlier. Policies that restrict or eliminate harmful substances have helped reduce the exposure. See cdc.gov for new reports on body burdens.

Hormone Disruptors and Endocrine Disruptors

Hormone and endocrine disruptors are chemicals that mimic hormones in the endocrine system and interfere with natural hormones in humans and animals. Potential hormone and endocrine disruptors can be found in a variety of materials. Health concerns from low-level exposure include neurodevelopmental disorders, reproductive abnormalities, cancer in women, and decreased sperm count in men (saferchemicals.org 2009).

Many products have been identified as containing potential hormone- and endocrine-disrupting chemicals including pesticides, PCBs, surfactants (contains nonylphenols), epoxy, plastics (many contain phthalates and bisphenol A), and flame retardants (PBDE-47 and others). The Centers for Disease Control and Health has more information on IAQ at cdc.gov.

> Dust and mold cause the majority of indoor air quality problems. Common allergens and irritants include smoke, dust mites, pollen, pets, fungi/molds, endotoxins, VOCs, dust, and radon.

Volatile Organic Compounds (VOCs)

Volatile organic compounds (VOCs) are "emitted as gases from certain solids or liquids. VOCs include a variety of chemicals, which may have short- and long-term adverse health effects (Figure 13-6). Concentrations of many VOCs are consistently higher indoors (up to ten times higher) than outdoors. VOCs are emitted by a wide array of products, including paints and lacquers, paint strippers, cleaning supplies, pesticides, building materials and furnishings, copiers and printers, and glues and adhesives....VOCs can cause eye, nose, and throat irritation; headaches; loss of coordination; nausea; and damage to liver, kidney, and the central nervous system. Some organic compounds (carbon-based) can cause cancer in animals; some are suspected or known to cause cancer in humans. Key signs or symptoms associated with exposure to VOCs include nose and throat discomfort, headache, allergic skin reaction, nausea, fatigue, and dizziness....Studies have found that levels of several VOCs average 2 to 5 times higher indoors than outdoors. During and for several hours immediately after certain activities, such as paint stripping, levels may be 1,000 times more than outdoor levels" (epa.gov 2012).

Figure 13-6: VOCs may have short- and long-term adverse health effects.

Nail Salons

Health hazards from chemicals in nail salons are serious. Adequate ventilation, MSDS sheets, protective gloves, masks, and numerous chemicals, including the toxic trio, are covered in *Health Hazards in Nail Salons* by the US Department of Labor, Occupational Safety & Health Administration at osha.gov (2012). Technicians working with hair chemicals should take similar precautions.

IAQ Best Practices include:

- Use green building materials and avoid toxic chemicals.
- Avoid irritating scents in products.
- Have good ventilation and change air filters regularly.
- Control and monitor humidity; monitor CO_2 levels.
- Clean and dust often.
- Check HVAC systems for sturdy ducts and good filter systems; check the location and efficiency of external vents.

FENG SHUI DESIGN

Interior design and layout take IEQ one step further with **Feng Shui**, the ancient Chinese practice of how the arrangement of the outer world affects our inner world. Our home or building environment should be arranged harmoniously so that health, prosperity, and happiness thrive. According to Feng Shui design, if the building or space is not aligned, energy does not flow as it should and our life reflects this by becoming stuck or unhealthy (ehow.com 2012). Feng Shui concepts correlate with standard interior design techniques.

Color balance, the four directions, yin and yang, and the five elements are all components of Feng Shui design. Feng Shui is about Chi flow and building energy (Figure 13-7). Everything is alive with Chi—our vital energy. It is the breath of life—buildings breathe as we breathe. Biologically compatible buildings are connected to the outside. For example, viewscapes, fish tanks and water fountains all give positive energy to rooms. Lighting, fresh air, and color choices are part of Feng Shui (fengshui.about.com 2012).

Another aspect of building energy is clutter. Clutter and chaos drain energy and creativity. A messy office is thought to clutter the mind. There is some definite truth to this messy desk idea when you are trying to be productive but are wading through papers. It is fun to pick up a reference book and make a bagua map of the home or office to reorganize the rooms for good Feng Shui. It can't hurt to have a good Feng Shui design and many people believe that the philosophy has made a difference in their lives and businesses.

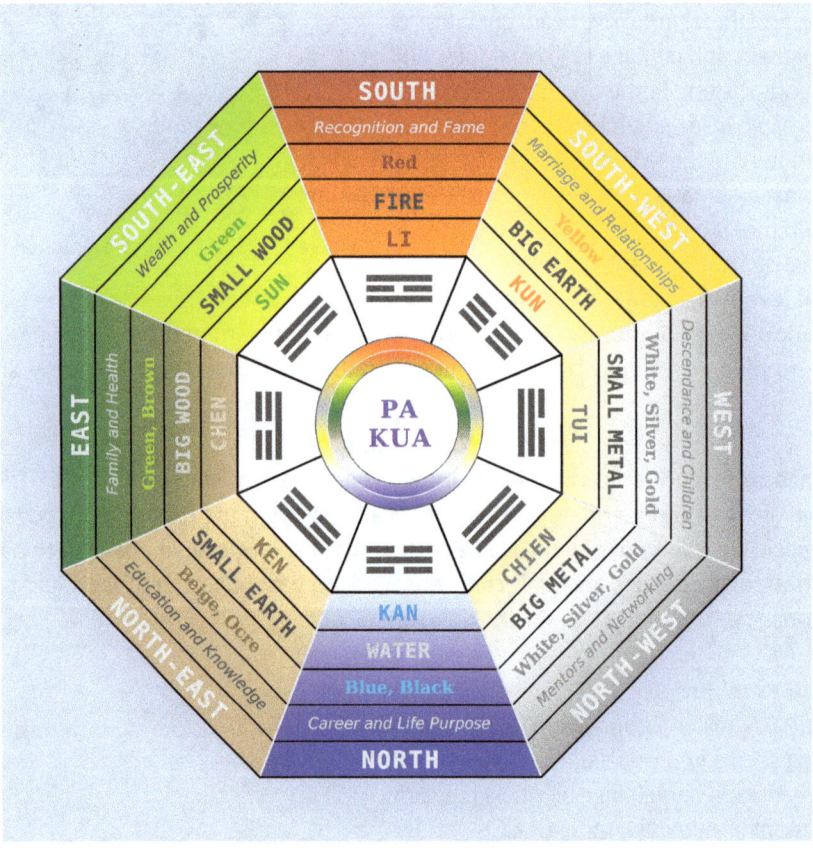

Figure 13-7: The Feng Shui Bagua Map.

SPA SPOTLIGHT

THE SPA AT CLUB NORTHWEST
The spa is all about philanthropy. It is a heart-felt mission that focuses on giving back to people.

Contact: Annette Draper, Owner, Spa Director (2012)

The Spa at Club Northwest/ Club Northwest LLC

2160 NW Vine Street, Grants Pass, OR 97526

www.thespaatclubnw.com

Facility size: Spa: 2600 sq. ft.

Number of employees: 21 (spa) 10 full-time.

Number of treatment rooms: 5: including a Synergie room, 5 salon/hair stations, 2 pedi, and 2 mani.

Established: added spa in 2007.

Facility Description
Italian villa-style spa plus fitness club, salt water pool, steam, sauna, food, and retail areas.

SPA GOALS AND VISION

What is your green business mission statement?
The focus is on people and giving back to the community: over $750,000 in cash and in-kind donations to date! The Club NW green team supports responsible stewardship of our environment for the wellness of the members as well as our planet. Our mission: as a leader in the fitness industry, one of our goals is to make the club as environmentally friendly as possible. With a 5-acre, 60,000-square-foot facility, serving thousands of members, it's a challenging but worthwhile task.

What is your spa image?
Full service, luxury wellness spa that is environmentally conscious. The Spa is thriving in a small town even with the recent recession due to the community focus and business savvy. The business is one of integrity and positive energy.

What are your sustainability goals?
Solar thermal water heating, motion activation of all lighting, auto flush toilets and urinals, using treadmills and bikes to make electricity, and solar power.

What is important to you regarding sustainability?
Lowering the carbon footprint and involving others in the process.

What business practices or areas would you like to make more sustainable?
In-house recycling and sorting, Blue Sky energy derived from sustainable means: wind, solar, etc.

What are the challenges in being green?
Cost and accessibility to established recycling centers in the area.

Is the staff interested in greening the facility?
Absolutely.

What business practices do you think your clients/members want to see with regard to sustainability?
Power generation from fitness equipment in the cardio theater.

Have you seen any positive effects from green practices you have implemented?
The Club has donated over $750,000 in cash and services since inception in 1997.

What positive benefits do you offer your staff?
Incentives, club membership, wellness benefits, exemplifying a LOHAS lifestyle.

Do you promote your green practices? What promotional methods do you use for this?
Yes, in-house signage, website, newsletter, club in-house TV, local editorials.

SPA ELEMENTS

The Menu
- Printed on recycled paper; use e-blasts to reduce paper use.

Face
- Natural, botanically-based products: Academie (France), MD Formulations, Cell Renewel Systems. Synergie® Vacuum massage facials, light therapy, microdermabrasion.

Body
- Synergie Elite™ cellulite body sculpting treatments, body wraps.
- Royal bamboo wrap and scrub using cocoa cups and bamboo sticks.

Hair
- Wella color, Pureology, Sebastian.

Nails
- Natural protocols are botanically-based; Zoya polish, gel nails.

Makeup
- Colorescience Pro, Bare Escentuals.

Hair removal
- Full waxing services offered.

Other
- Aroma journey featuring Young Living oils; massage: both therapeutic and medical are offered; acupuncture.

Service Sales and Retail
- Synergie body treatment: 60% retention; spa: 39% rebooking.
- Retail is equal to 95% of services (almost 50% of sales!).

Products
- Recycled packaging, refillable containers, no animal testing.
- *Face:* Academie (natural, botanical based), MD Formulations.
- *Body:* Young Living aromatherapy products and jojoba oil for massage.
- *Hair:* Wella haircolor (fewer chemicals), Pureology.
- *Nails:* gels, shellac, Zoya nail products.
- *Makeup:* Colorescience (refillable, recyclable packaging), Bare Escentuals.

Supplies
- We look for vendors who are as concerned about the environment as we are and have practices in place to make a difference.

Treatment Supplies
- Microfiber linens.
- Paper is recycled, use both sides of paper.
- Spa water is from filtered system, infused with lemons and mint from spa courtyard plants.
- We use glass and cornstarch cups for all beverages at the spa.
- Minimal plastic usage; recycled if used.
- All general cleaning products are all natural; Thieves cleaner from Young Living oils.

Facility
- The existing building is a remodeled former manufacturing plant; also utilized building materials salvaged from the Southern California earthquake: recycled bricks from the Loma Prieta earthquake in the 1980's were used for the exterior of the building.

Energy
- We purchase Blue Sky green power from the electric company.
- Full spectrum lighting, compact fluorescents, motion sensitive activation of lighting.
- Consumption is tracked and measured.

Building
- Built in 1961. Remodeled: 1996–present—we are always improving our facility to stay ahead of the curve.
- *Type of insulation:* Recycled denim in newly remodeled areas, R-value is 30 or greater.
- Weatherization is performed and ongoing by facilities staff; energy audits have been done on appliances by the utilities company.

HVAC system
- Electric heat pump; regulated temperature controls; thermostat settings: 69° to 72° F.
- Ventilation system: fresh air and filters.

Appliances
- High efficiency washer and dryer; paid spa staff does all laundry for the facility (called "spa angels").

Hot water heating
- Radiant floor heating in spa treatment rooms.

Type of lighting
- **Fixtures:** 277 fluorescents; bulbs are full spectrum and compact fluorescent. Full spectrum lights are used for health aspects.
- Lighting controls and dimmers, some occupant sensors, solar tube lighting in some newly remodeled areas.

Water

Quality/filtration
- Use Aqua Pure on-site water filtration.
- Salt water pool uses limited chemicals.
- **Hot water:** Uses instant hot water taps, Energy STAR gas water heaters.
- **Fixtures:** Photo activated/motion.
- **Sinks, faucets, showers:** Many are low-flow with aerators.
- **Steam/sauna:** Thermostatically-controlled.

Green Materials

- Natural, botanically-based/biodegradable amenities and cleaning products.
- Biodegradable, botanically-based cleaners and soaps, shampoos, and lotions provided in locker rooms.
- **Carpet:** Recent carpeting: low-VOCs.
- **Equipment:** Maintenance performed for equipment longevity.
- **Interiors:** Floors, rugs, paint, fabrics, low-VOC paint in most areas, future paint will be no/low-VOC.

Indoor Environmental Quality (IEQ)

- **Ducts and filters:** High micron HVAC filters and duct disinfecting.
- **Ventilation:** Fans everywhere applicable, fresh air: some operable windows.
- **Cleaning products:** Some essential oils, MSDS sheets on chemicals, disinfectants.

Purchasing

- Vendors are vetted.
- Retail bags are recycled.
- **Cups:** Cornstarch (Greenstripe by Ecoproducts: compostable), corn gluten cups.

Waste Reduction

- In-house recycling center for cardboard, paper, glass, plastic, aluminum, and steel.
- Paperless billing and e-marketing, double-sided copies.
- Sorting: Store used materials and equipment for future use.
- Reuse packing materials, reuse cardboard boxes; use old towels for cleaning rags.
- Customer recycling incentive program: clients bring in 6 empty makeup containers and receive discounts off their purchase.

- Marketing is electronic, and the club also uses an in-house club TV for promotions.

Outdoors/Landscaping:
- Drip systems, xeriscaping, and low-water-use trees.
- Soil is amended by Jo-Grow (locally made recycled wood waste compost).
- ***Outdoor areas:*** Outdoor tennis courts, sand volleyball, basketball, picnic area and BBQ.
- The beautiful courtyard has an original wall mural by local artist Janet Gogué, multiple outdoor fountains, and Corsican mint ground covering.

Transportation
- Company uses a ZAP electric vehicle.

Food Service
- We buy local food.
- ***Farmers market:*** Local grower's market delivery and pick up point at the club.
- Wheatgrass is grown on-site.
- Juice bar, organic coffee served, Talbot bulk teas.

Marketing
- Chalkboard for daily available appointments in member view to fill up the day's schedule, club TV, text club TV, radio, e-blasts, print and EVENTS!!!

People
- Health benefit reimbursements, club memberships, service trades, 401(k), on-going training, personal one-on-one corporate coaching available for leaders, a uniquely supportive environment.
- ***Spa events:*** Locks of Love for cancer, "Cut for a Cause" (an original event inspired by one of our stylists), to benefit abused women in our community supporting the Women's Crisis Center, Sparrow Club, Bright Future's "Goddess Event", Boys and Girls Club, "Girlfriends' Great Escape," and many others.
- Charity donations over $750,000 since inception: donations focused on families in need in the community.

Education
- Guest presenters, presentations by staff for club Green days.
- Green team meetings are open to the public.
- Our motto is "Inventing the Future."

CHAPTER 14

Energy Conservation

INTRODUCTION

Energy and electricity are essential to our quality of life. Energy fuels our economy and our ability to work in many ways. A secure, sustainable, and affordable future is dependent on resources, especially energy and water. As energy costs keep growing, this affects our lifestyle.

Conserving resources helps reduce the environmental effects from energy use. Protection from cost inflation by reducing consumption is imperative to keep businesses running. For the spa, it is good to have some knowledge of the facts and figures relating to energy issues. Energy is a vast subject, so only a brief overview of the resources and impacts from energy use are included here. Energy conservation and best practices for your business are continued in the planning chapters and in Chapter 24, Green Building Practices.

Energy Conservation Mantra
"The cleanest, cheapest, and most sustainable form of energy will always be energy efficiency."

BENEFITS OF ENERGY CONSERVATION

The benefits of energy conservation are the same as the sustainability benefits discussed in previous chapters. Saving energy is beneficial for prosperity, people, and the planet. Energy use and savings are easier to measure compared to other resources. Energy conservation is the number one green practice that businesses implement due to the direct cost savings. Heating, ventilation, and cooling systems are a major utility cost. Lighting is approximately 30% of electricity costs. Cost savings helps the bottom line and can in turn be used for other expenses or investments.

A primary focus of green building design is on energy conservation (Figure 14-1). A better building design saves a huge amount of energy use and reduces carbon emissions. A *smaller footprint* (building size) with better space design saves money and wasted space. Monitoring energy use and finding ways to conserve is a top priority for large businesses.

Many large hotel and resort properties are showing approximately a 30% reduction in energy costs after implementing conservation practices. This savings amount is typical for homes and buildings. Lighting retrofits can have a fast payback of one to two years, which means the cost to install is paid for by the energy savings within that time. Anything under five years is considered a fairly fast payback. The average annual return on investment for energy efficiency retrofits and weatherization is more than 20 percent.

Cleaner air quality and less pressure on the environment are two benefits of using less energy. Insulation from rising energy costs and global oil shortages is another major benefit of conservation and using renewable resources. New technology will also help to conserve energy as alternatives to outdated designs are implemented.

ENERGY CONSERVATION PRACTICES

The first step in implementing energy conservation is to analyze what your usage is and what you are doing now to save energy. An energy audit is sometimes free from state agencies, power companies or organizations. The cost involved in having an audit is worth the service, as you can save hundreds to thousands of dollars the first year after implementing conservation measures on older building systems.

Building and operations aspects include insulation, ventilation, windows, weatherization, lighting, appliances, HVAC systems, heating and cooling loads, and electronic devices. See Chapter 17 for conservation practices and the online resources for planning worksheets on energy conservation. Initial steps to implement conservation practices are listed here.

Determining heat loss from leaky buildings and analyzing lighting systems are the main items for your checklist. These should be assessed every few years to check for needed improvements and new technology. If you have a facility manager, they will normally take care of the energy management and the other operating systems. A good conscientious facility manager or building operator is a valuable asset.

You could have energy audits and broader sustainability audits done by professionals or it could be more budget-friendly to do your own tracking. All of the rates, usage, and dates appear on the utility bills, and that data can be entered into basic spreadsheets for analysis.

Figure 14-1: Energy conservation is the primary focus of building green.

Monitoring systems are another good way to track usage. Some larger companies have an interactive "green screen" display in the lobby that continually monitors the building's energy systems. Not only does the system show live temperature data and real-time calculations, it can also help boost efficiency. This is also an interesting way to share your green actions with staff and the clients.

"Energy Management Systems (EMS) are a combination of building management systems and software that manage the building functions in a more energy efficient way and provide demand response controls. The systems reduce energy usage, costs, and carbon emissions." HVAC, lighting, refrigeration, and other systems are automated and monitored, including daily occupancy schedules and peak loads (aceee.org 2012).

> See the EPA Green Building section for energy tips and resources at epa.gov.

Steps to Energy Conservation

- Establish a baseline by calculating the current energy usage.
- Analyze and track utility bills.
- Conduct an energy audit.
- Evaluate the facility room by room.
- Include the heating, cooling, lighting, equipment, appliances, and electronic devices.
- Determine potential conservation measures and calculate potential savings.
- Consider alternative renewable energy sources.
- Establish priorities by the easiest and most affordable solutions first (known as "low hanging fruit").
- Research incentives and tax credits for energy conservation measures.
- Set long-term and short-term goals with timelines.
- Monitor progress on a regular basis.
- Calculate and report the savings.

ENERGY CONCEPTS

Energy is central to our lifestyle and comfort. We do not consciously think about it, but daylighting from the sun, lighting, heat, and transportation are all part of the energy that we rely on. The physiological and psychological needs of people are affected by energy systems. For health, comfort, and productivity, the experiences of occupants should be considered throughout the energy design process. Energy systems work best when integrated into the whole building design. These concepts are discussed in Chapter 23, Building Green.

Impacts from energy use reach beyond the kWh used on our utility bills. Energy is expensive and has many external costs to society. The source, production, transportation, and international issues are all costs associated with energy. These could be measured by using a Life Cycle Assessment model that computes all the costs, but this is complicated and is not usually feasible or expected for small businesses.

We pay for infrastructure, land, roads, dams, transportation, and air pollution from energy production. Global gas and oil conflicts are additional energy issues. Like most resources, the main concerns are pollution, cost, and scarcity. Climate change and greenhouse gases are impacted by energy use, including heating and transportation. In industrialized countries, buildings are estimated to be responsible for approximately 40% of total energy use. The energy we use also accounts for most of the greenhouse gases in the atmosphere, primarily caused by cars and transportation sectors, which use the most gas/oil (epa.gov 2012).

Renewable energy (wind, solar) can provide much of our energy needs, but the upfront costs are still high so it is not always affordable. Hopefully, the cost will go down with increased market share and improved technology. Government incentives and rebates have helped make renewables more affordable.

Energy Sources

Energy sources are divided into two groups—*renewable* (an energy source that can be naturally replenished) and *nonrenewable* (an energy source that is depleted and cannot be replenished). Nonrenewable energy sources include oil and petroleum products, gasoline, diesel, heating oil, propane, natural gas, coal, and nuclear energy. Renewable energy sources include solar energy, wind power, geothermal energy, hydroelectric power, and biomass. *Biofuels* are ethanol, biodiesel, and other fuels made from biomass.

Oil demand continues to increase steadily. "Current projections foresee a 70% increase in oil demand and a 130% rise in CO_2 emissions by 2050. Such an increase in CO_2 emissions could raise global average temperatures by 6°C or more, resulting in significant impacts on all aspects of life and irreversible changes in the natural environment" (worldenergyoutlook.org 2011). New clean energy technology and conservation measures are the main ways to help ensure the energy supply and reduce the negative effects on the environment.

Solar Power

Solar power includes *photovoltaics* for electricity and solar thermal systems for heating buildings and water (Figure 14-2). *Solar thermal systems* use solar collectors to absorb solar radiation to heat water. In warm climates and in other countries, solar hot water units are common and have a simple, affordable design. Photovoltaic (PV) systems use solar electric cells, which convert solar radiation directly into electricity. The cost has come down on PV systems, but the ROI or payback in years still makes it a long-term investment.

Passive solar design for buildings takes advantage of the free heat from the sun. In colder northern climates, windows are designed to face south for solar heat gain. Getting to net zero energy use is a goal for many people and companies. The most efficient energy is the energy that is not used—this is the first step of conservation. See Chapter 23 for more information on renewables and passive solar design.

Renewable Energy Incentives

Investment in and use of renewable energy is both encouraged and required by a range of federal, state, and local government legislation and utility incentives. As noted on eia.gov, there are tax credits and incentives that businesses and homeowners can take advantage of, but these change constantly. The major types of programs currently in place include Federal Renewable Energy Tax Credits, Renewable Energy Certificates (RECs), State Financial Incentives, Net Metering Programs, Feed in Tariffs (FITs), and Green Power Programs.

US Energy Use by Sectors

- Transportation: 27.5%
- Industrial: 30.1 %
- Residential: 22.2%
- Commercial: 18.2%

(measured in Quadrillion BTUs: British thermal units, census.gov 2012)

Energy Consumption in the US

- Oil: 36%
- Natural gas: 25%
- Coal: 20%
- Nuclear power: 8%
- Renewable energy: 9%

(mainly biomass and hydro)

(measured in Quadrillion BTUs: British thermal units, US Energy Information Administration, eia.gov statistics, 2012)

Figure 14-2: Solar power includes photovoltaics and solar thermal systems.

Greenhouse Gases

Climate change occurs when long-term weather patterns are altered. Global warming, a rise in the average global temperature, is a result of climate change. Today's atmosphere contains over 32 percent more carbon dioxide than it did at the start of the industrial era. Extreme weather events are becoming more common with these climate changes.

"We can reduce greenhouse gas (GHG) emissions in many different ways. Most of the solutions involve increasing the efficiency of our energy use to reduce fossil-fuel demand. Many of the potential solutions have benefits beyond GHG reduction, such as increased employment, stimulation of the green technology manufacturing sector, and reduced urban air pollution" (davidsuzuki.org 2012). ***Greenhouse Gases (GHG)*** are those gaseous constituents of the atmosphere, both natural and anthropogenic, that reflect back infrared radiation (heat) emitted by the Earth's surface (Figure 14-3).

Renewable energy sources from the sun are under-represented in our accounting—for instance, free daylighting and solar heat gain.

Carbon Offsets

Many people and organizations are going carbon neutral with carbon offsets. A *carbon offset* is a certificate representing the reduction of one metric ton (2,205 lbs) of carbon dioxide emissions. "If you develop a project that reduces carbon dioxide emissions, every ton of emissions reduced results in the creation of one carbon offset. Project developers can then sell these offsets to finance their projects. There are hundreds of different types of carbon reduction projects. For example, wind farms generate clean energy, which reduces carbon emissions from coal-burning power plants. In order to finance its operations, a wind farm can sell these reductions in the form of carbon offsets" (terrapass.com 2012).

Figure 14-3: Greenhouse gases.

Greenhouse gas components:
Water vapor (H_2O), carbon dioxide (CO_2), nitrous oxide (N_2O), and methane (CH_4), are the primary greenhouse gases in the Earth's atmosphere.

(EPA, Intergovernmental Panel on Climate Change 2012)

SPA SPOTLIGHT

SPA MOANA AT HYATT REGENCY MAUI
Local Hawaiian healing in tune with Mother Nature and the ocean.

Contact: Rachael McCrory, Spa Director (Michael Lanzo, 2011)

Hyatt Regency Maui Resort & Spa
200 Nohea Kai Drive, Lahaina, HI

www.maui.hyatt.com

Facility size: 15,000 sq. ft. (plus 5000 sq. ft. fitness center below the spa)

Number of employees: 65 to 70

Number of treatment rooms: 15 and 2 oceanside cabanas

Established in: April, 2000

Facility Description
Ocean view relaxation lounge, locker rooms, steam, sauna, and Jacuzzi. Full of aloha spirit and ohana (family) in a relaxing, oceanfront setting.

SPA GOALS AND VISION

What is your business mission statement?
To embrace authentic practices and ingredients to care for the body, mind, and spirit. We encourage guests to take time for themselves by slowing down, relaxing, and enjoying the journey.

What is your spa image?
Hyatt Spas is a worldwide collection of spas. Each spa is custom-designed to embrace the local environment and culture to provide an authentic indigenous experience. Local Hawaiian healing is in tune with Mother Nature and the ocean, in harmony with the environment and culture.

What are your sustainability goals?
Initiatives from Hyatt: caring for our guests by encouraging healthy lifestyles and offering local and healthy cuisine options; support local business by using products made on Maui such as local cheeses and sugars, etc.

What is important to you regarding sustainability?
Conserving product and supply use, ordering from local vendors.

What are your current green practices?
We use Eco-products compostable cups, reusable linens in the services, rather than disposables. We also use post-consumer recycled materials for disposables. We use vendors that support a similar mindset on green practices. We are currently using iLike Organic Skin Care.

What are the challenges in being green?
Shipping burdens and costs.

Is the staff interested in greening the facility?
Yes, definitely. Hyatt trains the staff and hosts webinars on greening facilities.

What business practices do you think your clients want to see concerning sustainability?
Embrace a commitment to sustainable and renewable product lines and practices; pay mindful attention to the environment while honoring the guest's unique needs; use organic and recycled products whenever possible.

Have you seen any positive effects from green practices you have implemented?
Yes, economic savings of energy and water.

What positive benefits do you offer your staff? (health, wellness, incentives)
The staff benefits from receiving services, employee engagement, and training. We have low to no turnover, an ohana family dynamic, and health insurance.

Do you promote your green practices? What promotional methods do you use for this?
Every treatment that incorporates green practices or organic ingredients is mentioned in the spa menu. Our spa concept states that we utilize authentic practices and natural Hawaiian botanicals.

SPA ELEMENTS

The Menu
- The menu is printed on FSC paper.
- Services are focused on Island healing, nature, and local culture. Services are based on refreshing natural Hawaiian botanicals and scents.

Face
- Oxygenating facial delivers powerful results using an organic and sustainable product line.

Body
- Kaanapali coffee scrubs, sugar scrubs, ginger, volcanic clay for the detox wrap.
- **Lomi-Lomi:** The Hawaiian therapy massage using long, rhythmic strokes.

Hands and feet
- Manicures and pedicures: organic, homegrown Hawaiian products.

Hair removal
- Repurposing items lessens shipping needs and simultaneously lowers the supply cost.

Products
- Services are based on refreshing natural Hawaiian botanicals and scents such as kukui nut, Hawaiian noni, papaya, pineapple, coconut, citrus, Kauai volcanic clay, Maui Turbinado sugar, Hawaiian coffee berry, Big Island spirulina, Hawaii awapuhi (torch ginger), and macadamia nut.

- Cocoa Butter Bliss is made locally in Kihei.
- *Face:* Epicuren and iLike Organic Skin Care products.
- *Body:* Epicuren, iLike, Warren Botanicals (made on the Big Island), Lokahi (the Spa Moana Brand), Kaanapali coffee scrubs, sugar scrubs, volcanic clay from Kauai for the detox wrap, ginger mask from the Big Island, Kukui oil (a Hawaiian oil).
- *Hair products*: Moroccan Oil.
- *Hands and feet:* Island Essence products used in pedicures are made in Maui; Customized foot files are sourced through a local Maui vendor are designed and made for a spa setting.
- *Other Retail:* Alii Kula Lavender products from the local lavender farm in upcountry Maui.

Supplies
- Corn cups and bamboo plates are used for serving food and beverages.
- All copy paper used is Sustainable Forestry Initiative certified (sfiprogram.org).
- The plastic bags used by accounting for associates are Sentry Green and biodegradable.
- Green cleaning products used for cleaning spa windows.
- Esthetic supplies that are disposable are made with recycled products, such as the biodegradable cotton rounds.

Energy
- Engineering tracks consumption and strives for maximum efficiency in the operation throughout the property.
- The steam room, Jacuzzi tub, and sauna are on timers.

Building
- Built in 2000; remodeled in 2003.
- Building orientation and climate: window tinting to the west for shading.

HVAC system
- Computerized temperature controls.
- Ventilation system: fresh air; tropical breezes.

Type of lighting
- Timers are used on all house lights to prevent waste; energy efficient light bulbs.

Water
- Staff is trained to conserve water. The Island has a limited water supply.
- Landscaping uses recycled irrigation water sources.
- The hot water expelled from the air conditioning units in the hotel rooms is recycled and used in the pool.
- *Amenities:* Spa offers water with fresh fruit infused in the water.
- *Toilets:* Retrofitting in progress (2011).
- *Showers:* Vichy operations kept to minimal use.
- *Steam/sauna:* Timers used.

Green Materials
- Green purchasing is used as much as possible.

Indoor Environmental Quality (IEQ)
- Fresh air (operable windows): natural ventilation from fresh air open breezes; front door is left open.
- The staff asked for less toxic green cleaning products.

Waste Reduction
- Hotel utilizes recycling programs: glass, plastic, cardboard, massage product container recycling.
- Staff training for proper recycling bin disposal.
- *Paper:* Use smaller receipts, double-sided copies, reuse scratch paper.
- Compostable cups.

Landscaping, Exteriors (Tropical)
- Maintained by resort staff; ocean maintained by dolphins and whales.

Food Service
- Restaurant offers local, organic food choices; big emphasis on local ingredients for our healthy food offerings including Surfing Goat Dairy Goat Cheese made in Kula, Maui.

People
- *Fitness:* Hyatt has a *Stay Fit* program that provides guests with fitness options and running, walking maps.
- *Education:* Green education is given to the staff.

Green Conservation Achievements and Practices as of 2010:
- Recipient of the 2009 Green Business Award from the State of Hawaii Green Business Program.
- Recipient of the *Four Green Key Rating* from the Green Key Eco-Rating Program.
- Resort-wide greenhouse gas emissions: 11% drop since 2006.
- Resort-wide water consumption: 5.3% drop since 2006.
- Propane consumption: 10.7% reduction since 2008.
- Water consumption: 5.1% reduction since 2008.
- Electricity consumption: 5.1% reduction since 2008.

Guest and meeting room eco-friendly upgrades:
- Thermostats with occupancy sensors automatically lower A/C usage when room is not occupied. Guestrooms have a "GREEN" button, which allows guests to choose to reduce A/C usage while in the room.
- Low-flow showerheads and toilets lessen water consumption.
- LCD flat-screen information monitors installed at every meeting room, and in public areas for guest information throughout the resort reduce paper waste.

Maui property eco-friendly upgrades:
- Ümalu Restaurant focuses on local and seasonal products, as well as the use of recyclable and compostable to-go containers.
- Resort-wide use of eco-friendly compostable to-go cups (made from corn).
- 7,035 gallons of food waste per month recycled and utilized to nourish animals at a locally operated pig farm.
- 600 gallons of grease and oil per month recycled into biodiesel.
- Renovation of all elevators to improve energy efficiency.
- Replacement of lighting on guest floors, meeting rooms, and restaurants to more energy-efficient models.

Average monthly recycling metrics:
- Total recycled goods: 57,254 lbs per month:
  Green waste: 27,760 lbs per month; glass: 15,900 lbs per month.
  Cardboard: 11,940 lbs per month; mixed paper: 560 lbs per month.
  Aluminum: 558 lbs per month; plastic: 516 lbs per month; tin: 20 lbs per month.

Additional features:
- Will have green guest rooms for those with allergies.
- Retrofitting toilets in 806 guest rooms.
- Air conditioning systems are auto controlled with occupancy sensors in guest rooms.z

CHAPTER 15

Water Conservation

INTRODUCTION

Water is an integral part of the beauty industry. The healing power of water has been used by cultures for thousands of years. Social bathing in healing waters and natural hot springs has been practiced by the Mesopotamians, Egyptians, Greeks, Romans, Japanese, and others.

The word "spa" is derived from a number of sources. "Spa may originate from the Latin word *spagere* (to pour forth, sprinkle, or scatter) or may be an acronym of the Latin phrase *sanitas per aquas* (health through water). Spa was also thought to be the name of a mineral springs town in Belgium centuries ago (spafinder.com 2012). A timeless and relaxing therapy, there is nothing more soothing than soaking in hot water (Figure 15-1).

As spas are expected to have services and facilities similar to hot springs or baths, water is considered one of the most important elements of a spa. Jacuzzis, plunge pools, baths, and Vichy showers are common water therapies. Salon and facial services also require large amounts of water. Maintaining the spa atmosphere and services is important, but how do we do it while using less water?

In order to understand and communicate the whys of sustainability, it is good to review the facts and statistics regarding this precious resource. Fresh water is becoming more scarce and conservation is going to be even more crucial in coming years. The global issues and benefits of water efficiency are included here. Best practices for conservation are continued in the planning chapters.

Figure 15-1: Spa bath therapy.

BENEFITS OF WATER CONSERVATION

The benefits of conserving water are similar to the other natural resources. The most important benefit is environmental sustainability because life depends on fresh water. Social equity and the impact on people from lack of fresh water and food are big issues. Living lighter by using fewer resources so that others have enough is part of social responsibility.

The cost of water is generally not as expensive as other resources, but water and sewer bills are rising. Water rationing is used in some areas when there are droughts. The infrastructure costs of water supplies, storm

Water is Life
"When the well is dry, we know the worth of water."
~ Benjamin Franklin

water piping, and sewer treatment facilities are very high, so reducing these saves on public fees and taxes.

In addition to cost savings, letting clients know that your facility is trying to save water will show a commitment to sustainability. Educating people on the therapeutic benefits of water helps build appreciation and respect for the spa beyond the treatments. *Balneotherapy*, water therapy, is considered part of a healthy lifestyle, not just a wasteful luxury with no consideration for the effects on people or the planet.

WATER CONCEPTS

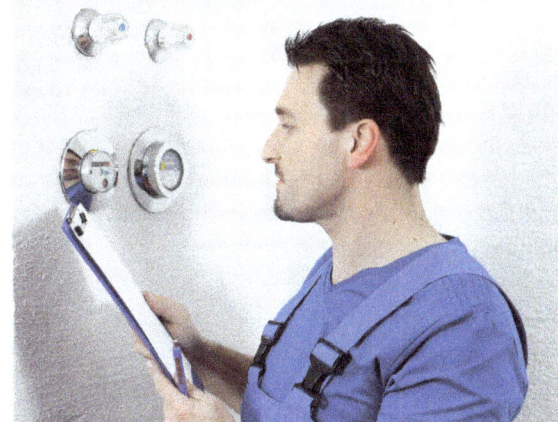

Figure 15-2: Water strategies and footprints will soon be as common as carbon footprints.

Water issues will have a major impact on our business and personal lives. Much of corporate sustainability reporting has been focused on carbon and energy. Many companies have strategies for these, which have a significant impact. Water strategies and footprints will soon be as common as carbon footprints (Figure 15-2). Water is becoming *Blue Gold* or "blue oil" as authors and activists have written.

As with the other sustainability concepts, it is good to have some background knowledge about the issues. The water crisis is predicted to be the biggest issue facing our world in the near future. Food production and our way of life will be impacted by this shortage. Conservation and better water management is needed as population growth, pollution, development, and chemicals/pesticides have all taken their toll on land and water everywhere.

The infrastructure for transporting, treating, and maintaining water is part of the supply issue. Water today is relatively cheap and poorly managed. Municipal water pricing does not include the true cost of using the water supply. Conservation is not always rewarded. Public storm water and piping costs are paid for by taxes and development fees and can be made more affordable with low impact development. Reducing consumption and protecting water quality are less expensive than creating or expanding new supply systems. It is predicted that supplies in the US will become more scarce every year. More efficient planning can save a large part of the development fees as discussed in the green building chapter.

Water Statistics
- 97% of the earth's water is salt water
- 2.5% of all water is freshwater
- Only 1% of the earth's fresh water is available for human use (potable)
- 70% of the world's water withdrawals are for irrigation (farming and landscaping)

(Source: unep.org)

GLOBAL WATER IMPACTS

Global water statistics are included here to help bring awareness to the facts. Water is cited as essential for all socio-economic development and for maintaining healthy ecosystems. Future conflicts over equitable distribution of clean water is a real concern. Another issue is water privatization. As depicted in documentary films such as *Flow*, corporations are buying global water supplies and privatizing them as a commodity. The problem is especially acute in poor countries where people cannot afford to pay for water that should be a free resource necessary for survival.

Water Quality and Health

The ecosystem is interdependent and one domino affects the next one. Land use affects our water.

Pollution in our waterways is caused by many factors including pesticides, development, wastewater discharge, animals, and manufacturing. Wastewater is part of the water problem. Making sure it does not get into fresh water sources is a constant battle and not always managed properly. Furthermore, dumping waste into the ocean is not healthy or ethical. Seafood is scarce and filled with toxins. Deforestation and storm runoff also affect streams, rivers, and the ocean. Buffer zones and tree cover are necessary for streams and aquatic life (usgs.gov 2012).

Storm water management is important to protect waterways and water quality, prevent flooding, and to conserve water. Toxins from fertilizers, pesticides, pharmaceuticals, and hazardous waste from sinks, toilets, drains, and sewers end up in the water. Streams tested by the US Geological Survey were found to be hormonally and pharmaceutically active. This is a huge problem for aquatic life and our water supply.

Nonpoint Source Pollution comes from a non-discernible point of origin; it cannot be traced to a particular pipe or ditch. These types of pollution include "excess fertilizers and herbicides from agricultural lands and residential areas, oil and toxic chemicals from urban runoff, sediment from construction sites, and eroding stream banks." It is widely recognized that these pollutants have harmful effects on drinking water, recreation, fisheries, and wildlife (nepis.epa.gov 2012).

There are many unregulated contaminants in the US. The Environmental Working Group (EWG) analysis of city water utility test data from 2004–2009 found 316 contaminants in the nation's tap water, of which only 115 have regulated safety standards. Other chemicals are unregulated (ewg.org 2009).

Pharmaceuticals and Personal Care Products as Pollutants (PPCPs) are "products used by individuals for personal health or cosmetic reasons or used by agribusiness to enhance growth or health of livestock. PPCPs include thousands of chemical substances—prescription and over-the-counter drugs, veterinary drugs, fragrances, lotions, and cosmetics" (epa.gov 2010). Studies have shown that PPCPs are present in our water bodies, which causes ecological harm (Figure 15-3). This is one more reason to use fewer chemicals in our products.

Figure 15-3: PPCPs cause ecological harm.

Water scarcity is an issue of poverty: 2.6 billion people have no access to sanitation; 1.1 billion people have no access to clean water. (worldwatercouncil.org 2012)

Water and Food Production

According to the Food and Agriculture Organization (FAO), it takes 2400 liters of water to produce 1 hamburger; 200 liters of water to produce 1 glass of milk; 70 liters of water to produce 1 apple; and 25 liters of water to produce 1 potato (unwater.org 2012).

WATER CONSERVATION PRACTICES

Water conservation practices are relatively easy to implement. Indoor and outdoor water use considerations for spas include water therapy equipment, fixtures, appliances, and laundry. An audit can be conducted and there are

many rebate and incentive programs to help businesses install water saving products. Visit the EPA WaterSense website and check with your local and state agencies for more information. Water conservation measures and landscaping best practices are discussed further in later chapters.

Indoor Water Conservation Solutions
- Being mindful of not leaving the water running unless necessary is an easy, free first step in conservation.
- Install low-flow fixtures and aerators for faucets and showers.
- Install low-flow toilets and consider waterless urinals.
- Look for low-water-use appliances.
- Install on-demand water heaters on taps for instant hot water.
- Reduce linen use and use an energy efficient washer.
- Turn off hot tubs and steam rooms when not in use.
- Use water filtration at the faucet or countertop units, whole-house filters or distillers, or small filter pitchers. Do not use bottled water.
- Consider greywater systems to reuse sink or laundry water for landscaping or outdoor use.
- Look into alternatives for chlorine use in pools and soaking tubs. Many are switching to saline pools.

Outdoor Water Conservation Solutions
- Use native plants and low-water-use plants (xeriscaping).
- Reduce chemical use.
- Water wisely outdoors with appropriate systems (drip or sprinklers).
- Install rainwater catchment systems off roofs.
- Use greywater systems.
- For new buildings, low impact development catches more water on-site and uses less storm water infrastructure.
- Match the water source to the appropriate use. For example, use reclaimed water or catchment systems for irrigation and save cleaner potable water for drinking.

BOTTLED WATER ISSUES
Many salons/spas are switching back to filtered tap water, saving a lot of money and helping lighten the environmental problems from bottled water. Use BPA-free stainless steel water bottles and reusable glasses. Many facilities now provide staff and clients with reusable bottles. You can also encourage the staff to bring their own bottles, just as we do shopping bags.

The bottled water industry has exploded in recent years. It is estimated to be a $100 billion industry worldwide and has produced millions of tons of refuse in US landfills. Fifty percent of profits from the water industry market are made in the US. Selling potable bottled water has become big business as bottled water sells for hundreds of times more than what it costs to get straight from the tap (cleanwateraction. org 2012).

The plastic bottle is a huge environmental problem (Figure 15-4). Plastics are not biodegradable and are a hazard to oceans and marine life, including our fish supply. The huge garbage patches in the ocean are full of plastic debris.

According to research, bottled water is not necessarily better than tap water. Surprisingly, bottled water is less regulated and is not tested for E.coli, sourcing, disinfection, asbestos, or phthalates. It is not necessarily filtered nor are there any other certified testing or regulations on bottled water that tap water must meet. It is estimated that 20 to 40 percent of bottled water is actually tap water disguised as special (nrdc.org 1999).

Tap Water
- Tap water is delivered to homes and offices for $0.002 a gallon. Bottled water, which can cost as much per gallon as gasoline, is a thousand times more expensive (Cruz, R. 2008).
- Use a reusable container filled with filtered tap water, but do not reuse single-use water bottles. This can expose you to bacterial build-up and carcinogens leached from the plastic.
- Food and Water Watch has a *Take Back the Tap* report that gives a detailed overview of the issues surrounding tap water versus bottled water.

Figure 15-4: The plastic bottle is a huge environmental problem.

SPA SPOTLIGHT

SUNDARA INN AND SPA
Respect for the natural resources is at the soul of Sundara's green practices.

Contact: Tara McKinley,
Sales and Marketing (2012)

Sundara Inn and Spa

920 Canyon Rd, Wisconsin Dells, WI

www.sundaraspa.com

Facility size: 41,600 sq. ft. (spa 13,000 sq. ft.)

Number of employees: 100

Number of treatment rooms: 16 treatment rooms plus 4 manicure and pedicure stations

Established in: 2003

Sundara is drawn from the Sanskrit word for beautiful. We interpret that as beauty flowing from wellness.

Facility Description
A destination spa nestled in a pine forest on the scenic outskirts of Wisconsin Dells, Wisconsin. Our 26-acre parcel is lush with sky-high pine trees and natural stone outcroppings. Respect for natural resources is at the soul of Sundara's green practices. Our heated outdoor infinity edge pool, sculpted fireplace, waterfalls, and curving deck connect seamlessly with the tranquil environment. The main building is representative of some of the most striking organic-style architecture in the Midwest. Inside, the principles of Feng Shui contribute to a soothing environment.

Our spa treatments incorporate the finest organic products from around the world. The Sundara Spa signature collection even draws ingredients indigenous to the area for an authentic experience. Our spa cuisine features the fruits of labor of fresh, local, and seasonal ingredients sourced from Wisconsin organic farms.

SPA GOALS AND VISION

What is your green business mission statement?
Before Sundara even opened its doors, we felt strongly about our role as a steward of the environment, so much so, in fact, that we wrote that sentiment into our overarching mission statement: We set an example of love and respect for the earth. That single sentence set the tone for specific operational and building practices; equally important, it also established a core principal of how we hope employees lead their lives.

What is your spa image?
Our image is inextricably tied to the land. We are tucked back in a pristine 26-acre pine forest. Not for a day do we take for granted how fortunate we are to work in this setting. Guests appreciate the solitude and recognize the important role the natural resources play in their experience too. All one needs do is reflect back on the Native American culture of the area and the farming heritage of the state to see how genuine our environmental mission is.

What is important to you regarding sustainability?
Respect for the natural resources is at the soul of Sundara's green practices—reducing our footprint on the planet locally and globally. We are dedicated to partnering with like-minded local businesses to create an authentic experience. Our spa cuisine features items sourced from local Wisconsin organic farms, cheese makers, and wineries.

What business practices or areas would you like to make more sustainable?
Water conservation and energy consumption reduction.

What are the challenges in being green?
In most cases, cost and practicality are the largest factors.

Is the staff interested in greening the facility?
Our staff is dedicated to our green practices and often bring ideas to us for consideration.

What business practices do you think your clients want to see with regard to sustainability?
We make all of our efforts transparent, and even list them on a dedicated green page on our website, as we believe strongly in being true to our guests and employees.

Have you seen any positive effects from green practices you have implemented?
We have realized energy and water savings and a decrease in consumption based on the programs we have in place. We feel socially responsible by having the programs in place that we do and our guests appreciate our efforts.

What positive benefits do you offer your staff?
Sundara offers generous discounts on spa services and use of the facility to our staff and their immediate family. Health insurance and wellness programs are available. Sundara is smoke-free for health. Additionally, discounted employee meals are available to promote healthy eating habits.

Do you promote your green practices?
We created a web page dedicated to our green practices. We participate in Earth Day and encourage our guests to partake and make pledges as well.

 SPA ELEMENTS

The Menu
- Guests may select from a complete series of organic spa treatments and product lines.
- The menu itself is printed using a local printer located 45 minutes away, using recycled paper and vegetable-based inks. The printer uses FSC certified paper and repurposes outdated ink.

Products
Face
- Eminence: Organic products with environment-friendly packaging.

- Amala: Produced by organic farming, packaging printed on recycled paper, carbon neutral global headquarters.
- Organic Male: FDA Organic, fair trade, cruelty free, Whole Foods premium standard.
- Medik 8: Recyclable packaging.

Body
- An ancient Cambrian-era sand discovered at the spa's excavation site is used as the exfoliating agent in the Sundara signature Sandstone Body Polish product.
- Deserving Thyme: Product contains no synthetic color or fragrance. Packaging is recycled paper with soy-based inks.
- Voya: 100% organic hand-harvested, Soil Association organic, recyclable packaging.
- Farmhouse Fresh: Recyclable packaging.
- *Hair:* John Masters: No parabens, DEA's, artificial colors, or fragrance.
- *Nails:* Spa Ritual: Certified organic, vegan, and made with bamboo, all free of paraben, formaldehyde, toluene, and DBP. Packaging from responsible sources using renewable energy, and printed with soy ink.
- *Makeup:* Jane Iredale: All natural minerals and recyclable packaging.
- *Hair removal:* Nufree is wax-free.
- *Retail:* We retail all of the above named products in our boutique and online. Other products in our boutique are carefully selected.

Supplies

Treatment supplies
- Bulk products are preferred for our professional spa products and in our guest lounges.

Paper/glass/plastic/single-use items
- When possible, glass is used in both the spa and suites to reduce paper and plastic waste.
- We separate paper, cans, and plastic and contract with a nearby company for our paper recycling. Our participation in this program saved many trees last year.
- Containers are reused when possible to reduce waste.

Linens
- Spa linens are cotton.
- Overnight guests participate in the green practices with simple measures such as requesting less frequent laundering of linens.

Cleaning
- Our cleaning supplies are provided by a local company that is committed to creating a partnership that minimizes waste by developing clean, safe, and sustainable practices and products on-site. Products are purchased in bulk and we reuse cleaning containers.

Facility Supplies
- Whenever possible we partner with local Wisconsin or Midwest vendors and seek out partnerships that promote an eco-conscious vision and are like-minded in our respect for the earth.

Energy
- We use exhaust to heat our radiant heating system.

Building
- Built in 2002; remodeled in 2006: addition of the villas.
- Construction type: block and wood frame; type of insulation is batt and blown in.
- Energy audit in 2011.

HVAC system
- Temperature controls are manual in guest rooms, regulated the public areas.
- **Ventilation system:** Energy recovery unit for guest rooms.

Type of lighting
- Fixtures: incandescent, CFLs, fluorescent.
- Lighting controls: automatic, dimmers, occupant sensors.
- The special outdoor lighting system controls light pollution and protects nocturnal animals.

Building Materials
- Trees that had to be removed were recycled and used by the contractor for timbers and retaining walls for other projects.
- Site disturbances were kept to a minimum during the construction of Sundara, dramatically reducing the development footprint by preserving as many pine trees and other indigenous plants as possible.
- Pine straw and pine cones collected from the forest floor were used for natural mulch.
- The stone retaining walls are natural stone harvested locally.
- In our villas: low fuel-emitting materials for flooring and paint were selected; wood used in the construction was harvested as a renewable resource; placement of the windows reduces the need to turn on lights; overhangs stop direct light from coming in during the summer, keeping the space naturally cool, while other sun shading is angled to allow the winter sun to stream in, lending natural warmth.

Water
- Sinks, faucets, toilets, and showers low-flow; most fixtures have aerators.
- Rainwater is collected from downspouts in rain barrels for use in watering plants.
- Our outdoor pool and indoor and outdoor soak baths use a minimum amount of purification chemicals required by state law.

Indoor Environmental Quality (IEQ)
- Proper chemical management.

Waste Reduction
- Always purchase in bulk, cuts down on waste.
- Proper recycling.

Food and Beverage
- Purchase from local vendors during individual growing seasons. Provides mostly organic produce and cuts down on emissions (short distance shipping).
- Primarily using companies that follow the same "green" thinking (Testaproduce.com).
- We use green cleaning chemicals in the kitchen.
- Low temperature water saving dishwasher.
- We will be expanding our own gardens from 4 to 12.
- We are constantly talking about nutrition in the culinary department.
- Our culinary team grows herbs and vegetables in our own garden right here on the grounds.
- We participate in a Community Supported Agriculture partnership with nearby Orange Cat Farm.
- We source all of our milk, butter, eggs, cream, and yogurt from Organic Valley headquartered in Wisconsin, and it's all 100% Certified Organic.
- We source our whole fruit locally whenever possible and it's organic too.

Landscaping, Exteriors
- Plants: we have a lot of native plants that require less water.
- Water: we catch rainwater for our gardens.
- We have sandy soil and try to let mulch go back into the soil.
- Gardens for food production.

Nature/outdoors

During the winter months, guests enjoy snowshoeing and cross-country skiing on the grounds adjoining Sundara—these are gentle on the earth and silent sports. There are three state parks nearby that are sanctuaries for hiking, canoeing and kayaking—again, gentle on the earth and silent sports.

Marketing
- We created a web page dedicated to our green practices so that all of our efforts are transparent.
- Sundara participates in Earth Day events and encourages guests to partake and make green pledges each year.
- We are members of the Green Spa Network and certified *Travel Green Wisconsin*.

People
- We believe each of our efforts and practices benefits our guests and staff, no matter how big or small. We are committed to growing our efforts while staying true to our mission, the guest experience, and providing a positive and healthy work environment. We look to partner with like-minded businesses and local businesses.

Education
- Sundara is a founding Seed Spa member of The Green Spa Network and is certified *Travel Green Wisconsin*. Our management and staff participate in several webinars and attend conferences annually.

CHAPTER 16

Staff Needs and Green Teams

INTRODUCTION

A shared vision of connecting beauty, the environment, and a balanced lifestyle is part of the green spa culture. What is your global culture? Your global culture includes clients, local cultures, and your staff. What do they care about and what are their opinions? Companies and managers who truly care about their coworkers and mission are more successful.

As mentioned in the economic and social equity sections, taking care of the staff is vital to the success of any service-based business. Many employees care about being appreciated and valued, not just about their paycheck. Supporting the staff beyond a paycheck through benefits and wellness programs is part of social equity. Providing a healthy environment and indoor air quality also benefits the staff. A positive atmosphere builds loyalty. Green teams and sustainability training are necessary to build collaboration around green policies (Figure 16-1). Chapter 17, Exploring Green Steps and Practices, starts the planning part of greening your staff and facility.

Figure 16-1: Green teams build collaboration.

What does your staff think about greening the facility? How does it benefit them?

WORDS OF WISDOM

~ A leader is best when people barely know he exists, when his work is done, his aim fulfilled, they will say, "we did it ourselves." (Lao Tzu)

~ A favorite quote from Ted Ning, Executive Director, LOHAS—Lifestyles of Health and Sustainability, lohas.com

HAPPY EMPLOYEES

Employee wages are the highest expense of most businesses. Employee retention saves time and money because training new employees is expensive and time-consuming. Green-minded individuals will want to stay with a company that shares those same values. Additionally, staff members who are physically, mentally and spiritually healthy radiate that positive energy to others. Promoting a holistic lifestyle at work is part of today's spa world (Figure 16-2).

Staff benefits and wellness programs are expensive, but are worth the cost of happy employees, reduced sick leave and turnover rates. Profits, however, do have to support these benefits. In a small business with one owner, the staff may not realize that the owner has a small profit margin. It may be helpful to share some of this profit and loss information with employees for transparency and to build trust and support.

Providing education and training is another benefit that is undervalued. Product and treatment protocol training may be expensive but the staff will appreciate it. Product and service discounts and trades are other perks in the beauty industry. Putting a value on these will help staff members see the value in these benefits, which is worth hundreds of dollars per year.

Figure 16-2: Healthy employees promote a holistic lifestyle.

Share sustainability information with your staff and educate them on green practices. More savings in one area equals more pay and bonuses for the staff. A common purpose and atmosphere where people feel valued builds a solid team.

Spa Staffing

As ISPA notes, the spa experience is strongly people-oriented, with a diverse range of client needs. Ensuring a positive spa experience depends on having staff with the necessary skills and experience. The industry is also a significant employer, with over 330,000 people working in US spas.

The most frequently cited benefits provided to staff by a majority of spas are discount programs and flexible work schedules. Less than 50% of spas said they provided benefits such as health insurance, a 401(k) plan, paid vacation, or disability insurance. The resort/hotel and other spa sectors were exceptions, with a majority of such spas providing the health insurance and other benefits listed above. These same sectors also provide the widest range of benefits. The main human resource challenges were a shortage of qualified candidates applying for open positions and low staff morale (experience ispa.com 2010). According to labor statistics, massage training and other beauty industry professions predict growth over the next few years.

> A new work model is emerging in companies where flexible work areas and employee lounges are enjoyable places to hang out and connect with others. People want to come to work if it is a fun, supportive environment. Outdated models of separated workspaces and cubicles are being replaced with group areas for creativity and collaboration. New generations work differently than older generations so changes are needed to meet the needs of the different working styles.

GREEN TEAMS

Many spas have volunteer green teams that are composed of employees. Others have an additional sustainability coordinator or a department head as part of the team. Resorts and hotel green teams may include the facility manager, marketing person, spa director, and other department managers. Sometimes employees start the greening process or it is part of the company policies such as Corporate Social Responsibility and Sustainability Reporting.

Green teams can outline a green operations plan. The team objectives usually consist of researching existing practices, coordinating meetings, defining goals, and creating and implementing a green action plan. Green team activities include brainstorming sessions, planning, contests, and employee training/education. See Chapter 18 for a list of brainstorming and meeting suggestions.

Involve the Staff

Planning begins with including staff in the greening process. They are the ones who carry out the vision. Get the staff involved so they feel a sense of ownership and are part of the process. A team effort generates better ideas and success. Share communication through employee training and meetings (Figure 16-3).

It can be a challenge to encourage reluctant participants, but meetings are a great opportunity to get everyone involved and motivated. Speak to what they care about. Team participation creates buy-in and saves money on outside consultants. The staff know how things work on-site and including them is the best approach in implementing new policies, green or otherwise.

Paying the staff for the meetings and providing food and drinks is a small price to pay for the savings generated from future green operations. Participating in green teams can be fun and keeps things fresh and interesting. Monthly meetings and communications are vital to keep staff engaged and informed. Include sustainability updates in your messages.

STAFF TRAINING

Depending on the facility, staff training on sustainability could be done as part of initial training and periodically during regular meetings. Including green policies and expectations in employee handbooks is a good idea. Bulletin board reminders and signage are also helpful for additional staff communications.

> Green team planning meetings for building projects are known as eco-charettes.

Figure 16-3: Share green communications with the staff.

Green Team Planning Steps

- Communication is important—share the vision and plan.
- Have a brainstorming session and get everyone involved.
- Designate a Sustainability Coordinator.
- Coordinate employee training for sustainable practices.
- List and communicate the sustainable goals.
- Outline the plan with timelines and action steps.
- Implement the green practices.
- Monitor the progress and track the savings.
- Analyze the plan and make adjustments to it.
- Include green procedures in your policy manual.

Staff Participation

- Engage the staff.
- Share the benefits of conservation and recycling efforts.
- Staff needs to be eco-conscious, as many clients will expect that level of understanding.
- Staff needs to understand environmental issues, company facts (how much waste is generated, cost, etc.), resource use, and impacts.
- Use role-playing or questions to review the concepts in meetings.
- Get participation and feedback.
- Provide education and training.
- Check their understanding and use of green practices.

Staff Questionnaire

Some green spas are asking about green preferences in interviews during the hiring process or as part of staff training. This is a good way to assess the training needs and get ideas from the staff.

Questions to ask staff members regarding green topics:

- Do you currently use sustainable practices?
- What are the green issues that you care about?
- Do you have an understanding of spa impacts and resource use?
- Where can the spa improve green practices?
- What green practices would you like to see the company use?
- Are you interested in being on a green team?

Education and Training Tips for Green Practices

- Have an engaging mission statement.
- Include training in orientation.
- Post your expectations: motivational signage.
- Share facts and data.
- Include initiatives in the student/employee handbook with procedures and policies.
- Create awareness.
- Identify challenges and opportunities.
- Include all departments.
- Communicate expectations.
- Set specific, measurable goals and action steps.
- Use consistent messages.

A fun way to encourage green habits in the workplace is to have a contest designed to reward green practices and ideas.

- Have follow up meetings and track results.
- Share the plan and achievements with the entire staff.
- Recognize contributions.
- Plan educational or award events: Make it fun, have contests and food.
- Give incentives for conservation ideas.
- Communication: Use internal and external messaging.
- Share the progress with the staff and clients and report progress in meetings and newsletters.

WEIGHT LOSS AND WELLNESS HAVEN SPOTLIGHT

THE NEW WELL
A nationwide women's wellness franchise dedicated to providing women with a variety of holistic health resources.

Contact: Scott Draper, President (2012)
The New Well, LLC
2160 NW Vine Street, Grants Pass, Oregon
www.thenewwell.com
Facility size: 1700 sq. ft.
Number of employees: 7
Number of treatment rooms: 2
Established in: 2009

Facility Description
The New Well is a nationwide women's wellness franchise, with plans to open over 200 centers over the next nine to ten years. The business is dedicated to providing women with a variety of holistic health resources, including weight loss services, wellness counseling, an individualized nutrition program, and beauty/relaxation treatments.

SPA GOALS AND VISION

What is your green business mission statement?
Our centers are consistently fun, clean, earth friendly, and inviting.

What is your spa image?
Our passion is empowering women to be well.

What are your sustainability goals?
To continue to lead the sustainability conversation within the franchise space.

What is important to you regarding sustainability?
We see the whole as greater than the sum of the parts and celebrate when everyone wins through lifestyles of health and sustainability.

What are your current green practices?
Offering a basic sustainable center build out to franchises and an upgraded Earth Steward
Level build-out through our partners, Sustainability Matters.

What are the challenges in being green?
The cost.

Is the staff interested in greening the facility?
Yes.

What business practices do you think your clients want to see with regard to sustainability?
Clients love it when we share the stories of the green materials and companies we have chosen.

Have you seen any positive effects from green practices you have implemented?
Yes, we are beginning to.

What positive benefits do you offer your staff? (health, wellness, incentives)
Connections to local food sources, sustainable lifestyles, and working in a wellness environment.

 SPA ELEMENTS

The Menu
- Weight loss, facials, makeup, and Synergie body treatments.

Products
- *Face:* Botanical-based, no animal testing, recycled packaging.
- *Body:* Synergie.
- *Makeup:* Colorescience Pro makeup is all natural, mineral-based, with refillable containers.
- *Other:* Essential oils are local from a private vendor.

Treatment Supplies
- *Linens:* Microfiber.

Facility
- In franchising, we focus on the interior. We are currently developing ideas and practices to encourage locations in green-built shopping centers.

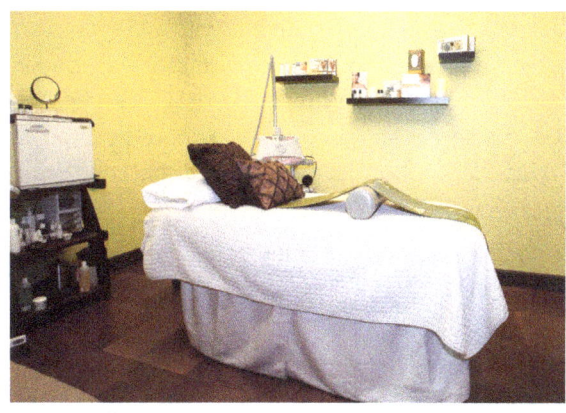

Green Materials
- A sustainable interior materials package was important to the owners as members of the wellness industry from an environmental and social perspective, and key in developing a consistent brand and marketing message.
- Sustainability Matters Inc., by Kristen Victor Design, improved the sustainability and aesthetics of the interior building materials, within a budget comparable to the previous standard build-out package.

Sustainable Building Materials:
- Manufactured from 100% recycled content core materials with no added urea or formaldehyde, and a Greenguard-certified laminate containing recycled content.
- *Wall ledge accent band:* Redesigned from the original spec to include 100% sustainable materials. The accent band was made from 100% recycled content, including newspaper, cardboard, and agricultural waste. The backing was made from FSC wood, and the piece was lined with LED tape lights.
- *Signature light fixture:* Fixture was handmade in the United States, with aluminum parts containing the highest available recycled content, and finished with hand applied beeswax, using no paint or

lacquer. The fixture was designed exclusively for CFLs using HPF electronic ballasts. The shade was covered with organic decorative paper, making it a truly unique piece!
- *Signage:* Made from 100% postindustrial recycled material, using water based inks, and Greenguard-certified adhesives. This was an innovative alternative to the previous spec, which was plastic signage with standard VOC emitting paints.
- *Wall coverings:* zero-VOC paints and wood stain was used throughout the project. Decorative paper made from 100% organic material used to highlight accent wall; Zero-VOC wood stain.

Flooring
- *Carpet:* 25% pre-consumer and 3% post-consumer recycled content by weight, with a PVC-free backing.
- Carpet does not require adhesive, eliminating VOCs, reducing raw material and chemical usage. CRI Green Label Plus Certified.
- Border carpet has 33% pre-consumer recycled content backing.
- *Cork flooring:* Over 95% pre-consumer recycled material, Greenguard Certified.
- Flooring is extremely durable with a 15–year warranty.
- Porcelain tile manufactured domestically, containing 6% post-industrial recycled content (SCS Certified).
- Glass accent tile manufactured domestically, containing at least 50% pre-consumer recycled content.

Accessories
- Stainless steel washrooms' accessories have 60% recycled content.

Plumbing
- Low-flow toilets and faucets, reducing water consumption.

Other
- Materials were drop shipped directly from the manufacturer in bulk to reduce carbon emissions.
- The construction crew was instructed to donate materials left at the site by the previous tenant, including tables, chairs, kitchen equipment, and to reuse existing items, such as lighting, kitchen storage racks, rough plumbing, and electrical when possible.

Purchasing
- Earth friendly cleaning products, paper, and supplies are suggested to franchisers.
- FSC paper is purchased from an all-wind-powered facility.
- *Well food bars* are organic and produced in a solar-powered facility.
- Waste reduction: We encourage the use of reusable containers, no disposable water containers.
- Food service: Organic well bars. Food plans encourage local foods.
- Marketing: Green features are marketed and shared with franchisers and clients.

People
- The no-VOC build-out benefits peoples' health and environment.
- The majority of the staff are on the lifestyle program.

CHAPTER 17

Exploring Green Steps and Practices

INTRODUCTION

Let's explore examples and ideas for specific green practices. Chapters for planning, creating, and implementing your own action plan and specific steps to achieve these goals will follow this chapter. The categories listed below are connected, as purchasing decisions have material, waste, and health considerations. Each table lists green practices and columns to note costs, savings, and benefits. These tables will have blank columns here (and in the next chapters) for you to fill in your own answers. The first table here is partially filled in to give you an idea of how it can be used to compare costs and benefits.

These lists are extensive and it is not expected that you will be incorporating everything discussed here into your facility operations. Most spas choose a few items to start with. Choose which of these practices you would like to use for your goals. See the online resources for planning worksheets and checklists.

Spa Categories:

- The Service Menu
- Retail and Service Products
- Purchasing and Green Materials
- Waste Management
- Indoor Environmental Quality
- Energy
- Water
- Landscaping
- Transportation
- Staff
- Clients

> **Table Key for symbols $, R, P**
> $= Economic: financial *Savings*
> R= Environmental: natural *Resource* savings
> P= Equity: good for *People*

Use the following categories and tables to explore green ideas for the different areas in the facility:

TABLE 17-1: THE SERVICE MENU

Green Menu Ideas	Cost to Implement (with examples)	Long-Term Savings (with examples)	Benefits & Resource Savings $=Ec, R=Env, P=Eq
Evaluate the service menu for green features.	*Time*	*Efficiency, streamlining services*	*Beneficial for: $, R, P*
Use natural, organic products.	*Product costs*	*Possibly, price dependent*	*$: client demand* *R: less chemicals, manufacturing* *P: healthier for people*
Add health and wellness focused services.	*No additional costs*	*Potentially more long term clients*	*$: increased business* *P: better health*
Incorporate pure essential oils into treatments.	*Quality oil costs more*	*Cost recovered by blending with bulk products*	*R: fewer synthetic chemicals* *P: health*
Promote local treatments (local culture, products).	*Product cost*	*Promotes local businesses, good PR*	*$: less shipping* *R: less fuel, pollution* *P: supports local economy*
Offer more waterless body treatments.	*New service/training*	*Saves $, water*	*$: saves time, water cost* *R: saves water*
Use recycled paper, eco-friendly ink, and less paper for menu printing and marketing materials.	*Higher paper, printing cost*	*Offset by fewer print materials*	*R: saves trees, ink* *R & P: fewer chemicals in manufacturing*
Serve local, organic food and beverages.	*More expensive*	*Cost offset by pricing and demand*	*R: fewer chemicals used in farming* *$ & R: less shipping* *P: healthier food*
Add green measures in fitness centers.			P

| TABLE 17-2: RETAIL AND SERVICE PRODUCTS ||||
Examples of Green Product Ideas	Cost to Implement	Long-Term Savings	Benefits & Resource Savings $=Ec, R=Env, P=Eq
Use green criteria and supplier questions to rate product lines.			
Use organic products and ingredients.			
Buy from local suppliers.			
Look at fair trade/sustainable sourcing.			
Ask about green chemistry.			
Look for green packaging features.			
Ask if the vendor uses sustainable practices.			
Ask about third party certification.			
Order bulk products.			
Consider other green retail items.			
Sell locally made accessories: jewelry, scarves, etc.			
Sell organic cotton or other sustainable textiles and apparel.			

TABLE 17-3 : PURCHASING AND SUPPLY USE			
Examples of Sustainability Practices: Supply Use	**Cost to Implement**	**Long-Term Savings**	**Benefits & Resource Savings** $=Ec, R=Env, P=Eq$
Evaluate vendors and the supply chain for green practices. Refer to the green materials checklist.			
Guest Services and Treatment Rooms			
Use natural materials for treatment linens and towels: organic cotton, wool, microfiber linens.			
Reduce use of robes or slippers for clients going straight to treatment rooms.			
Use more towels and less disposables in treatments.			
Use smaller towels if applicable (will a washcloth work rather than a hand towel for cleaning?).			
Use washable bowls and containers rather than plastic ones.			
Use fewer disposable cotton for facial treatments.			
Wash and disinfect reusable implements, rather than throwing them away (plastic and non-porous items).			
Use bulk refills for amenities.			
Recycle all soaps and amenities.			
Gyms and fitness: Encourage towel conservation.			
Promote the use of reusable glasses and stainless steel water bottles. Avoid bottled water.			

| TABLE 17-4: PURCHASING SPA EQUIPMENT ||||
Equipment Suggestions	Cost to Implement	Long-Term Savings	Benefits & Resource Savings *$=Ec, R=Env, P=Eq*
Choose vendors with green and CSR practices.			
Evaluate equipment and make a list of inventory throughout the facility.			
Buy quality service equipment.			
Assess energy use of towel warmers, hot packs, and bed warmers.			
Put equipment on timers and turn off when not in use.			
Buy high efficiency, quality appliances: washer/dryer, dishwater.			
Buy Energy Star rated appliances.			
Perform regular maintenance and repairs.			
Look for massage beds that are made with sustainable materials.			

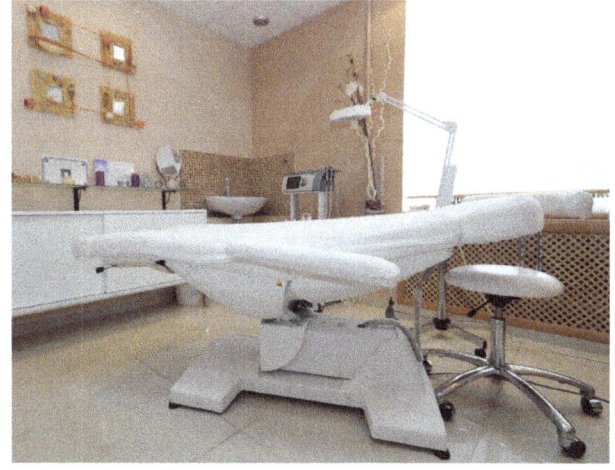

TABLE 17-5: WASTE REDUCTION			
Waste Reduction Practices	**Cost to Implement**	**Long-Term Savings**	**Benefits & Resource Savings** $=Ec, R=Env, P=Eq$
Assess your waste generation, cost, disposal and recycling needs.			
Recycling			
Install paper, glass, and plastic recycling bins with good signage.			
Use recycling bins for cardboard, e-waste, and yard waste/composting.			
Purchasing			
Use the LCA checklist and green criteria for purchasing guidelines.			
Look for recycled, renewable, and recyclable items.			
Reduce plastic use.			
Buy reusable dishes, cups, and cloth napkins.			
Buy cups with recycled content or other compostable material rather than plastic cups.			
Use recycled content and unbleached paper products for the facility.			
Office and Communications			
Have more communications and marketing through email and social media.			
Post or circulate staff communications and announcements via email.			
Use less print materials and smaller marketing materials.			
Use double-sided copies, smaller margins, and smaller font (but legible).			
Invest in a double-sided copier.			

TABLE 17-5: WASTE REDUCTION *(continued)*			
Waste Reduction Practices	**Cost to Implement**	**Long-Term Savings**	**Benefits & Resource Savings** $=Ec, R=Env, P=Eq$
Do not use individual tip envelopes.			
Make note pads from scratch paper and reuse envelopes and shipping supplies.			
Purchase refillable or re-inked printer cartridges.			
Retail			
Ask guests if they would like a bag for small purchases, rather than automatically giving them one.			
Use envelopes rather than gift certificate boxes.			
Use smaller retail and gift bags with recycled content.			
Other R's to remember: Reimagine, reject, repair, reduce, reuse, recycle, repurpose.			
Reduce magazines, junk mail, and catalogs.			
Donate, exchange, and give away useful items such as linens or magazines.			
Use rechargeable batteries.			
Compost organic yard or food scraps.			

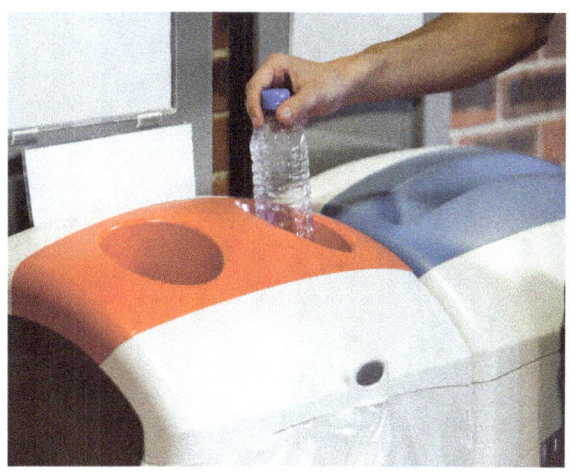

172 GREEN SPAS AND SALONS

TABLE 17-6: PACKAGING			
Examples of Sustainability Practices for Packaging / Waste Reduction	**Cost to Implement**	**Long-Term Savings**	**Benefits & Resource Savings** $=Ec, R=Env, P=Eq$
Specify sustainable guidelines and practices from vendors and in service contracts.			
Reduce purchasing and on hand inventory.			
Look for recycled content packaging.			
Look for soy ink for printing.			
Use glass bottles for products (vs. plastic containers).			
Ask for better shipping packing material if Styrofoam is used.			
Order bulk products and supplies to reduce packaging.			

| TABLE 17-7 GREEN MATERIALS FOR INTERIORS ||||
Purchasing Green Materials *(see the green building chapters for more on materials)*	**Cost to Implement**	**Long-Term Savings**	**Benefits & Resource Savings** $=Ec, R=Env, P=Eq
Use the green materials checklist to evaluate materials for interiors, building, and other purchasing needs.			
Check for third party certification.			
Consider the LCA and manufacturing of materials.			
Use or renovate what is there. Repaint or restore décor to keep the fresh spa look and quality on a budget.			
Use locally accessible décor and elements from nature.			
Choose natural fabrics for curtains (cotton, silk) and furniture (rattan, bamboo).			
Use washable slipcovers.			
Use wood products instead of plastics or concrete.			
Look for recycled materials.			
Buy low-VOC paint and other green materials made with fewer chemicals.			
Choose sustainable flooring: Marmoleum or eco products in treatment rooms (avoid vinyl). Use natural carpeting and rugs such as wool. Salvaged hardwoods are the greenest choice for many building materials.			

TABLE 17-8: INDOOR ENVIRONMENTAL QUALITY (IEQ)

Examples of Sustainability Practices for IEQ and IAQ	Cost to Implement	Long-Term Savings	Benefits & Resource Savings $=Ec, R=Env, P=Eq
Evaluate indoor environmental quality and air quality.			
Avoid VOCs and chemicals.			
Address IEQ for occupant comfort.			
Make sure there is adequate ventilation—especially for areas with humidity, chemical use, and required cleaning disinfectants: salons, services, tubs, steam rooms.			
Designate space and ventilation for chemical use (hair, nail services) away from other areas.			
Replace and maintain air filters as recommended.			
Monitor humidity and CO_2 levels as needed.			
Use natural cleaning supplies.			
For laundry soap: use fragrance free, with fewer chemicals; do not use fabric softener.			
Consider natural chlorine generators or saline systems for pools and whirlpools.			
Appeal to the 5 senses: visual, scents, music, touch, taste: create a healthy atmosphere, use good lighting, natural scents, and organic food.			
Store and dispose of hazardous materials properly.			

TABLE 17-9: ENERGY CONSERVATION STEPS			
Examples of Energy Conservation Practices *(also in the online resources)*	**Cost to Implement**	**Long-Term Savings**	**Benefits & Resource Savings** $=Ec, R=Env, P=Eq
General			
Monitor the current energy use and do a cost analysis from the utility bills.			
Have an energy audit performed to determine building insulation, perform weatherization, and check windows for leaks.			
Seal and insulate any building or window leaks with weather stripping.			
Building and Design			
Evaluate passive solar, site, location, climate, and shading needs.			
Use awnings and trees for shading and windows for solar gain where needed.			
Install good insulation and double pane windows. (See the green building chapter for more on green building design and retrofits).			
Lighting			
Take advantage of natural lighting and use window shades/coverings to control light needs.			
Use LED, CFL and T-5 fluorescents and fixtures.			
Switch T-12 fluorescents to more efficient T-8's.			
Convert ballasts from magnetic to electronic.			
Install reflectors to increase the effectiveness of fixtures.			
Use automated controls such as occupancy motion detectors and light sensors.			
Use dimmers. (3 way fixtures)			
Use task lighting instead of overhead lighting where appropriate.			
Use efficient LED exit signs.			
Use solar lighting for outdoor walkways.			
HVAC			
Check ducts and change air filters regularly.			

TABLE 17-9: ENERGY CONSERVATION STEPS *(continued)*			
Examples of Energy Conservation Practices *(also in the online resources)*	**Cost to Implement**	**Long-Term Savings**	**Benefits & Resource Savings** $=Ec, R=Env, P=Eq
Insulate and check ducts for leaks.			
Use a heating recovery ventilation (HRV) or energy recovery system (ERV) to recapture heat.			
Use variable speed controls on HVAC systems to save energy.			
Use a programmable thermostat on HVAC systems.			
Heating and Cooling			
Turn down hot water tank temperatures and insulate pipes.			
Use natural ventilation and fresh air from screened windows and doors instead of air conditioning.			
Use reversible fans to move air and save energy (reversible fans pull hot air up in the summer and push hot air down in the winter).			
Close off vents and doors to unused spaces.			
Equipment and Appliances			
Buy EnergyStar-efficient appliances.			
Use timers for waxers, warmers, steamers, saunas, etc.			
Use power strips and turn off electronic equipment and computers at night.			
Upgrade old equipment to new energy efficient equipment.			
Use energy monitors to assess use.			
Clean and maintain equipment.			
Renewable Energy			
Consider a solar thermal water heater.			
Consider solar PV or other renewables (wind, biomass, geothermal).			
Calculate your carbon footprint and buy carbon offsets.			

TABLE 17-10: WATER CONSERVATION MEASURES			
Water Conservation Measures	**Cost to Implement**	**Long-Term Savings**	**Benefits & Resource Savings** $S=Ec, R=Env, P=Eq$
Assess water use and goals.			
Monitor water consumption and monthly bills to track usage. *(see tracking sheet in Chapter 18)*			
Maintenance			
Check for leaks and monitor the water meter.			
Repair pipes or fixtures and replace seals regularly.			
Fixtures			
Install efficient low flow sink fixtures and aerators.			
Install low flow showerheads with aerators.			
Replace inefficient toilets or fit with toilet dams in the tanks.			
Consider automatic shut off faucets.			
Water Heating			
Consider a solar water heater.			
Install on-demand instant water heaters.			
Wrap pipes and water heater tanks.			
Water Quality			
Use filtered drinking water for staff and guests (infused w/ lemon, fruit, or cucumber).			
Use less chlorine and chemicals.			
Make sure chemicals and hazardous materials are disposed of properly and do not enter the water system through drains or outdoor run-off.			
Clean and maintain equipment.			

TABLE 17-10: WATER CONSERVATION MEASURES *(continued)*			
Water Conservation Measures	**Cost to Implement**	**Long-Term Savings**	**Benefits & Resource Savings** $=Ec, R=Env, P=Eq$
Equipment and Appliances			
Consider water usage for treatment equipment purchasing.			
Use best practices for commercial equipment such as cooling towers or food service equipment.			
Use water efficient pedicure equipment.			
Monitor tubs and steam rooms for energy and water efficiency.			
Kitchen and laundry: use high efficiency appliances on water saving settings.			
Reduce linen use and buy lighter weight linens to reduce the laundry volume.			

TABLE 17-11: LANDSCAPING			
Examples of Sustainable Landscape Practices	**Cost to Implement**	**Long-Term Savings**	**Benefits & Resource Savings** $=Ec, R=Env, P=Eq$
Analyze landscaping, irrigation needs, and water usage.			
Use xeriscaping with drought tolerant plants (dry landscaping design requires minimal water).			
Design irrigation systems to conserve water (drip systems, timers).			
Use mulch and other landscape methods to conserve water.			
Use native plants.			
Put the right plant in the right place for best results (soil, sun).			
Use organic gardening and pest control methods.			
Water landscaping early in the morning to reduce evaporation.			
Plant flowers and herbs and use on site for treatments or décor.			
Compost organic waste (food scraps and landscaping materials).			
Reduce turf (grass) and mow grass height taller (3" or higher) leaving clipping on the lawn to conserve water and chemical fertilizer needs.			
Use rain gardens, pervious pavement, and other low impact development methods to reduce run off and storm water needs.			
Consider rainwater catchment or greywater systems to reuse water.			

TABLE 17-12: FOOD AND BEVERAGE CHOICES

Healthy Food and Beverage Choices	Cost to Implement	Long-Term Savings	Benefits & Resource Savings $=Ec, R=Env, P=Eq
Offer organic, local food.			
Consider on-site gardens.			
Have a healthy choice menu (fruit).			
Consider water and tea amenities.			

TABLE 17-13: SUSTAINABLE TRANSPORTATION AND TRAVEL

Examples of Sustainable Transportation and Travel	Cost to Implement	Long-Term Savings	Benefits & Resource Savings $=Ec, R=Env, P=Eq
Promote biking and walking through education and incentives.			
Provide bike and electric vehicle parking.			
Support mass transport and bus passes for staff.			
Support car pooling.			
Use a hybrid or electric vehicle.			
Reduce trips and use webinars or conference calls to cut travel costs and time.			
Determine carbon footprint and buy carbon offsets for travel.			
Use more eco-friendly transportation and hotels.			

CHAPTER 17: Exploring Green Steps and Practices   181

TABLE 17-14: STAFF CARE			
Staff Care	**Cost to Implement**	**Long-Term Savings**	**Benefits & Resource Savings** $S=Ec, R=Env, P=Eq$
Involve the staff and form a green team.			
Educate staff and encourage green practices.			
Add sustainable policies to the employee manual and training program.			
Provide benefits.			
Address staff needs and provide a healthy atmosphere.			
Provide a wellness program and other classes.			
Provide incentives and performance bonuses.			
Pay for advanced training classes and meetings.			
Host an annual company party.			
Recognize achievements.			

TABLE 17-15: CLIENTS AND THE COMMUNITY			
Clients and the Community	**Cost to Implement**	**Long-Term Savings**	**Benefits & Resource Savings** $S=Ec, R=Env, P=Eq$
Make a list of community priorities and goals.			
Donate to charities.			
Provide education to the community.			
Host events.			
Share your green practices with clients.			
Implement a green marketing plan.			

Note: This information was compiled from many resources. See the references for more information on the green practices included here.

SPA SPOTLIGHT

VDARA SPA AND SALON
A Green Oasis In Las Vegas.

Contact: Shannon L. Mariani, Director of Recreational Services, Spa, Salon & Pool (2012)

Vdara Hotel and Spa
2600 W Harmon Ave, Las Vegas, NV
www.vdara.com
Facility size: 18,000 sq. ft.
Number of employees: 92
Number of treatment rooms: 11
Established in: December, 2009. A LEED Gold-certified property, part of CityCenter.

Facility Description

Large reception, smoothie bar, fitness center; separate and co-ed lounges, meditation room; outdoor pool, private cabanas for treatments. Solidifying CityCenter's commitment to sustainability, Vdara has achieved LEED Gold certification by the US Green Building Council. It is a non-smoking, non-gaming property.

Steps to achieve this goal include the use of wood products from responsibly managed forests; high efficiency water use, both inside the building and outdoors; alternative fuel options for limousines; and an improvement of more than 30 percent in energy efficiency over standard building codes.

Vdara is also honored to have received a *"5 Green Keys"* rating, the highest honor possible from the Green Key Eco-Rating Program. This organization is an international program evaluating sustainable hotel operations. The spa atmosphere has a boutique feel, with natural, earthy materials, and natural light. The boutique size saves space and cost, so extra high-end finishing touches could be added, such as the wood and marble.

SPA GOALS AND VISION

What is your green business mission statement?
As part of the overall mission statement for Vdara and CityCenter, we have made a commitment to social and environmental responsibility. The core mission statement is to provide distinctive, personalized experiences to every owner, guest, and employee.

What is your spa image?
We spotlight holistic health and well-being in an intimate environment.

What are the challenges in being green?
Rising costs for natural supplies and ingredients.

Have you seen any positive effects from green practices you have implemented?
Yes, many customers come here specifically based on our green practices. Also attracts a certain type of employee, which has proven to be very beneficial.

What positive benefits do you offer your staff?
Internal incentives, discounts, on-going training for all, and a positive work environment.

 SPA ELEMENTS

The Menu
- Holistic health supported by the healing power of nature is the focus of the spa menu.
- Body treatments focus on holistic health and utilize high-grade, natural ingredients derived from herbs, flowers, fruits, vegetables, and oils.
- Personalized, holistic spa services include treatments that celebrate the purity and organic freshness of nature, including the Indian Jasmine Flowers Hold Life Ritual.
- Naturopathica products are featured in many of the services.
- The menu includes the Green Statement for the hotel and spa.

Products
- Botanic-based products free of synthetics include essential oils and herbs.
- We strategically seek out vendors that practice green measures from the product or their packaging.
- *Face:* Naturopathica, Skin Authority.
- *Body:* Naturopathica, RedFlower and Akhassa.
- *Hair:* Loreal Kerastase, Aveda, Morrocan Oil.
- *Nails:* Spa Ritual and Farmhouse Fresh.
- *Makeup:* Being True.
- *Other retail:* Chocolate Sun for Sunless Bronzing.

Supplies
- All collateral used in the spa/salon is recycled, as well as retail packaging.
- Supplies in locker rooms and treatment rooms are purchased (when applicable) with green considerations.

Treatment supplies
- Linens: Natural fibers.
- Single-use items (cotton, plastic): organic cotton from Universal Company.

Facility
- LEED Gold certification: The main building points in construction included efficient energy systems and lighting, windows and glazing, computerized energy monitoring, low- low fixtures, low-VOC building products, construction waste management, salvaging, and local building sources.

Energy

Building
- Efficient systems include a light colored reflective roof, window coating/glazing; energy is reused to heat water.

Equipment
- Each locker room has a eucalyptus steam room, plunge pool/Jacuzzi, and redwood dry sauna.
- Fitness center has a low energy mode for equipment.

Type of lighting
- Lots of natural light in lounge/waiting area.
- Fixtures and bulbs are energy efficient.
- Lighting controls: dimmers.

Water
- Low-flow fixtures throughout the property.
- Laundry: outsourced.

Green Materials
- Impressively, 80% of the original existing building was used in the construction of CityCenter, rather than demolition to the landfill.
- Interiors: seppeli wood for floors and walls and marble counters give a feeling of warmth.
- All paint, glues, composites, and carpets are nontoxic and low-VOC.

Indoor Environmental Quality (IEQ)
- Nontoxic materials and cleaning products.
- Efficient ventilation systems.

Purchasing
- The spa tries to use local vendors for goods and services.
- Glasses and cups are used for water and tea.

Waste Reduction
- All retail packaging and spa collateral are recycled.
- Recycling program includes food scraps, cardboard, glass, and paper.
- Recycled paper content is used for brochures, cards.

Landscaping, Exteriors
- Plants are drought-tolerant.

Transportation
- Bike parking and storage, mass transit accessibility and rewards, and preferred parking for electric vehicles are all part of the transportation considerations.

Food Service
- Smoothie bar naturally has healthy options.

Marketing
- The website highlights the green features and design of the property.

People
- Eight out of ten potential employees are attracted to the green aspects of the spa.

CHAPTER 18

Green Planning and Assessments

VISION

INTRODUCTION

This section begins the actual planning and assessment phase of your current green practices. Defining goals and green team participation starts here. The subsequent Chapters 19 and 20 are designed for creating specific goals and the actual implementation steps. The online resources include a set of useful action plan checklists and worksheets compiled from all of the chapters.

The first order of business is to make a plan. Without specific goals or a timeline, changes are hard to implement. Involve the staff and share the plan. Education and training are important to get everyone on the same page. Keeping track of progress will keep you moving forward. While the information is extensive, starting with one or two items can break the project down into manageable pieces. It is easier to start with small steps and choose a few items on the checklists to focus on in the beginning of the greening process. You may only need to improve a few areas or analyze your current practices. Either way—choose whatever works for you.

Creating a Sustainability Plan
- Make a commitment and create a plan.
- Develop goals and a timeline to track progress.
- Document your plan for transparency and communication.
- Make it part of the spa culture.
- Incorporate sustainability into each team meeting.
- Encourage ideas, set a good example, and reward participation and success.
- Motivators in the work place will make it fun and competitive. Provide incentives and reward actions.
- Use checklists and focused discussions to facilitate changes.
- Enlist collaborators and partners.
- Use a green self-assessment and score card.
- Communicate that sustainability is everyone's job.

DEFINE YOUR GOALS AND THE VISION

Most businesses have a mission statement and vision in place. Your image and values will set the tone for your sustainability goals. What can be accomplished is ultimately determined by the policies and the staff's desire to support the vision. Before implementing new practices, consider these aspects of your business:

Spa Planning Considerations:
- Theme or image: What is your image and how does that relate to your values?
- Mission statement: What is your business mission statement and vision?
- Staff: How will the staff participate in the green policies?

- Clientele: How will practices affect and benefit your clients?
- Goals: What are attainable goals?
- Budget: What type of investment or budget is available to green the facility?

Exploring the Vision and Goals

Ask questions such as:
- What is your green mission statement?
- What is your green image?
- What are your sustainability goals?
- What business practices or areas would you like to make more sustainable?
- What are your current green practices?
- Is the staff interested in greening the facility?
- Have you seen any positive effects from green practices you have implemented? (economic, environmental, social equity impacts)
- What positive benefits do you offer your staff? (health, wellness, incentives)
- Do you promote your green practices? What promotional methods do you use for this?

PLANNING STEPS

After defining the goals and vision, get the staff involved and evaluate the current practices (Figure 18-1). Another approach is to get the staff involved to help review or refine the goals and vision. Either approach works, but staff input is invaluable and encouraged. Green teams can lead the planning and assessments.

Figure 18-1: Get the staff involved to evaluate current practices.

Involve the Staff

As discussed in previous chapters, get the staff involved early so they are part of the process and feel a sense of ownership. A team effort generates great ideas and accomplishments. Share information and communicate through employee training and meetings. Prior to green team meetings, share the facility's current green facts and statistics with the staff.

Green Team Training
- Have a meeting and get everyone involved.
- Have a brainstorming session.
- Ask the team what is important to them. What would they like to see?
- Assign team members for implementation and research.
- Have a contest designed to encourage green practices (healthy competition).
- Communication is important—share the vision and plan.
- Coordinate employee training for sustainable practices.
- Designate a Sustainability Coordinator.

> Just as recycling has become a habit, other green practices will also become habits. In order to change habits, it needs to be convenient.

Group Brainstorming Sessions

Brainstorming is a creative and fun way to create a common vision for a sustainable organization (Figure 18-2). Encourage participants to say what comes to them naturally, not to think about if it is a good idea or how it would work. Use all the ideas generated by your participants to create a vision that will inspire people. Create a storyboard, or an outline that captures your common ideas. Let this be your guide as you develop your action plan. This process can also be used for other business planning sessions. Use a whiteboard and have someone type up the final notes (always print double-sided) to share (via email saves paper, ink, and time).

Figure 18-2: Brainstorming is a creative way to create a common vision.

Questions for the Staff

These can be asked in the meeting and you could give a questionnaire out on these beforehand. These questions and answers can be brainstormed or reviewed during the meeting.

Initial Team Questions
- Who would like to facilitate the green team meeting?
- What is important to you regarding sustainability?
- What green practices would you like to see?
- What is our green image? Do we have one?
- What are our sustainable values?
- How can we conserve resources?
  (Use the various spa categories.)
- What are our sustainability goals?
  (See worksheets for this.)
- What are clients interested in and asking about?
- How do we promote our green practices?
- Who would like to volunteer for help with research and implementation?

Figure 18-3: Ask meeting participants to share their ideas on green practices.

Other Staff Questions
- What are examples of our current green practices?
- How are resources used in our facility?
- Is the recycling bin system working?
- What are staff expectations and responsibilities in the greening process?
- What should the green policies include?

Meeting Ideas

In a future meeting, ask participants to share their ideas on green practices (Figure 18-3). Have note-takers capture all of the responses on a computer or on flip chart paper. Be as specific as possible. Your ideas could be listed by category or just randomly. You could then prioritize and hold another planning meeting to follow up later. Meanwhile team members could research specifics such as costs or vendor options. After deciding on the action plan, assign responsibilities and timelines (see next chapters for this). Try to add refreshments and fun, creative activities for more interesting and energetic meetings.

Suggestions for Green Team Meeting Agendas

1. Brainstorming
- Ask questions, review current practices, brainstorm new ideas.
- Record and share answers, assign and perform research.

2. Goal Setting
- Review information from first meeting to prioritize goals and planning steps.
- Assign responsibilities and set timelines.

3. Review Progress and Plan Training
- Review progress and make adjustments as needed.
- Communicate practices and policies to staff and clients.
- Incorporate into the employee policy manual, plan education and training.

4. Assess and Monitor Progress in Subsequent Meetings
- Review and assess progress.
- Track and report benefits and savings.
- Communicate progress to staff and the community.

EVALUATE THE SPA'S CURRENT PRACTICES

The first step in greening the business is to evaluate the current practices (Figure 18-4). This can be a quick walkthrough or overview. It is helpful to know what is already green and what needs work. Then you can go through it more specifically. Use the questions below and fill in Table 18-1 to assess your current sustainable practices.

Spa Elements

Think about your current green practices. Use the following categories to analyze the different areas in the facility. In meetings, put these up on the board and give handouts for participants to record their ideas. Some of these areas may overlap and fit into more than one category.

- **The Service Menu:** What are the green features of the service menu (organic, local, etc.)?
- **Products and Retail:** Do products and retail items have any green features?

Figure 18-4- The first step in greening the business is to evaluate the current practices.

- **Purchasing and Supplies:** Are supplies for treatments or operations purchased with green considerations? Are there any green aspects considered in making purchasing decisions (recycled paper, etc.)?
- **Waste Reduction:** Are there measures to reduce waste (such as less packaging or disposables)? What recycling practices are used?
- **Green Materials:** Consider items such as supplies, linens, and cleaning products. Does the facility or operations use any healthy green materials (recycled, nontoxic, etc.)? What is green about the overall facility or building?
- **Indoor Environmental Quality (IEQ):** What healthy IEQ features does the facility have? Are there green materials used? Consider indoor air quality, acoustics, visual aesthetics, and scents.
- **Energy:** What current energy measures and practices conserve energy? What heating system is used (gas, electric, heat pump, boiler)? Is consumption tracked or measured? Assess energy use and factors to consider in the facility, such as equipment, lighting, and ventilation.
- **Water:** What current water measures and practices conserve water? Assess water use, fixtures, and equipment.

- ***Landscaping, Outdoors:*** Are there any landscape conservation practices used?
- ***People:*** What sustainable practices benefit people (staff, clients, community)?
- ***Marketing:*** How are your green features marketed or shared with staff or clients?

Current Sustainable Practices

What are your current sustainable practices? Table 18-1 is left blank to fill in answers. Continue to Chapter 19 for creating specific sustainable goals.

TABLE 18-1: ASSESS YOUR CURRENT SUSTAINABLE PRACTICES			
Category	**Current Sustainable Practices**	**Benefits** $=Prosperity, R=Resources P=People	**Challenges** ($, Time, Management)
Service Menu			
Retail & Service Products			
Purchasing, Supplies			
Waste Reduction			
Green Materials			
IAQ/IEQ			
Energy			
Water			
Landscaping/Outdoors			
Food/Beverage			
Transportation			
Staff Policies			
Clients/Community			

Assessments

When planning and implementing goals, it is important to check the progress along the way, and evaluate the results. The first step is to identify what to measure. When it comes to economics, evaluation is more quantitative: the dollar amounts and percentages often speak for themselves. When it comes to the other two E's, the relevant quantities may not be as easy to identify, and quantifying the results may not be straightforward. For example, when measuring employee satisfaction, the criteria may be more subjective: some people are hard to please, while others are thankful by nature.

The next step is to get the current values for each of the quantities you are measuring: that is the baseline. For example, look up the monthly amounts from your current water bills. You may also want to check the seasonal variations, and decide to compare same months: June to last June. Alternatively, compare the same months over the past few years. In deciding the degree of detail, it is good to keep in mind that there is a point (or a fuzzy line) of diminishing returns—too many details in the analysis may not be useful or practical.

Setting realistic goals is the next step. For example, reduce the water usage by 10% in the summer months and 5% in the winter months. In setting the goals, it is important to get some strategies on how to achieve the goals. For example, an action step is to water plants in the early morning rather than midday to reduce the water use for landscaping. The next step would be to collect your data (monthly usage, in the case of water) for the duration of your plan, and check against the target values and goals. The worksheets are included in the online resources to track and assess energy and water use.

ENERGY TRACKING SHEETS

Fill in the following information as needed for your specific assessment needs. Disregard the areas that do not apply to your facility. This information can be used to determine energy use based on a set time period or by the number of occupants. You can use more than one sheet to analyze seasonal variations. It is also helpful to calculate the occupancy rate to track client visits. There are many software tools available for these assessments.

TABLE 18-2: OCCUPANCY HOURS		
Occupant Needs and Hours of Operations	Example	Data
Number of employees	10 (part-time and full-time)	
Number of clients/month	700	
Average total occupancy (per day, week, month)	710/month (or use 700 for clients only)	
Hours of operations:		
Days per week	6	
Hours per day	8	
Hours per week	48 (days x hours)	
Hours per month	192 (48 hours/week x 4 weeks/mo.)	
Days per month	24 (6 x 4)	
Occupancy per week (clients)	175 (700 divided by 4 weeks/mo.)	
Occupancy per day	29.16 (175 divided by 6 days/wk.)	
Occupancy per hour	3.64 (29.16 divided by 8 hours/day)	

Table 18-3: This information helps monitor energy systems and determine your energy needs.

TABLE 18-3: BUILDING SPECIFICATIONS	
Building Specifications	**Data**
Energy types/sources	
Year built	
Remodeled	
Type of insulation Roof, wall, attic R-values	
Weatherization performed?	
Energy Audits? When?	
Sealed leaks? When?	
Climate factors/considerations	
Heating/air conditioning units	
Type of ventilation, filter system	
HVAC, filter maintenance schedule	
Controls, timers, fans used	
Thermostat settings: Heat (winter) Air con (summer)	
Hot water needs	
Appliances	
Equipment	
Type of lighting	
Bulbs	
Lighting controls (Auto? Dimmers? Occupant sensors?)	
Renewable E (solar, green energy purchasing?)	
Other	

Table 18-4: Use utility bills to monitor energy costs and fluctuations on a spreadsheet. You can use similar worksheets to assess other practices, such as recycling assessments.

TABLE 18-4: ENERGY CONSUMPTION WORKSHEET							
BENCHMARK DATA							
Facility Location	**Electricity (in kWh)**		**Natural Gas (therms)**		**Other: fuel oil, kerosene, propane (in gallons)**	
Year	Amount Used	Cost	Amount Used	Cost	Amount Used	Cost
January						
February						
March						
April						
May						
June						
July						
August						
September						
October						
November						
December						
Monthly Average						

Monthly electricity use per square footage and operational hours:

Square footage:_____

Monthly kWh per square foot:_____

Monthly operational hours (from Table 18-2):_____

kWh per operational hour _____

Table 18-5: This data may be difficult to calculate, but some businesses may want to zoom in on specific equipment or areas to determine energy loads or track equipment use.

TABLE 18-5: ENERGY ASSESSMENT WORKSHEET: EQUIPMENT USE						
Location	Equipment, fixtures, devices	Model Specs (and Watts)	Energy Use (kWh) per hour	Daily Usage (Number of hours/day)	Energy Use (kWh) per month	Energy Use (kWh) per year
Reception, Retail Area						
Private Treatment Rooms						
Open Stations						
Client Locker Rooms						
Bathrooms						
Lounge Areas						
Offices						
Fitness Center						
Other Spaces						
Outdoor Areas						
Totals:						

Note: Use the watts/month to find the kWh per month. One kilowatt is equal to 1000 watts. Divide the watts used by 1000 to calculate the kWh used/month. For example: a 60 watt lamp used for 10 hours/day and 20 days/month is 200 watt hours/month. Energy use is 60 W x 200 = 12,000. Divide this by 1000 and this is 15.6 kWh per month.

WATER ASSESSMENT SHEETS

| TABLE 18-6: WATER CONSUMPTION WORKSHEET |||||||
| Facility Location | Water Usage ||| Sewer, Stormwater |||
Year	Amount used (gallons/month)	Cost	Avg. Gallons (per day)	Amount used (per month)	Cost	Avg. gallons (per day)
January						
February						
March						
April						
May						
June						
July						
August						
September						
October						
November						
December						
Monthly Average						

Note: Water bills may be measured in CCF, which is 100 cubic feet (equal to 748 gallons).

TABLE 18-7: WATER ASSESSMENT WORKSHEET FOR SPAS					
Location	Equipment, Fixtures, Appliances	Model, Specs	Flow rate (gallons per minute)	Usage (number of hours/week)	Water use (gallons) per day
Reception, Retail Area					
Private Treatment Rooms					
Treatment Tubs, Showers					
Open Stations	Shampoo Sinks Pedi Tubs				
Client Locker Rooms	Sinks Showers Toilets				
Steam Room					
Jacuzzis					
Bathrooms	Sinks Toilets				
Lounge Areas	Drinking Water				
Offices					
Fitness Center					
Other Spaces					
Outdoor Areas, Landscaping					
Laundry					
Totals					

SPA SPOTLIGHT

WATERSTONE SPA
Services and products are inspired and energized by nature.

Contact: Deb Cleland, Spa Manager and Founder (2012)

Waterstone Spa and Salon
236 E. Main St., Ashland, Oregon

www.waterstonespa.com

Facility size: The upstairs spa is 2500 sq. ft.

Number of employees: 23 (4 full time, 19 part time)

Number of treatment rooms: 5 (1 wet room)

Established in: 2003

Facility Description
Waterstone Spa offers five private treatment rooms, a naturally lit solarium, Japanese Ofuro soaking tub, steam and saunas, as well as couples' favorite, the Duet Suite. The spa has a fresh clean look with influences of nature and the botanical world in its décor. The salon is not included here as a case study and is a separate facility downstairs. Located in a historic building in the heart of downtown Ashland, Waterstone Spa strives to become Southern Oregon's wellness destination. The spa is now part of the historic Ashland Springs hotel.

> *Remember that we are in the Health and Wellness Business. It is our responsibility to set the example of what that means. Because we want the best possible outcome of the work we perform with a client, be it giving a facial or a spa treatment or a massage, it is imperative that we use the most therapeutic and healing ingredients. This means that we find products that are pure, unprocessed, and of the Earth. It is so important to utilize only organic, fresh ingredients because the organ of the body we are dealing with is the skin, which is absorbing everything. If only healthy ingredients are used, the body can go so much further in its continual quest to maintain homeostasis, rejuvenate, and heal itself.*
>
> ~ Deb Cleland, Spa Manager, Waterstone Spa

 ### SPA GOALS AND THE VISION

What is your vision?
Our vision for becoming a "green spa" is that we become certified as green (which means that we complete all that is needed to qualify), join the Green Spa Network for support and ideas, and become the best example in Ashland of walking our talk.

What is your spa image?

We offer services that support wellness, renewing, and healing. There is a local focus: Northwest nature is the theme of the historic hotel and spa/salon. We care deeply about the health and well-being of our guests and our staff—therefore we use materials and products that are good not only for them, but healthy for the planet as well. Our products are effective and many are organic, resourced locally, and from Oregon.

What is your green mission statement?

We are inspired by Oregon's natural abundance and are dedicated to sharing it with our guests. We are committed to integrity, quality, and building loyalty by empowering our employees, supporting our community, and providing excellence to every guest.

What are your sustainability goals?

To evaluate all the ways we use resources from office supplies to linens to utilities to determine if there are ways to be more efficient, sustainable and green. Order more local products, use less disposable items, use recycled paper, better building weatherization and ventilation, evaluate fixtures for water conservation, more recycling, and green education for staff.

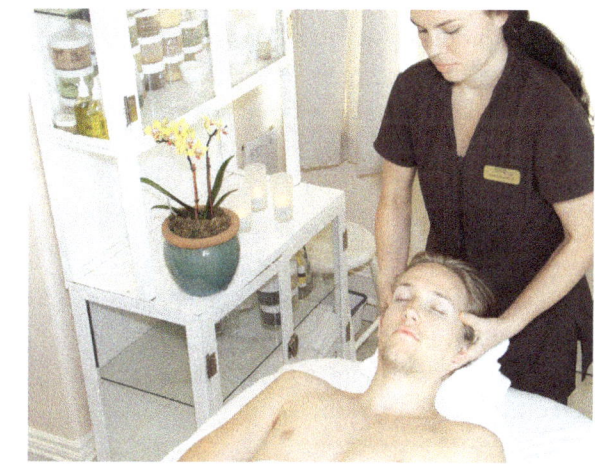

What is important to you regarding sustainability?

Because our service is about healing and wellness, our choices of products and materials need to be healthy choices also. We are not part of a thoughtless destruction of our planet and need to be making decisions that help sustain the livability of our planet for the next generations.

What business practices or areas would you like to make more green?

We should look at energy savings, office functions, and evaluate where our products come from and the total overall impact of that.

What sustainable business practices do you think your clients want to see?

That we take this idea seriously enough to not just apply it in a few obvious areas, but take the time and effort to apply in all phases or aspects of the business.

SPA ELEMENTS

The Menu

Our services include La Stone Therapy, foot reflexology, Ayurvedic body treatments, iLike facials, and solarium foot treatments, essential oils, vinotherapy, and soaking tubs.

- Natural, organic products; focused on health and wellness.

Products

- Healthy, organic, local.
- We look for fair trade/sustainable sourcing.
- All our products offer healing and medicinal benefits of herbs and flowers, such as lavender, jasmine,

rose, and calendula, which nourish and beautify the body, mind, and spirit.
- Ilike and Jurlique organic skin care; Sacred Earth Botanicals (organic from Eugene, OR); Young Living essential oils.
- Buddha Blends body and chocolate products are local from Ashland, some organic.
- Applegate Botanicals vino body lotion is local from the Applegate Valley.
- Banyan ayurvedic oils and sandalwood; order bulk products (salt); switching seaweed from French to Canadian sourcing: Seaflora.
- Some recycled content packaging, printed with soy ink.
- There is less of a shipping footprint with local products.

Supplies
- Paper products have recycled content.
- Soap refills save containers and space.
- Retail bags have recycled content.
- Soy candles.

Treatment Supplies
- Cotton, wool, microfiber linens.
- Laundry is done by the hotel with eco products; optional robes and slippers save laundry and time.
- Towels are used more instead of disposable cotton for facial product removal.

Energy

Building
- Brick historical building built in 1910; remodeled and weatherization performed in 2000.
- Energy Audit performed in 2006 by the city.
- Acrylic was placed inside historic single pane windows in the treatment rooms.

HVAC systems
- Electric heat pump and programmable thermostat.
- Treatment rooms have existing radiant wall units heated with a central high efficiency hot water heater.
- Fans in treatment rooms circulate air and help balance temperatures.

Equipment
- Wax equipment is on timers.
- Sauna, steam room, towel warmers, hot packs turned off when not in use.

Lighting
- Bulbs are replaced with new CFL's as they burn out; lighting controls: dimmers.

Water
- Filtered water for staff and guests (w/ lemon, cucumber, or mint).
- Hotel staff does the main laundry.
- Energy Star dishwasher.
- Fixtures: Low-flow aerators on sinks, faucets, showers, high efficiency toilet: 1.6 gpf.

Green Materials
- Local décor, elements from nature (rocks, sea sponges).
- Natural fabrics for curtains and furniture (rattan), washable slip covers.
- Marmoleum™ floors in treatment rooms.
- Use or renovate what is there—repaint or restore décor.

Indoor Environmental Quality (IEQ)
- Fans for air circulation.
- Cleaning: non-toxic laundry soap and natural cleaners are used.
- Natural furnishings and décor.
- Fewer chemicals are used whenever possible, replaced with healthier products and natural scents.
- LED-powered "candles" for safety and cleaner air quality.

Purchasing
- All purchasing, products, and supplies are considered for green aspects.
- No disposable cups.

Waste Reduction
- Recycling: paper, glass, and plastic recycling bins.
- Communications through email, e-news, and computerized booking cuts paper use.
- Operations: we make note pads from scratch paper.
- Printing: marketing and promotional specials are written on dry erase boards.
- Not using individual tip envelopes saves paper.
- Soap refills cuts down container waste.
- The hotel recycles soap and room amenities for recycling and distribution to communities and countries in greatest need through the efforts of Clean the World Foundation, a charitable organization.

Transportation
- Downtown location is good for guest and pedestrian access.

Food Service
- The hotel restaurant focuses on using local and seasonal food sources.
- The restaurant recycles fryer oil used in our kitchen and composts all food scraps.

Marketing
- The green features of the products are attractive to clients.

People and Staff Care
- The spa is owned by Ashland Springs Hotel, which offers health care, staff discounts, and generous educational opportunities.
- They recognize Employees of the Month and have an annual appreciation event for the entire staff.
- Provide a Wellness Program and classes for staff and the community.
- Provide extra work hour opportunities if possible.
- Ayurvedic classes, Hawaiian classes, and salon charity fundraisers are some of the events.

Education
The staff is trained to use more green practices.

CHAPTER 19

Creating Your Green Action Plan

INTRODUCTION

Think about specific goals and changes for your business. Here are blank tables to outline a customized sustainability plan. Refer to Chapter 17 for recommended green practices. After beginning with planning and assessments from Chapter 18, you can outline your summarized goals and ideas here. Then in Chapter 20, Implementing Your Green Practices, you can refine the goals with action steps, timelines and checklists. The online resources include blank worksheets and checklists from all the chapters together in one place to use for planning purposes.

CREATING SUSTAINABILITY GOALS

Before outlining your goals, review your current practices, as discussed in Chapter 18.

Ask your team what the pros and cons are to the suggested green practices—are they feasible?

Here is a list of steps for goal setting:

Goal Setting Steps:
- Complete a current business analysis.
- What are the current practices?
- Explore examples and ideas for changes.
- List the pros and cons to decisions.
- Perform a cost/benefit analysis and use comparison tools (such as LCA).
- Outline proposed changes.
- Record the goals, steps, and timeline.

Planning Recommendations

When deciding which practices to implement, first go for the "low hanging fruit." These are the easiest, least expensive options. Compare the options and decide what changes you want to make. What are the priorities?
- Low Hanging Fruit: Go for the easiest, less expensive options first.
- Light green versus dark green changes: Are you making major or minor changes?
- Different possibilities and scenarios: Consider a variety of options for each decision.
- Defining goals: What are the priorities?

Spa Sustainability Goals

Use this condensed table with all categories listed here together for brainstorming the initial goals. Subsequent tables have each category separated into individual tables for more detailed planning. Once these goals are decided, transfer these to a new table with a timeline and steps to achieve these (see Chapter 20).

Table Key for symbols $, R, P
$= Economic: financial *Savings*
R= Environmental: natural *Resource* savings
P= Equity: good for *People*

TABLE 19-1: SUSTAINABILITY GOALS FOR EACH SPA CATEGORY			
Spa Category	**Initial Sustainability Goals**	**Benefits** ($, R, P)	**Challenges**
Service Menu			
Retail & Service Products			
Purchasing, Supplies			
Green Materials			
Waste Reduction			
IEQ			
Energy			
Water			
Landscaping			
Food and Beverage			
Transportation			
Staff			
Clients, Community			

SUSTAINABILITY PLANNING TABLES

Now use the following categories and tables to explore more specific ideas for the different areas in the facility. These are also found in the online resources. Fill in your own answers in the blank tables. Remember that some categories overlap, so it is okay to have duplicate items in different tables. These can be refined later. These lists are extensive so you can just choose a few items to start with.

Table Key for symbols $, R, P
$= Economic: financial *Savings*
R= Environmental: natural *Resource* savings
P= Equity: good for *People*

TABLE 19-2: THE SERVICE MENU GOALS

Green Menu Goals	Cost to Implement	Long-term Savings	Benefits and Resource Savings to Consider $= Ec, R= Env, P= Eq

TABLE 19-3: RETAIL AND SERVICE PRODUCT GOALS

Green Product Goals	Cost to Implement	Long-term Savings	Benefits and Resource Savings $= Ec, R= Env, P= Eq

TABLE 19-4: SUPPLY USE GOALS

Supply Use Goals	Cost to Implement	Long-term Savings	Benefits and Resource Savings $= Ec, R= Env, P= Eq

TABLE 19-5: EQUIPMENT GOALS

Equipment Goals	Cost to Implement	Long-term Savings	Benefits and Resource Savings $= Ec, R= Env, P= Eq

TABLE 19-6: WASTE REDUCTION GOALS

Waste Reduction Goals and Targets (Recycling, purchasing)	Cost to Implement	Long-term Savings	Benefits and Resource Savings $= Ec, R= Env, P= Eq

TABLE 19-7: PACKAGING GOALS

Packaging/Waste Reduction Goals	Cost to Implement	Long-term Savings	Benefits and Resource Savings $= Ec, R= Env, P= Eq

TABLE 19-8: GREEN MATERIAL GOALS

Green Material Goals (Interiors, Building, Purchasing)	Cost to Implement	Long-term Savings	Benefits and Resource Savings $=$ Ec, R= Env, P= Eq

TABLE 19-9: INDOOR ENVIRONMENTAL QUALITY (IEQ) GOALS

IEQ Goals (Interiors, Building, Purchasing)	Cost to Implement	Long-term Savings	Benefits and Resource Savings $=$ Ec, R= Env, P= Eq

TABLE 19-10: ENERGY GOALS

Energy Conservation Goals and Targets	Cost to Implement	Long-term Savings	Benefits and Resource Savings $=$ Ec, R= Env, P= Eq

TABLE 19-11: WATER CONSERVATION GOALS

Water Conservation Goals and Targets	Cost to Implement	Long-term Savings	Benefits and Resource Savings $= Ec, R= Env, P= Eq

TABLE 19-12: LANDSCAPING CONSERVATION GOALS

Landscaping Goals	Cost to Implement	Long-term Savings	Benefits and Resource Savings $= Ec, R= Env, P= Eq

TABLE 19-13: HEALTHY FOOD AND BEVERAGE GOALS

Healthy Food and Beverage Goals	Cost to Implement	Long-term Savings	Benefits and Resource Savings $= Ec, R= Env, P= Eq

TABLE 19-14: SUSTAINABLE TRANSPORTATION AND TRAVEL GOALS

Transportation Goals	Cost to Implement	Long-term Savings	Benefits and Resource Savings $= Ec, R= Env, P= Eq

TABLE 19-15: STAFF CARE GOALS

Staff Care Goals	Cost to Implement	Long-term Savings	Benefits and Resource Savings $= Ec, R= Env, P= Eq

TABLE 19-16: GOALS FOR CLIENTS AND THE COMMUNITY

Goals for Clients and the Community	Cost to Implement	Long-term Savings	Benefits and Resource Savings $= Ec, R= Env, P= Eq

Education and Building Green Awareness

One way to build awareness is to have a sustainability education event:
- Include presentations and workshops.
- Share the vision.
- Rethink business methods, products, and services.
- Engage peoples' values.
- Promote the use of the triple bottom line philosophy.
- Foster a culture of involvement and continual improvement related to sustainability.

The event can include both internal staff presenting their sustainability efforts along with some of the other key business partners.

Here are some ideas for contests to promote green practices:
- Best green idea.
- Best energy savings idea.
- Best recycling or waste reduction idea.
- Best cost savings conservation idea.

TABLE 19-17: CONTEST AND EDUCATION IDEAS		
List Contest / Education Ideas	**Timeline, Dates**	**Awards/Prizes/Recognition**
1.		
2.		
3.		

CHAPTER 20

Implementing Your Green Practices

INTRODUCTION

This chapter consists of tables with timelines and action steps to use for your finalized goals from Chapter 19. Check off tasks as you apply your practices in your operations. After implementing each new practice, measure and assess the progress. Results can be recorded by monetary savings and percentages or by other means.

IMPLEMENTING SUSTAINABILITY PRACTICES: Action Steps and Tables

TABLE 20-1: THE SERVICE MENU PRACTICES					
New Green Menu Practices	**Action Steps**	**Timeline and Schedule**	**Monitor and Measure Progress**	**Results:** Resource and cost savings or increased profits
Table Example: Switch product lines	Research, order, advertise, change menu	By a set date	Increased sales by 8%	Note by the month and the year

TABLE 20-2: RETAIL AND SERVICE PRODUCTS					
Green Products Practices	**Action Steps**	**Timeline and Schedule**	**Monitor and Measure Progress**	**Results:** Resource and cost savings or increased profits

CHAPTER 20: Implementing Your Green Practices 209

TABLE 20-3: SUPPLY USE PRACTICES				
Supply Use	**Action Steps**	**Timeline and Schedule**	**Monitor and Measure Progress**	**Results and Cost Savings**

TABLE 20-4: EQUIPMENT CHOICES AND PRACTICES				
Equipment Choices and Practices	**Action Steps**	**Timeline and Schedule**	**Monitor and Measure Progress**	**Results and Cost Savings**

TABLE 20-5: WASTE REDUCTION PRACTICES				
Waste Reduction Practices	**Action Steps**	**Timeline and Schedule**	**Monitor and Measure Progress**	**Results and Cost Savings**

TABLE 20-6: PACKAGING PRACTICES				
Green Packaging Choices and Practices	Action Steps	Timeline and Schedule	Monitor and Measure Progress	Results and Cost Savings

TABLE 20-7: GREEN MATERIAL PRACTICES				
Green Material Practices	Action Steps	Timeline and Schedule	Monitor and Measure Progress	Results and Cost Savings

TABLE 20-8: INDOOR ENVIRONMENTAL QUALITY (IEQ) PRACTICES				
Healthy IEQ Practices	Action Steps	Timeline and Schedule	Monitor and Measure Progress	Results and Cost Savings

TABLE 20-9: ENERGY PRACTICES				
Energy Conservation Practices	**Action Steps**	**Timeline and Schedule**	**Monitor and Measure Progress**	**Results and Cost Savings**

TABLE 20-10: WATER PRACTICES				
Water Conservation Practices	**Action Steps**	**Timeline and Schedule**	**Monitor and Measure Progress**	**Results and Cost Savings**

TABLE 20-11: SUSTAINABLE LANDSCAPING PRACTICES				
Landscaping Practices	**Action Steps**	**Timeline and Schedule**	**Monitor and Measure Progress**	**Results and Cost Savings**

TABLE 20-12: HEALTHY FOOD AND BEVERAGES				
Healthy Food and Beverage Choices	**Action Steps**	**Timeline and Schedule**	**Monitor and Measure Progress**	**Results and Cost Savings**

TABLE 20-13: SUSTAINABLE TRANSPORTATION PRACTICES				
Sustainable Transportation Practices	**Action Steps**	**Timeline and Schedule**	**Monitor and Measure Progress**	**Results and Cost Savings**

TABLE 20-14: STAFF CARE				
Staff Care	**Action Steps**	**Timeline and Schedule**	**Monitor and Measure Progress**	**Results and Cost Savings**

TABLE 20-15: CLIENTS AND THE COMMUNITY				
Green Practices to Benefit Clients and the Community	**Action Steps**	**Timeline and Schedule**	**Monitor and Measure Progress**	**Results and Cost Savings**

CHAPTER 21

Marketing Green

INTRODUCTION

The marketing of green products and services is an area that keeps changing based on consumer interests. Why do consumers buy green products? Why do they care? Business trends are one of the marketing factors to keep in mind. It is both interesting and useful to study marketing demographics and what appeals to buyers.

Branding your business image is a primary focus in marketing. The emphasis on e-marketing and social media has definitely changed the way we promote our business, so having a social media marketing plan is necessary in today's world. Additionally, Greenwashing in marketing campaigns is prevalent so it is important to make sure your services and products are truly green if they are promoted that way. Specific marketing plans and ideas are discussed in Chapter 22.

The natural and organic personal care market is one of the fastest growing segments of the cosmetics and toiletries industry in the US and internationally (klinegroup.com 2010). Spas are experiencing this major lifestyle shift. While consumers are confused or skeptical about green products, the sale of green products has increased. In 2010, Mintel marketing surveys and the Green Gauge Global Report found that over 50% of consumers think environmentally friendly products are too expensive (gfkroperpulse.co.uk, 2010; mintel.com). On the other hand, consumers care about such benefits as natural and free of chemicals. Some people put too much faith in marketing claims, while others are skeptical about what they read.

MarketLine research shows that more than 30% of consumers now look for natural products. Over 10% of new products are advertised as paraben free. Packaged Facts reports "the US natural and organic hair care, makeup and skin care market expanded by more than 60% in the five-year period ending in 2010. The industry was worth close to $8 billion and is forecast to hit the $11 billion mark in 2016" (reportlinker.com 2012).

WORDS OF WISDOM

The sustainable community is passionate and ideally suited for social media. Conversations on social platforms are shoring up customer retention and brand loyalty. Businesses that quickly learn how to master the art of attracting and retaining customers using real-time social media will be ready to generate growth and will end up winners in the globally connected world.

~ Beverly Macy, CEO of Gravity Summit and Co-Author of *The Power of Real-Time Social Media Marketing,* www.gravitysummit.com

MARKETING AND LOHAS

Clients have numerous choices and want value for their dollar. Consumers also want to spend money in places aligned with their values (Figure 21-1). As discussed in Chapter 1, these potential clients are Lifestyles of Health and Sustainability (LOHAS) consumers. There is an estimated "$290 billion dollar US marketplace for goods and services focused on health, the environment, social justice, personal development, and sustainable living (2010). Approximately 20 percent of adults (41 million people of the 215 million adults in the US) are considered LOHAS consumers." This is one in five Americans.

The LOHAS market is expanding rapidly (Figure 21-2). The future social, environmental, and economic changes will be affected by these progressive, forward thinking individuals. It is a good marketing tool to understand these LOHAS consumers who care about personal, community, and planetary health. The green consumer marketplace could quadruple by 2015 reaching over $800 billion (lohas.com 2012). This is a very motivating opportunity for businesses to expand into the green market.

Figure 21-1: Consumers want to spend money in places aligned with their values.

This market is significant to the future of your business. Consumers want to visit salons and spas that are more natural and that use fewer resources. They want to feel they are making a difference while taking care of themselves. Not indulging, but receiving holistic self-care while caring for the environment at the same time.

The core values of consumers are expressed differently depending on the local culture where you live. LOHAS markets are booming in some parts of the world as values of nature and respect are interwoven facets of sustainable lifestyle choices. In contrast, US consumers have a stronger focus on personal health and well-being (lohas.com 2012). This focus is the heart of the beauty industry.

LOHAS defines a lifestyle and philosophy of a holistic world view. Similarly, the body, mind, and spirit interconnections are what a spa's philosophy embraces. This trend of mainstream cultural awareness is evolving and the ever-changing beauty industry is set to embrace the evolution.

Companies that address these sustainable values will achieve success with innovative products and services. LOHAS businesses are attracting significant interest from investors. There are many exciting opportunities for niche markets beyond the retail sectors.

Another useful marketing study defines five consumer segments: LOHAS, Naturalites, Drifters, Conventionals, and Unconcerned. Check out *Understanding the LOHAS Consumer: The Rise of Ethical Consumerism, A Strategic Market Research Update* from The Natural Marketing Institute (NMI) Consumer Trends Database at nmisolutions.com (2011).

- LOHAS market sectors include personal health, natural lifestyles, green building, alternative transportation, eco tourism, and alternative energy.
- The beauty industry is part of the personal health sector that includes natural and organic products.
- The health and wellness (personal health) sector reached $118 billion in 2010.

BUSINESS TRENDS FOR TODAY'S MARKETPLACE

Many professionals agree that current spa trends complement the green market. A focus on offering simple, well-priced products and services, engaging clients, using social media, and supporting local products are part of the new business model. Healthier products, green chemistry, and natural practices are in vogue.

Spa Trends

Give Value

According to SpaFinder's 2011 Trends, customers want value and return on their investment—not necessarily inexpensive, but more value for their dollar spent. This trend is observed for other industries as well. Excellent customer service and competitive pricing are essential.

Offer Real Therapy

Think health and wellness. "Corrective" skin treatments, rather than "anti-aging" treatments are being offered. Pain relief services, such as hydrotherapy and infrared saunas are popular for the aging population in the US.

Brand Yourself

A business trend is global branding. Getting on the spa "brand wagon" is focused on making global brands and services consistent at each geographic location. Eco-friendly and lifestyle branding is a growing movement (Figure 21-3). Signature spa journeys give spas a unique individuality to set them apart from others. What is your brand image?

LOHAS in Chinese and Japanese cultures means *good life, happy living*, or *harmonious light*.

Figure 21-2: The LOHAS market is expanding rapidly.

Simplify the Menu

A simpler, affordable spa menu caters to clients with limited time and budgets. Express menus are popular for those on the go. Clients can still get their spa fix, but it is time efficient and more affordable. Mini facials, manicures, and foot treatments are common services. These mini procedures also save natural resources.

Go Local

There is a local, regional focus on using products and food from local suppliers indigenous to the region. A spa's unique place and culture should be shared. Facility design and décor based on local flavors feels like the salon belongs there. Serving local food and bringing in a connection with the natural environment makes sense for the ultimate guest experience. It also supports the local economy and saves resources by cutting down transportation needs.

Get Social Using E-Marketing

Mobile appointment booking and social media outlets are growing segments of marketing. Giving exclusive, real values to bring in customers is important to stay competitive. Blogging, Facebook, YouTube, and tweets are all marketing avenues necessary in today's messaging world. Worldometers.info shows the live, real time numbers of people currently on the Internet measured in seconds. More than half of all Americans are now on Facebook.

Engage and Communicate

Client and employee retention and engagement are key elements in the sustainable business world. Use engaging interactive messages and communication to stay in touch with clients and staff. Surveys and votes are popular, engaging methods on the Internet that are part of a comprehensive marketing plan.

Offer More

Spa programming is another addition to regular services. Lifestyle coaches, yoga, wine parties, wellness programs, and educational classes can add other interesting features or connections for clients. Events bring interest beyond regular spa services.

Be Real

Transparency and authenticity are two elements discussed often regarding green business practices. Honesty about business practices is known as transparency. An example of transparency is reporting the actual impacts on the environment. Real, or authentic, practices are what a business truly represents. Honesty in business is respected and valued.

> Your products and services are a reflection of who you are. Make sure it is quality. Stand out among the competition.

Share Your Passion

What excites you? Share what you are passionate about in your business practices or share your values and milestones. Even sharing ideas with those in your industry is a sustainable practice. Sharing knowledge and resources benefit everyone. People are attracted to those who share their positive stories and interests.

Highlight the Rejuvenation Benefits

We are bombarded with a massive amount of information, which is increasing with more computer time, sound bites,

Figure 21-3: Eco-friendly and lifestyle branding is a growing movement.

and fast moving technology. This is information overload. The beauty industry caters to providing the down time to unplug, recharge our batteries, and rest our busy minds. A massage is not a luxury, but a therapeutic, healthy alternative to combat stress. Most people would rather see a massage therapist than a doctor. It is more affordable too! Spas are havens away from daily stress for both clients and the staff.

DEMOGRAPHICS AND DIFFERENT GENERATIONS

Another facet of marketing is the *generational demographics*. Generational population studies give a better understanding of society and how we interact with each other. What are the generational differences and what do they care about? What experiences will the next generation be exposed to? Generations do not have a set pattern of years and are defined more by the major changes and a significant spike or decline in birth rates at the time.

Beyond traditional demographics of income, gender, and lifestyle habits is the generation we were born into. For example, those of us born before the Gen Y generation have to train ourselves to keep up on social media and Internet marketing. Marketing strategies have changed from the old standard newspaper ads. In order to stay competitive, new marketing plans need to be used.

- **New Silent Generation or Generation Z:** Born from 1995 through the present (a 16 year range as of 2011, although some statistics say this starts in the year 2000).
- **Millennials or Generation Y:** Born between 1981 and 1995 (a span of 14 years or more).
- **Generation X:** Born between 1965 and 1980 (a span of 15 years).
- **Baby Boomers:** Born between 1946 and 1964 (a span of 18 years).
- **The Silent Generation:** Born between 1920 and 1945 (a span of 25 years).
- **The Greatest Generation:** Born between 1900 and 1920 (a span of 20 years).

(Source: Johnson, M. & L. Generations, Inc. 2010)

*Note: Other sites, including geography.about.com (2012), and the population reference bureau have different dates regarding Gen Y and Gen Z ending and starting in the year 2000.

Figure 21-4: There are currently 6 US generations.

The six US generations are the Greatest Generation, Silent Generation, Baby Boomers, Generation X, Generation Y, and Generation Z (Figure 21-4). There is some inconsistency with regard to details of the generations and the exact years associated with those births. It is an extensive and interesting subject that goes beyond marketing and also impacts the staff expectations and work habits in the workplace.

Each generation is known for their unique experiences, values, lifestyles, and other demographics that influence their beliefs and buying decisions (Figure 21-5). Generational history includes the economy, scientific progress, politics, technology, and social shocks that have impacts on each generation. The person's age, stage of life, and different segments within the generations are also factors to consider, according to various studies (aabri.com 2011). Any business can benefit from using these generational demographics and characteristics. This information covers broad marketing strategies and research and is not limited to salons and spas. Check out the chapter references to research interesting and useful details on generational marketing.

Figure 21-5: Generational demographics influence beliefs and buying decisions.

Website Marketing

Use something like Google Analytics to measure how many people come to the website, where they are from, how they found your site, and what pages they found to be most useful. This initial tracking then can serve as a benchmark to compare with future metrics.

> **How would you market to these different generations?**
> *What would the selling points be?*

ETHICS AND GREENWASHING

Greenwashing means misleading consumers (Figure 21-6). Many companies have jumped on the green bandwagon. It is estimated that a high percentage of green claims are false and there are no enforced regulations or standards for green claims. Misinformation is rampant and has given green products a bad name. Be authentic and transparent in your marketing. Make sure your claims are true and do not believe everything the vendor says. Who is the third party certifier of the product? Do your homework. Is it credible? How green is it and why?

Green Product Certifications

It appears that product labels and certifications are designed for marketing more than verification purposes. Certifications and standards for products, labeling, and building are clearly over-saturating the market. Most certifications are reliable and examples include Ecocert for products and LEED for buildings. See corresponding chapters for the list of product standards and ecolabels.

> Remember to note multicultural diversity, mature clients, and men's preferences in targeting your market.

The Seven Sins of Greenwashing

According to TerraChoice Group Inc., the Seven Sins of Greenwashing are:

Sin of the Hidden Trade-off:

A claim suggesting that a product is green based on a narrow set of attributes without attention to other important environmental issues. Paper, for example, is not necessarily environmentally preferable just because it comes from a sustainably harvested forest, which could be a mono-crop tree farm. Other important environmental issues in the paper making process, such as greenhouse gas emissions, or chlorine use in bleaching, may be equally important.

Sin of No Proof:

An environmental claim that cannot be substantiated by easily accessible supporting information or by a reliable third-party certification. Common examples are facial tissues or toilet tissue products that claim various percentages of post-consumer recycled content without providing evidence.

Sin of Vagueness:

A claim that is so poorly defined or broad that its real meaning is likely to be misunderstood by the consumer. "All-natural" is an example. Arsenic, uranium, mercury, and formaldehyde are all naturally occurring, and poisonous. All-natural is not necessarily green.

Figure 21-6: Greenwashing means misleading consumers.

Sin of Worshiping False Labels:

A product that, through either words or images, gives the impression of third-party endorsement where no such endorsement exists; fake labels, in other words.

Sin of Irrelevance:

An environmental claim that may be truthful, but is unimportant or unhelpful for consumers seeking environmentally preferable products. "CFC-free" is a common example, since it is a frequent claim despite the fact that CFCs are banned by law.

Sin of Lesser of Two Evils:

A claim that may be true within the product category, but that risks distracting the consumer from the greater environmental impacts of the category as a whole. Organic cigarettes could be an example of this, as might the fuel-efficient sport-utility vehicle.

Sin of Fibbing:

Environmental claims that are simply false. The most common examples are products falsely claiming to be Energy Star certified or registered.

(*Seven Sins of Greenwashing Source: Courtesy of Terrachoice Group, Inc., terrachoice.com 2010)

Marketing Tools

- Website
- Brochures
- Newsletters
- Articles
- Press Releases
- Direct Mail

- Social media sites: Facebook, Twitter, LinkedIn
- Blogs
- Videos, YouTube
- Podcasts
- Surveys
- Signage

- Ads
- TV
- Radio
- Public Relations
- Event Planning
- Charities and community events

* More information on marketing tools and planning ideas are given in Chapter 22.

CHAPTER 22

Planning Your Marketing Communications

INTRODUCTION

When planning marketing communications, clearly outline and define your green message (Figure 22-1). Are you adapting your current marketing plan to include green features or are you revamping your image and brand? How well do you know your clients? Think about the answers to the questions included in this chapter before designing your communications strategy.

Marketing can be a full-time job and does not always get the attention or funding needed to keep businesses thriving. Successful businesspeople adapt to trends and keep their message consistent, yet innovative. This chapter is a brief overview of green marketing tools and ideas.

> As always, word of mouth advertising from satisfied clients is the best promotion.
> Customer service and communications with existing clientele should be the primary marketing focus.

Figure 22-1: Clearly define your sustainability message.

MARKETING ASSESSMENT WORKSHEET

In order to plan your messaging, answer the following questions.

TABLE 22-1: CLIENT DEMOGRAPHICS Who are your clients? What are the demographics? Is this current information?		
Demographics	**Answers**	**Notes**
Age ranges		
Gender (%'s)	Female: Male:	
Culture, ethnicity		
Income ranges		
Lifestyle habits		
Values		
Career, interests		
Other		

- Define your customer: Who is your customer? What are their interests?
  _____

- What is your core, concise green message?
  _____

- What key services or products are you offering that are green?
  _____

- What unique words or language do you use to describe your products and services?
  _____

- What are the primary benefits of your services to clients? Is it health, or wellness?
  _____

- What are current trends in the industry? What do you offer that is relevant today?
  _____

- What are your competitors offering? Is it working for them?
  _____

GREEN MARKETING IDEAS

Make your message unique to promote your sustainable practices and corporate social responsibility (Figure 22-2). People love stories—telling a story about the history of how something got started or about a person who created something sparks interest and discussion. Additionally, sharing information through education is one of the best ways to promote green practices. Educating staff and clients on your green ideas builds support and awareness. There are many ways to increase your spa's visibility. The number one goal is to keep clients and potential clients engaged and interested. Social media is a primary way to do this.

Are you on brand?
*"On brand" is a set of expectations for your brand.
Are you living up to your clients' expectations?*

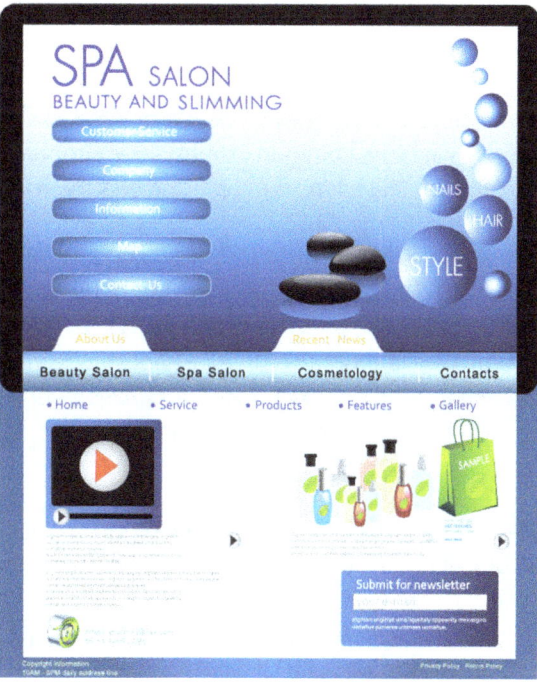

Figure 22-2: Make your message unique.

Marketing Tips
- Hire a marketing professional who is experienced and up on current trends.
- Join a green business organization.
- Promote third-party ecolabels and standards for products.
- Promote your green practices.
- Get your entire staff involved in marketing.
- Increase leads by capturing information from Internet avenues and social media sites.
- Increase the Internet conversations.

Where does your customer look for information?
That is where you want your messages to be located.

THE SOCIAL MEDIA REVOLUTION

The online community is described as a "virtual" community. Using social networking sites to connect with customers is a part of marketing strategies. E-marketing, e-ads, Google, social sites, Facebook, blogs, and Twitter are common media platforms. These are the current communication tools for personal and business messages. What is the return on investment from these sites? Some marketing professionals say whoever has the most leads and "likes" wins. Make sure communications are appropriately timed and the content interests people and gets them to act, call, or engage (Figure 22-3).

Figure 22-3: What interests people and gets them to act, call, or engage?

As Beverly Macy discusses in *The Power of Real-Time Social Media Marketing*, there are now dedicated *community managers* for taking care of the business's social media needs (2011). Using *search engine optimization* (SEO) and lead generation tools are two examples of e-tools. *Customer relationship management* (CRM) is both in-house and online. Another aspect of the Internet is *reputation management* to track online feedback from consumer reviews. Aim for quality, trust, popularity, and timeliness for marketing messages. Keeping the content fresh is key.

MARKETING TOOLS

Marketing tools include the following:
- Brochures and the menu: Include green logos, products, and services.
- Website: Include green features and a sustainability statement or educational page.
- Surveys: Use customer surveys via email or websites.
- Newsletters: Include green news and education.
- Articles: Promote green practices and products.

> Social media expressions include *conversation, community, engagement, transparency,* and *authenticity*, which are the same terms applied to green and sustainable subjects.

- Press Releases: Announce any green news, charities, or events.
- Direct Mail: Highlight green products and services.
- Social media sites: Play up green features and utilize the Facebook fan page, Twitter, and LinkedIn.
- E-commerce: Get on e-commerce sites and green websites.
- Blogs: Share green news or sustainability education.
- YouTube: Make a video about the health aspects of green products and services.
- Videos: Have an educational website as an "authority" on different subjects.
- Local search directories: Get listed in these directories and monitor the sites.
- Reviews: Manage reviewer feedback and websites (city sites, Yelp, travel review sites).
- SEO's, Google search and tracking: You can track who searches for you and monitor web searches.
- Text messages: Use to send promotional messages (with client approval).
- Signs: Add green information to in-house signage, show and post your green features.
- Ads: Use print and web banner ads.
- TV spots: Convey your brand.
- Radio announcements: Advertise specials or events.
- Public Relations: Promote your sustainable message.
- Event Planning: Hold fun evening or educational events.
- Charities and community events: Host fundraising or give donations based on sales.
- Networking: Attend community meetings and green business groups.

K.I.S.S.:
Keep it sustainable and social.

MARKETING REVIEW CHECKLIST

Use the following questions to help you review your marketing plan:

- What is your core message and brand?
- What are your monthly and seasonal promotions?
- Is your current plan consistent and getting results?
- What marketing tools are you using?
- Are you tracking responses?
- What is your budget?
- Is your graphic artist or web designer working well for you?
- Who are your strategic partners? (Suppliers, other local cross-promotional companies.)
- What organizations, websites, or individuals are giving you positive and credible endorsements?
- Do you need to hire a dedicated staff person or marketing person?

For readability, use bigger print for clients whose eyesight is not 20/20 for labels, signs, forms, etc.

Marketing Ideas

- Give special offers for local members and segments of the community.
- Offer last-minute discounts through social media.
- Have a customer loyalty program.
- Offer something extra or unique.

TABLE 22-2: MARKETING PLANNING					
Marketing Tools	**Placement, Venue**	**Monthly Schedule Timeline**	**Frequency, Number**	**Budget, Cost**	**Response, Tracking**
Website, blogs, reviews					
Social media sites					
E-banner ads, other "e" promotions					
Newsletters (e and print)					
Direct mail					
Public Relations, networking					
Print ads					
TV, Radio					
Specials and promotions					
Events, charities					

CHAPTER 23

Building Green

INTRODUCTION

Green building methods can save a tremendous amount of money and resources in the long run. Basic building design concepts for new construction and remodeling projects are an interesting area of study. It is also helpful to analyze your existing facility for efficient operations or to get potential renovation ideas. The methods described here can be used for both small and large facilities. Not all will be feasible or applicable to your business, but understanding building and operations management is definitely beneficial. Some of these concepts have been discussed in previous chapters and apply to building best practices. Building concepts are introduced here and building best practices are found in Chapter 24.

Interest in green building has been growing very quickly in the past decade. New materials and methods have made it easier than ever to build more sustainably with healthier materials. The cost of green materials is becoming more affordable and there is a renewed focus on building quality, rather than quantity. *Integrated design* considers the whole building as one system and is the preferred design method used for green building.

Building codes and standards are increasingly more stringent (such as minimum energy savings requirements). Green building certifications exceed these standards and include a range of national and state programs. Many companies are taking advantage of federal and state incentives for building green, but these incentives change constantly. Commercial incentives have been generous in the recent past.

Building green can be challenging, but the return on investment is worth the effort. Green building is predicted to be the standard method within the next decade. Building appraisal values are positively influenced by green features, so it is important to keep facilities and operations up to date. Invest wisely in your future building or remodeling projects to save on spa operational costs and increase future resale values.

WORDS OF WISDOM

It is easier than ever to influence a project with sustainable features and stay within a client's budget. Many aspects of green building are becoming mainstream. It is gratifying to be part of the solution, rather than part of the problem.

~ Gina Heckley, CSBA, Design and Resource Consultant, Idea House Consulting, ideahouse.net

Green Building Components

- Site design
- Energy systems & renewable energy
- Daylighting and lighting
- Green materials and products
- Indoor environmental quality
- Water conservation and landscaping
- Green building standards
- Operations and maintenance

THE GREEN BUILDING PROCESS

So what is green building? Building green incorporates materials and methods that are healthy for people, the planet, and prosperity (Figure 23-1). The main building considerations are site, energy, water, materials, and indoor air quality. The first step in green building/remodeling is to put together a great team. Traditional building has many separate components and players, where sustainable building brings all of the components and players together. This is probably the main challenge—a coordinated team project. Green building starts at the design phase with a good architect who is experienced with green projects.

Green Team Meetings (Eco-charettes)

The owner, builder, architect, facility manager, and others (subcontractors) involved in the building project should have team meetings referred to as *eco-charettes*. This process is similar to the green team planning for implementing your facility operations and practices. Everyone should be on the same page and work together to create an integrated whole building approach that works as one system. For example, it makes no sense if the plumber and electrician come in and do their thing without coordinating what the other person is doing or why except for the basic scheduling or necessary communication. Cutting holes through the expensive insulation installed the day before or installing the wrong pipes are expensive and permanent mistakes. Making sure everyone is on board with the goals, is aware of the expectations, and agrees to the specifications are key to finishing the project successfully on time and on budget.

Figure 23-1: Building green incorporates materials and methods that are healthy.

Choosing Contractors

Green builders need experience and continuing education to keep up with current methods. It is difficult to change years of traditional habits. Many are stuck in doing things the same way over and over and will get left behind in the marketplace as new green builders emerge. Most building education is now focused on green methods.

> It is estimated that "by 2020, about 80% of green-certified building space will be in the commercial building sector, up from 73% today."
>
> (pikeresearch.com 2012)

It is very important to choose your contractors wisely, ask questions, and get references. Get solid written bids based on green specifications (Figure 23-2). Look for enthusiasm and be wary of any reluctance in specifying green materials and building methods. It is not uncommon for contractors to say later that such and such material was not available so the less expensive item was substituted. If possible, have a project manager who checks the sourcing and availability of materials prior to construction deadlines.

It is helpful to have an unbiased third party helping with research, tracking, and project management, such as a Certified Sustainable Building Advisor who has no affiliation with the contractors or architects. It is money well spent and saves time and oversights in the unavoidable stressful process of building or remodeling. Additionally, Greenwashing is prevalent regarding building materials and products so research is important to verify claims.

Figure 23-2: Get written project bids based on green specifications.

Building Impacts

"Buildings have a huge ecological impact—consuming between 30 and 40 percent of all energy used, adding 30 to 40 percent of atmospheric emissions, and using up 30 percent of all raw materials in the US. Further, it is estimated that one-third of all buildings have serious indoor air quality problems, making them unhealthy environments for occupants and expensive for businesses."

(usgbc.org 2012)

What is the Cost of Green Building?

Generally the overall cost of green building is approximately 10% more than conventional building with an ROI and operational savings of over 30% (Figure 23-3). The cost depends on the chosen materials and building footprint. High performance efficiency systems costs can be offset by a more compact building size. You can analyze the cost as either simple payback, Life Cycle Assessment, Life Cycle Cost Analysis, or Triple Bottom Line Accounting. Incentives such as rebates and tax credits can also help offset the costs. Federal, state, and local programs for renovations and weatherization may be available to help pay for energy saving measures. Third party certifications add to the cost of building, but the long-term operational savings outweigh the cost.

Figure 23-3: Green buildings give an ROI and operational savings of over 30% (www.eere.energy.gov).

Biomimicry **is a new science that uses nature as a model.**

By studying nature's models, these "forms, processes, systems, and strategies can be emulated to solve human problems sustainably." The biomimicry philosophy can be used in building and material design (biomimicryinstitute.org 2012).

SITE DESIGN

The first aspect to consider in building is *site design* (Figure 23-4). Clearly, a good location is the number one factor in businesses that rely on customers coming in. Convenience and location is a big part of a client's decision to visit a salon or day spa. Once the location is chosen, site considerations are sometimes overlooked. The project goes right into the building design without considering the land where the building sits. The building orientation, climate, topography, water runoff, soil type, and solar access are all site considerations. Zoning and adjacent neighboring developments are also factors in planning. Transportation and mixed-use development are interconnected to site design. Existing facilities can still be analyzed for potential green factors regarding landscaping and building/site issues.

Figure 23-4: The first aspect to consider in building is site design.

Transportation

An accessible location close to public transportation is desirable for sustainable building and development. A commercial business should be convenient, address the demographics of the clientele, have good visibility, be pedestrian friendly, and have easy parking. The best thing to reduce the ecological footprint is to reduce vehicle use. Transportation can be the second highest cost in the household budget and there are many externalized costs to society such as greenhouse gases, pollution, wasted land, and transportation infrastructure. Eco transportation options are electric vehicles, bikes, car share, and mass transit light rail and buses.

Mixed-use Development

Smart Growth is a concept of strategies for compact development and mixed land use. Smart Growth strategies combine residential and commercial areas together. These mixed-use areas can utilize existing buildings and infrastructure and make areas pedestrian-friendly and attractive with a sense of place. Smart Growth concepts include more open space, mass transportation, and affordable development. Compact development benefits are open space, less driving, better health, cleaner air, a better local economy, and community stability (smartgrowth.org 2012).

New Urbanism promotes compact, vibrant, mixed-use communities. These are great locations for spas and salons.

Living and doing business in a mixed-use area is considered a better lifestyle with less commuting time. A pedestrian area gives more vitality to a place. Studies show that mixed-use developments consistently outperform standard real estate in many ways, including office and retail lease rates, residential prices and rents, retail revenues, hotel occupancy rates, and property values. Businesses thrive in these areas.

Low Impact Development (LID)

Low Impact Development (LID) is decentralized storm water management. By returning water to the ground on site, maximizing vegetation, and protecting soils, less storm water pipe infrastructure is needed. Planning drainage patterns and minimizing impervious surfaces slows drainage. Rain gardens, pervious paving, biofiltration from plants in bioswales, green roofs, and using less pavement are all LID methods that also save water. LID saves 25% of infrastructure costs, so it is a significant savings (lowimpactdevelopment.org 2012).

> **The Whole Building is an interconnected system**
>
> Site data, climate, daylighting, the building envelope, HVAC, plug loads, renewables, appliances, and lighting are all parts of the energy design. Site design, daylighting, and passive solar are among the first components in design. Next, the building envelope and energy systems for heat, cooling, electricity, and hot water needs are determined. Water conservation, green materials, and indoor air quality are part of the whole system equation (wbdg.org 2012).

ENERGY SYSTEMS

Energy considerations include insulation, ventilation, windows, weatherization, lighting, appliances, HVAC systems, heating and cooling loads, and electronic devices. Reducing systems needs and the system size save on installation, equipment, and operational costs.

Build for the Local Climate

The benefits of energy-efficient building design are lower operating costs, lower initial first cost of downsized equipment, improved occupant experience and productivity, and long-term energy reliability and independence. Initial *building commissioning* is done by an independent third party who checks and verifies the building systems. Ideally, in large facilities, maintenance is performed by the facility management team. For energy design, controls such as thermostats and fans are used. Monitoring systems and energy audits help track efficiency. A big part of *operations and maintenance (O & M)* by facility managers is energy management.

Passive Solar Design

Passive solar design is the most important feature in building design (Figure 23-5). Building a structure facing the wrong way with the windows on the wrong side is a recipe for never ending out of control energy costs. This is why site design, solar exposure, and microclimate analysis are vital first steps in building.

For colder climates in the northern hemisphere, the most important design feature is elongating the building to face south and putting the right amount of windows on the south side for solar gain in the winter (sustainablesources.com 2012). This includes shading and properly designed overhangs to avoid overheating in the summer. The energy savings from this design can save over 50% of energy costs. In warm climates, the design is the opposite to provide more shade from the sun and more north facing windows. This is a simplified description and there are many other design factors to consider, such as ventilation and humidity (wbdg.org 2010).

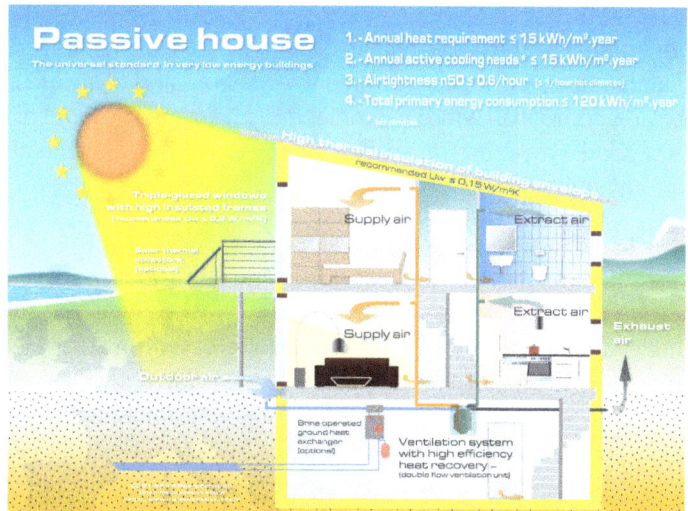

Figure 23-5: Passive solar design is the most important feature in building design (P. Billery-Schneider).

The Building Envelope

The building envelope is the exterior shell that connects the interior with the exterior. Components of the Building Envelope are the foundation, frame, roofing, doors, and windows/skylights (glass areas are referred to as glazing). Unwanted airflow and heat leakage through the building envelope leads to energy loss. Thermal energy loss from infiltration and leakage relates to pressure balance and temperatures. Thermal energy flow also comes from heat gain through occupant activities, lighting, and equipment. Radiant heat and solar gain come through windows and skylights. Weatherization focuses on sealing leaks for a tighter building envelope. There is a saying in building that reminds us to *"Eat your conservation veggies before your expensive dessert,"* which means first use all the conservation measures and fix the basic building problems before installing fancy expensive systems.

Heating, Ventilation, and Air Conditioning (HVAC)

HVAC systems include furnaces, heat pumps, boilers, chillers, radiators, and wall units. HVAC design is based on the climate, weather, and temperatures. Local weather patterns and the temperature ranges for *Heating Degree Days* (HDD) and *Cooling Degree Days* (CDD) are thermal comfort considerations in buildings (greenbuildingadvisor.com 2012). Heat and cold air transfer through walls, doors, windows, attics, and the foundation. Insulation efficiency values are based on thermal resistance and measured in R-values (R: resistance). A high R-value for insulation is good and means the resistance to thermal transfer is high.

For windows, the rating uses U-values, which rates the ease by which heat or cold transfers or passes through the window (conductance). The inverse, or opposite, of conductance is resistance. A low U-value is good and means thermal conductance is low (so thermal resistance is high). Look for these product ratings before purchasing materials. The recommended values are location and climate dependent.

Renewables: Sun, Fire, Air, Water, and Earth Sources

Investment in and use of renewable energy is both encouraged and in some cases required by a range of federal, state, and local government regulations and utility incentives. Renewable energy systems include solar, geothermal, wind, hydroelectric, and biomass. Purchasing green power from power companies is a good way to use renewable energy when on-site generation is not feasible. See epa.gov for more information on renewables.

Solar Power

As noted in Chapter 14, solar power includes photovoltaics for electricity and solar thermal systems for heating buildings and water. Solar thermal systems use solar collectors to absorb solar radiation to heat water. Photovoltaic (PV) systems are based on solar electric cells, which convert solar radiation directly into electricity. The cost has come down on PV systems, but the return on investment (ROI) or payback in years still makes it a long-term investment. Technology continues to advance on solar cells and panels. Solar thermal systems for hot water and radiant floors are the most cost effective and the fastest payback for solar. Since salons and spas use a tremendous amount of hot water, thermal hot water systems are recommended.

What are EMFs?

Electric and magnetic fields and electromagnetic radiation are referred to as EMFs or EMRs. EMFs are invisible lines of force created whenever electricity is generated or used (niehs.nih.gov 2012). There is scientific debate on whether EMFs and EMR from everyday devices in buildings have detrimental health effects. When building, consider the location of wires on blueprint schematics and use conduit to wrap electrical wires if EMR is a concern. Some individuals are affected by EMFs.

Lighting Design

Lighting is considered one of the most important aspects of building and interior design. Daylighting, passive solar, and electric lighting are elements in the design. Fixtures and bulbs are increasingly becoming energy efficient. Efficient lighting output has a high lumens per watts rating. Efficiency is determined by the lumens per watts so lumens or watts separately are not indications of efficiency. Lighting controls such as dimmers, timers, and occupant sensors save energy. Sunlight is the most natural light and it is free, so daylighting is a central part of building design.

Daylighting

A proper *daylighting* design can reduce energy use by 50% (wbdg.org 2012). Quality daylighting enhances people's performance, moods, sales, and health. Full spectrum natural light is necessary for people's moods, and stimulation from the light and changing variability during the day is good for the body's biological and chronological systems (light changing from day to evening). Daylighting design includes using interior windows to reach interior spaces, minimizing glare, and operable blinds. Views, good building orientation, and more light for visibility are preferred and lead to higher lease rates for buildings.

Daylighting
Good daylighting from natural light and windows has shown to improve test scores and retail sales (h-m-g.com 2012).

Interior Lighting Design

The right light for the right place is key to lighting (Figure 23-6). Glare, contrast, balance, color, and surface light can be analyzed in lighting design simulation software. Use of natural light and the right lighting for retail, tasks, and ambience are many times overlooked. Retail space lighting should be natural light and bright, but not glaring. LED is best for low ambient lighting. See resources such as energystar.gov and designlights.org (2012) for more information on lighting design.

GREEN BUILDING MATERIALS

As discussed in Chapter 11, the criteria for green building materials are that they are made from environmentally sustainable materials, lack hazardous materials, have a reduced environmental impact, reduced operational impacts, and healthy indoor environmental quality. Materials science is continually improving material properties and performance. There are some informative websites on comparing building materials, such as Building Green.com and Pharosproject.net.

Figure 23-6: The right light for the right place is key to lighting.

Materials selection takes into account the material's performance, service life, cost, and aesthetics. Added factors to consider are toxicity, durability, and quality. The virgin material quantity, embodied energy in the entire LCA, operational resource requirements, maintenance needs, and manufacturer policies/practices can also be assessed. Other considerations are packaging, transportation, installation, emissions, and end of life: is it cradle to cradle or cradle to grave?

"Defining whether a building material is green is not an exact science (Figure 23-7). Priorities need to be set when selecting specific products because each project and each person's reasons for building green are different" (globalgreen.org 2012). It is important to compare the characteristics of different products. There is no perfect green material so compromises are necessary.

When choosing materials, consider the costs and compare the materials using the following criteria.

Sustainable Building Materials meet the following criteria:

- Natural materials: saves chemicals used and processing
- Life cycle analysis and considering embodied energy (throughout the entire life of a product): saves initial resources and makes recycling easier
- Quality performance and a long service life: saves $ and saves resources (lasts longer, less maintenance costs and replacement)
- Durability of items, better quality (saves $, saves resources)
- Cost: affordability (saves $, good for the bottom line)
- Low toxicity: reduces health issues, liability, and chemical handling requirements (healthier staff and clients, higher productivity)
- Resource efficiency (saves energy, water, virgin materials, processing)
- Sustainable manufacturing and supplier company policies (reduces resource use and makes purchasing easier)
- Recyclable materials (may be reused again and extend the lifespan)
- Made of recycled content (uses resources efficiently)
- Locally made items (reduces shipping and packaging waste)
- Reduced carbon footprint (reduces pollution)
- Reduced operational/maintenance time and costs

Building Material Tools and Databases

The following resources are available for materials research, but most require membership to access the information.

GreenSpec: Published by Building Green, Inc., GreenSpec is a database of environmentally-friendly building products and screens products based on standards and testing procedures established by third-party groups. Building Green, Inc. has an extensive amount of information on green materials, including GreenSpec (buildinggreen.com 2012).

Figure 23-7: Defining whether a building material is green is not an exact science.

BEES (Building for Environmental and Economic Sustainability): Developed by the National Institute of Standards and Technology (NIST) Engineering Laboratory, BEES software evaluates environmentally-preferable building products. BEES measures the environmental performance of building products by using the life-cycle assessment approach specified in the ISO 14040 standards. Economic performance is measured using the ASTM standard life-cycle cost method, which covers the costs of initial investment, replacement, operation, maintenance and repair, and disposal (nist.gov 2012).

Pharos Project: Pharos emphasizes transparency in the building materials market. It is a tool to find the best materials with detailed product scoring. It is designed to help cut through the prolific Greenwashing and to show manufacturers what supports the best environmental, health, and social equity practices.

Pharos online tools include the *Building Product Library* (BPL) and the *Chemical and Material Library* (CML), both available by subscription. The CML sources health hazard information from authoritative national and international bodies and includes over 10,000 chemicals and materials. Pharos provides direct links to the manufacturer's technical data sheets, specs, safety/MSDS, and other product literature (pharosproject.net 2012).

Sustainable Materials Institute: A non-profit, the Sustainable Materials Institute has LCA-based design tools for buildings and assemblies. The *Impact Estimator* and the *EcoCalculator* are two tools available at AthenaSMI.org (2012).

> When researching materials, watch out for Greenwashing and verify third party testing. If applicable, ask for *materials safety data sheets* (MSDS) for toxicity and chemical information (OSHA 2012).

Waste Reduction in Building

Construction creates a lot of wasted materials that end up in the landfill (Figure 23-8). Waste management is now considered an important part of the building process. Salvaging used materials and recycling on the job site save an enormous amount of materials that can be reused or recycled. This also saves money by reducing landfill costs. Ordering the exact amount of materials at the right time during the project also cuts waste. Construction materials that are recycled include paper, plastic, wood, and drywall (gypsum). Gypsum can be shredded and used on site in the gardens and landscaping. The materials most frequently recovered and recycled are concrete, asphalt, metals, and wood (epa.gov 2012).

INDOOR ENVIRONMENTAL QUALITY

Healthy IEQ components include good air quality, thermal, visual, physical, and acoustical comfort. Key space features to consider for IEQ are visuals, daylight, fresh air, good lighting, thermal controls, and nature. As discussed in Chapter 12, using nontoxic green materials is a big part of healthy air quality. Giving occupants personal control over lights, temperatures, noise, and air flow (as much as possible) is also part of good design. The benefits to good IEQ are many as IEQ is central to people's comfort and health, which affect people's performance and moods.

"Indoor environments are highly complex and building occupants may be exposed to a variety of contaminants (in the form of gases and particles) from products, chemicals, cleaning products, carpets and furnishings, smoke, machines, water-damaged materials, microbial growth (fungal/mold and bacterial), insects, and outdoor pollutants. Other factors such as indoor temperatures, relative humidity, and ventilation levels also affect individuals" (cdc.gov 2012).

When choosing materials, avoid those containing VOCs, formaldehyde, polyvinyl chloride (PVC) and other toxic chemicals. These are prevalent in materials and the main source of indoor air quality (IAQ) pollutants. Many people are allergic to mold, mites, and chemicals and especially fumes and carpets. Ventilation systems, filters, and monitoring CO_2 and other pollutants are vital for indoor air quality (cdc.gov 2012).

Figure 23-8: Construction creates a lot of wasted materials that end up in the landfill.

WATER CONSERVATION

Water conservation methods include the site design aspects of building and landscaping. Indoor and outdoor water use considerations for spas include water therapy equipment, fixtures, appliances, and laundry. Choosing water efficient fixtures and appliances is easy to do. Water conservation measures are not that expensive to implement so it makes sense to prioritize these with the high amount of water that spas use. Cost and water savings are significant even with minor changes (Figure 23-9).

A water audit can be conducted and there are rebate and incentive programs to help businesses install water saving products. Visit the EPA WaterSense website and check with your local and state agencies for more information. Water conservation and landscaping best practices are also discussed in Chapters 15 and 24.

Landscaping and Outdoor Water Conservation

When planning water conservation methods for a home or commercial site, there are some alternatives to business as usual. The first consideration is the site. If it is new development, focus on low impact design and follow the natural flow of the land. Try to keep the natural habitat and vegetation intact and minimize disturbing the soil and slope. Practices such as rain gardens and permeable paving are smart choices to prevent runoff and save overtaxed storm drain systems. Other benefits of these methods are cooling the environment and the esthetics of green space. For landscaping, design for minimal water use and care.

Figure 23-9: Cost and water savings are significant even with minor changes.

Water Smart Devices

Automated landscaping can be a big water waster. Have you ever noticed sprinklers on when it is raining outside? According to the EPA, landscape irrigation can waste up to 1.5 billion gallons every day in the US (2012). Using *smart* irrigation controls that detect weather changes and soil conditions can save significant water usage. A Southern California study showed these controls can save as much as 42 gallons per day in a single-family home and non-residential sites saved 545 gallons per day. The reduction in runoff ranged from 64 to 71 percent.

Rainwater Harvesting

Rainwater management, also known as harvesting, is a practice that has been used for thousands of years. In ancient cities, cisterns and courtyards captured rain from aqueducts—and farming communities relied on rainwater for irrigation (unesco.org 2012). *Rainwater catchment* is becoming more necessary in modern times, especially in areas with drought conditions (Figure 23-10). Catching and filtering water from roofs and gutters into tanks can be used for outdoor landscaping and other needs.

GREEN BUILDING TRENDS

Recent trends in green building include zero net energy and water use, having a smaller footprint, reduced dependence on mechanical systems, water smart systems,

Figure 23-10: *Rainwater catchment* is becoming more necessary, especially in areas with drought conditions.

renewable energy technology, and LED lighting. Renovations of existing buildings and reusing salvaged materials are a big focus. More efficient use of space and open floor plans are popular in design. Other advancements include new technology for windows, textiles, and binders/glues. The use of green teams and sustainable building professionals is also more widespread.

A return to more natural and sustainable living practices with natural building materials (such as strawbale or cob) and reconnecting to the outdoors are popular movements. Another interesting trend is the lifestyle retirement village. Spas/salons are a definite asset to these communities. Eco spas and resorts use more natural materials such as bamboo and local wood sourcing. Building for the local climate with local materials (such as adobe in the Southwest) is both beautiful and practical. Green trends will continue to expand with the growing knowledge and demand.

Spa Building Trends

- Low-flow plumbing fixtures
- Tankless water heaters
- Energy Star appliances
- LED lighting
- Lighting controls
- Tubular skylights
- Built in recycle centers
- Low-VOC paints, caulks, sealants, adhesives
- Spray foam insulation for energy efficiency and sound absorption
- Formaldehyde-free wood products
- FSC-certified wood products
- Carpet with recycled content
- Glass and ceramic tile with recycled content
- Locally-sourced products
- Construction waste recycled
- On-site organic gardens
- Natural habitat preservation
- Chemical-free landscape maintenance
- Building materials with recycled content (roofing, steel framing, insulation)
- Solar and wind energy generation
- Bike lockers
- Geothermal heating
- Special parking for hybrid vehicles
- Car charging stations

Building Statistics

- About 30 percent of the energy consumed by US buildings is due to inefficiency or waste.
- Asset value increases by an estimated $3 for every $1 invested in energy efficiency.
- A 30 percent reduction in energy use can save $25,000 in operating costs per year for every 50,000 square feet of office space.

(Source: sustainableindustries.com 2012)

Green Leases

Green lease agreements for building owners and tenants address operations and management practices. A green lease includes specifications that follow the landlord's sustainability practices, including third-party certification requirements. The landlord may have an *Operations and Maintenance Manual* and require tenants to comply with it. Tenants can also negotiate for green features in the lease such as energy and water efficiencies or recycling centers (sustainableindustries.com 2012).

GREEN BUILDING CERTIFICATION AND STANDARDS

There are green standards for products, materials, manufacturers, and buildings. Building projects do not have to be certified to be green. There are many green buildings without certifications that are even more green than some with certifications. Certification is a good thing and may add value, but it can be expensive and time consuming, especially for smaller projects.

Why have a certification? Third party certification documents that the building is built to certain standards. It is a long-term investment and will pay off even more in the market resale value. Additionally, certification is good for public relations and has other benefits. Certification may also qualify the building project for rebates and tax credits or incentives. State and federal programs offer free consultations on building projects and assistance in navigating the maze of programs.

Keep in mind that using building methods such as natural building, *passivhaus*, and the *building biology* methods are even greener than the minimum certification standards, so certification is not necessary to remodel or build sustainably. Certifications are not always available for renovation projects, as they are generally designed for new construction, but that does not mean the remodel is not green. Keep documentation and receipts on materials and installation, and take photos during the building process to record the building techniques and materials used.

Incentives, Rebates, and Mandates

Federal, state, and city incentives encourage energy savings for purchasing new building materials, equipment replacement, solar installation, weatherization, and renovations. Tax credits and rebates are subsidized. Contact city and state agencies for information. Find a listing of incentives for your specific area on the Database of State Incentives for Renewables & Efficiency website (dsireusa.org 2012).

As discussed in Chapter 11, there are many certifications for buildings and building materials/products. Accreditations for professionals include LEED AP's (Accredited Professionals) and Certified Sustainable Building Advisors (CSBA's). Some programs are only available in certain states, while others are national and international. The following standards are well known in the green building world.

Building Research Establishment Environmental Assessment Method (BREEAM) is an international standard and rating system for sustainable building design, construction, and operation. It measures energy and water use, the internal environment, pollution, transport, materials, waste, ecology, and management processes. It is viewed as an international code for a sustainable built environment (breeam.org 2012).

> *ANSI* (American National Standards Institute) and *ISO* (International Organization of Standardization) both provide consensus standards for conformity assessment of products, services, and systems (ansi.org 2012).

What is your definition of sustainable building?

Building and Product Certifications and Standards include:

- Building Biology
- Built Green
- Certified Sustainable Building Advisor (SBA)
- CRI Green Label & Green Label Plus (Carpet)
- Cradle to Cradle Certification
- Earth Advantage
- Energy Star: USA
- Energy Performance Standards Ratings
- Forest Stewardship Council (FSC) Chain of Custody Certification (Wood and Paper)
- Green Globes
- Greener Product Certification Seal
- GreenGuard
- Green Seal
- High Performance Homes
- LEED Building Certification
- LEED Professional Credentials
- Living Building Challenge
- NAHB Certified Green Professional
- NAHB Green
- NPA Natural Standard (Home Care and Personal Care)
- NSF/ANSI 140 Sustainability Assessment for Carpet
- Passivhaus
- SMaRT Consensus Sustainable Product Standards
- Sustainable Forestry Initiative (SFI)
- WaterSense

(Note: all certifications are trademarks or registered trademarks.)

CHAPTER 24

Green Building Practices

INTRODUCTION

This chapter is an introduction to specific green building practices and an overview of what to look for when building or remodeling. Planning guidelines, best practices, and project checklists are included here. Many of these practices were introduced in previous chapters. Some of these ideas are applicable to either new construction or renovations. See the online resources for planning worksheets.

You do not have to be a building owner to implement green or energy efficiency measures. The rate of return on improvements for both new and existing buildings varies greatly depending on the technology. Any professional energy audit and/or project bid should include estimated rates of return for each recommended measure.

WORDS OF WISDOM

Operating a spa or salon in a green built environment is one of the most convincing ways to assure your clients you care about them and this earth we call home. So it is definitely good business. It is also absolutely appropriate for a business fostering the health and well-being of its customers to do the same for its employees.

~ Kathleen O'Brien, LEED AP, CSBA, Founder, Special Projects
Consultant: O'Brien & Company, obrienandco.com,
Author: *The Northwest Green Home Primer*

PLANNING FOR GREEN BUILDING

Whether you are building from the ground up or doing retrofits, it is helpful to consider the following questions to get clear on the project goals. Use the planning checklist and outline to help track the project.

Project Planning Questions
- What is the mission and vision for the building?
- What are the sustainable goals?
- What are your sustainable building priorities?
- What is your ultimate wish list for building or remodeling?
- What is the budget?
- Does the budget cover the estimated costs?
- What is the schedule?
- Who are your contractors and designers?
- Will you want third party green certification?
- What are your specifications and expectations?
- What is the architectural design?

Checklist of Project Planning Steps
- Create goals.
- Consider the design and type of building.
- Evaluate the budget.
- Decide on the mission and vision for the building.
- Decide on the sustainable goals and building priorities.
- Hire the designers and contractors.
- Have an integrated design meeting (eco-charrette; include architectural, mechanical, electrical, landscape designers, and other stakeholders).
- Decide on third-party certification.
- Review the design, and research materials.
- Document specifications and expectations in writing and get written bids with specifications.
- Plan the timeline and schedule.
- Sign contracts including change order agreements.
- Track and document certification.
- Utilize *building commissioning* for large projects (a third party that inspects systems).
- Post-building project steps:
  - Perform *Operations and Maintenance* (O & M).
  - Use *Best Practices*.
  - Train staff to operate systems and use green practices.
  - Make regular assessments on systems.
  - Implement a continual improvement program for operations.

Project Overview Outline
- Choose the builder, architect, and other collaboratives.
- Secure funding, decide on financial goals, ROI, and the budget.
- Plan the design.
- Lay out the planning steps and schedule.
- Apply for permits, research zoning and covenants.
- Plan utilities, infrastructure, roads: include transportation and land use.
- Plan outdoor spaces and landscaping.
- Building design and elements:
  - Site Design
  - The Building Envelope
  - Energy Systems and Renewable Energy
  - Daylighting and Lighting
  - Green Materials and Products
  - Indoor Environmental Quality
  - Water Conservation and Landscaping
  - Green Building Standards (LEED or others)

> It is estimated that retrofits can cost up to five times more than new construction, so if you are starting from the ground up, consider an integrated design process and plan ahead for future needs such as solar panel infrastructure. Some measures are impossible, or nearly impossible to implement once a building has been constructed (sustainableindustries.com 2012).

SITE DESIGN

There is more to site design than where to put the building for convenience. As mentioned in Chapter 23, the climate, topography, water runoff, soil type, and solar access are all site considerations. Zoning and adjacent neighboring developments are also considerations. Transportation and mixed-use development are interconnected to site design (usgbc.org). Good compact site planning can save on infrastructure costs with low impact development practices (Figure 24-1). Plan low maintenance landscaping and leave as much open space as possible to reduce costs and impacts on the land.

Figure 24-1: Sustainable site design saves infrastructure costs.

Site Assessment

Design professionals will assess the following features of the land and building site:

- Climate, latitude, microclimate: temperatures, precipitation, humidity, wind
- Solar exposure, sun paths (summer and winter)
- Soil and vegetation; topography/land features
- Water runoff and groundwater
- Natural habitat
- Zoning
- Existing infrastructure
- Transportation
- Neighboring developments and proposed future developments
- Site constraints/concerns (noise, location, water issues)

Low Impact Development (LID)

As noted in Chapter 23, LID saves infrastructure costs of approximately 25%. LID Decentralized Stormwater Management Best Practices include returning the water to ground close to discharge, maximizing vegetation, protecting soils, and minimizing impervious surfaces. A more natural landscape slows drainage. Use rain gardens, pervious paving, infiltration systems, good soils, biofiltration/*bioswales*, green roofs, and less pavement/smaller street widths for LID (lowimpactdevelopment.org 1999).

Location and Transportation Ideas for Business Owners

- Locate your business in a mixed-use development or town center.
- Be part of the neighborhood for increased foot traffic and a built-in clientele.
- Provide secure bike storage/parking.
- Offer incentives to true walk-ins or bikers: offer special treatments for walkers (pedicures), community gardeners (manicures), and local neighbors.

ENERGY CONSERVATION PRACTICES

As discussed in Chapters 14 and 23, the first step in implementing energy conservation for existing buildings is to analyze what your current kWh usage is and what you are doing now to save energy. An energy audit is sometimes free from state agencies, power companies, or organizations. Any cost involved in having an in depth audit is worth the service, as you can save hundreds to thousands of dollars the first year after implementing conservation measures on older building systems (Figure 24-2).

Building systems and operations energy considerations include insulation, ventilation, windows, weatherization, lighting, appliances, HVAC systems, heating and cooling loads, and electronic devices. One way to save energy is to install climate controls for seasonal conditions, such as controllers for lighting and shades for sun protection. Analyze the energy needs for occupants and then prioritize reducing energy loads beyond that.

CHAPTER 24: Green Building Practices   241

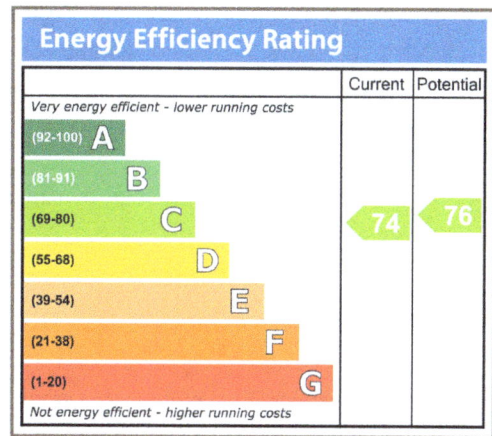

Figure 24-2: An energy audit is worth the cost.

The Core and Shell

The *core and shell* consists of the exterior and building envelope without interior finishing. This is all related to the building durability, quality, and energy use (nnsa.energy.gov 2002).

Components of the building envelope are:
- Foundation: Use energy saving techniques.
- Roofing: Use light colored, durable materials.
- Insulation: Use non-toxic materials with high R-values.
- Flooring: Insulate subfloors.
- Doors: Use insulated doors; make sure door gaps are sealed.
- Glazing/windows: Optimize the specifications, size, and orientation.
- Walls: High performance wall systems (i.e. SIPs, advanced framing, etc.) increase the amount of insulation.

Building mantra:
Build it right: build it tight and give it good boots (foundation) and a hat (roof).

Window Specifications

Window choices are based on the climate and which cardinal direction the window is facing.
- *Low U-value windows* have high energy efficiency and a greater resistance to heat flow.
- *Low-E windows* (low emittance coatings) are best where direct sunlight is a problem.
- *Solar heat gain coefficient* (SHGC) is the fraction of solar radiation admitted.
- *Visible transmittance* (VT) is the percentage or fraction of the visible spectrum that is transmitted. (efficientwindows.org 2012)

Passive Solar and Daylighting Design Tips

- Solar access: Determine the position of the building to take maximum advantage of natural solar resources for passive solar heating, daylighting, and photovoltaics (Figure 24-3).
- Sun and sky: Look at the site orientation. For cold climates elongate the building east and west and install most of the windows on the south side with shades.
- Narrow buildings have more natural light penetration to the center from both sides.
- Use the right size, type, and distribution of windows/glazing.

Energy System and passive solar design include the following components:
- *Collectors* (windows, walls, and sun spaces collect solar heat)
- *Absorbers* (a thermal mass such as concrete absorbs heat from the sun—dark surfaces absorb more)
- *Thermal mass* (spreads heat transfer time—for example, stone/rock collects and stores heat during the day and releases it at night)
- *Controls* (static: curtains, overhangs; dynamic: fans, dampers)
- *Insulation* (retains heat)

Passive Cooling
Minimize solar gain:
- Use insulation with a high R-value.
- Use correct window placement and overhangs.
- Use landscape vegetation for cooling.
- Use light colors for roofs, building exteriors, and interiors.

Ventilation:
- Install operable windows for natural ventilation and fresh air.
- Have windows upstairs that circulate and pull hot air out the top of the building (a stack effect).
- Have secure windows that open for night flushing of hot air.
- Use ceiling fans to circulate air.
- Use an energy recovery ventilator (ERV) to recapture waste heat.

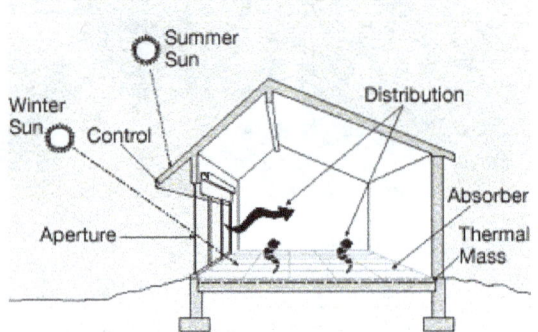

Figure 24-3: Passive solar design takes maximum advantage of natural solar resources for heating, daylighting, and photovoltaics (www.eere.energy).

Renewable Energy Choices
- Solar systems (for heat, electricity, and hot water heating).
- Wind (standard and vertical axis turbines).
- Hydro power (from water).
- Geothermal systems of wells: reservoirs for heat/cooling. These save energy by using the natural temperatures of the ground. The average US ground/earth temperature is 50–60°F, which balances cold and hot fluctuations (renewableenergyworld.com 2012).
- Biomass (organic materials: trees, waste, and sewage used for heat, methane gas, and biofuels).
- Purchase green power from a local utility company.
- Buy carbon offsets.

Steps to Energy Conservation for Existing Buildings Operations
- Establish a baseline by calculating the current energy usage.
- Analyze and track utility bills.
- Conduct an energy audit and evaluate the facility room by room.
- Include the building, heating, cooling, lighting, equipment, appliances, and electronic devices.
- Determine potential conservation measures.

- Consider alternative renewable energy sources.
- Establish priorities by the easiest and most affordable solutions first (the low hanging fruit).
- Research incentives and tax credits for energy conservation measures.
- Set long term and short term goals with timelines.
- Monitor progress on a regular basis.
- Calculate and report the savings.

Building Energy Conservation Tips
- Insulate the attic and crawl space as a "conditioned space."
- Install energy controls: windows, thermostats, fans, timers, sensor switches (CO_2, moisture), building management systems.
- Load reduction: smaller HVAC systems will recoup the additional cost of efficient features. System capacities commonly exceed the actual needs and can be downsized by using initial measures that reduce the energy load (www.energystar.gov 2012).
- Identify and eliminate phantom loads that use energy even when off. Unplug devices and use power strips.
- Integrate with natural energy flows (sun, wind).
- Ventilation systems: install a heat recovery ventilator (HRV) or energy recovery ventilator (ERV) to save up to 60% of energy costs.
- Energy audits (i.e. Blower Door Test): for air flow, the goal is 5 ACH (air changes per hour) for a tight building with adequate ventilation (ashrae.org 2012).

HVAC system ASHRAE recommended standards for temperatures and humidity
Set the heating/dry bulb temperature range at 68–74°F; set the cooling/dry bulb temperatures for 73–79°F. The comfortable relative humidity range is at 30–60%, depending on the season and your location. This is best for people's health and to avoid a too dry or too humid environment, which can promote mold growth (ashrae.org 2012). Use a hygrometer to test humidity levels.

Lighting Design
- Use interior windows through the building so light can reach interior spaces.
- Minimize glare, use operable blinds on windows.
- Plan spaces with light layers: general/ambiance, task, and accent lighting.
- Use correct fixtures and bulbs.
- Know your lumens and watts.
- Controls can be manual or automated: use switches, dimmers, and sensors.
- Use individual controls for each layer of lighting.
- Lightshelves: these shelves reflect light to the ceiling and deeper into spaces.

Plan Light Fixtures For Spaces
- Reception: Use CFLs, spotlights, and daylight.
- Retail and Makeup areas: Use daylight and product spotlights.
- Salon Stations: Use natural light, CFLs, and overhead fluorescents.
- Treatment Rooms: Design for ambiance, use LEDs and task lighting.
- Office: Use task lighting, CFLs, and fluorescents.
- Client lounges and locker rooms: Use T-8 high efficiency fluorescents and CFLs.

Lighting Measurement Terminology

Wattage: The amount of electricity consumed by a light source.
Lumens: The amount of light that a light source produces.
Efficacy: Lumens per watt (the efficiency rating).
Foot-candles: The amount of light reaching a subject.

(Source: americanlightingassoc.com 2011)

Building Statistics

- The commercial real estate industry spends approximately $24 billion annually on energy and generates 18% of US carbon dioxide emissions.
- Energy consumption and carbon emissions could be reduced by 10%, saving $400 million in energy costs and eliminating 6.6 billion pounds of carbon dioxide emissions if 2,000 buildings applied BOMA's Energy Efficiency Program's best practices for three years.

(Source: Building Owners and Managers Association (boma.org 2012))

GREEN MATERIALS AND INTERIORS

For many people, the most interesting part of the building project is choosing the interiors. There are many details to consider for interiors. Give yourself enough time to research options and make decisions before the construction schedule deadline (Figure 24-4). Material choices include counters, fixtures, floors, cabinets, and furniture.

Green Material Criteria and Life Cycle Assessment (LCA)

Choose materials based on:

- Performance and service life
- Durability and quality
- Cost
- Toxicity
- Resource efficiency
- Sustainable manufacturing
- Certification
- Recyclable materials and packaging
- Made of recycled content
- Locally made
- Reduced carbon footprint
- Reduced operational needs and maintenance
- Aesthetics, beauty, and style

Figure 24-4: Make sure you have enough time to research all of the interior design choices.

Choose Interior Finishes for Buildings

Think about the following building categories:

- Plumbing
- Flooring
- Lighting
- Electrical
- Paint or other wall coverings
- Caulking/adhesives
- Cabinets
- Countertops
- Appliances
- Furnishings
- Other Materials

Facility Interior Checklist

Consider each area for choosing interiors such as the furniture, materials, and equipment:
- Private treatment rooms
- Open stations
- Client lounges
- Changing rooms
- Front desk
- Reception
- Retail area
- Office areas
- Staff break room
- Bathrooms
- Fitness center
- Water therapies

INDOOR ENVIRONMENTAL AND AIR QUALITY

As noted in Chapter 13, indoor air quality concerns are chemicals (VOCs), particles, microbes, radiation (radon), CO_2, lead, and asbestos. Dust and mold are the main sources of IAQ problems (Figure 24-5). Common allergens are smoke, dust mites, pollen, pets, fungi/molds, endotoxins, and VOCs. See epa.gov and who.int for more information on these IAQ issues.

The main IAQ issues are:
- Moisture control (materials, walls, and carpets can absorb moisture).
- Microbes (humidity at 60% or greater is conducive to mold growth, which can grow within 24 hours).
- Chemicals (PVC, plasticizers, solvents, paints, wood binders, and insulation off-gas and release VOCs and chemicals for months and years).

Chemicals to avoid include:
- Benzene, formaldehyde, vinyl chloride, plasticizers.
- PVC: polyvinyl chloride.
- Formaldehyde (in glue/adhesive in pressed wood products, preservatives, coating on fabrics, paper, and insulation).
- VOCs (volatile organic compounds evaporate at ambient temperatures. Health symptoms from exposure: allergies, irritation, fatigue, dizziness).

> ### Spa/Salon Flooring
> Colored concrete, wood, natural stone/tile, and linoleum (not to be confused with sheet vinyl) are best choices. Marmoleum™ is a brand of linoleum. Avoid carpet due to hygiene issues and spills.

Figure 24-5: Dust and mold are the main sources of IAQ problems.

Reducing VOC Exposure
- Avoid materials and products that contain chemicals and off gas.
- Increase ventilation and filtration when using products that emit VOCs.
- Formaldehyde, one of the most common VOCs, is one of the few indoor air pollutants that can be readily measured. If not possible to remove, reduce exposure by using a sealant on all exposed surfaces of paneling and other furnishings (epa.gov 2012).

Carbon Dioxide (CO_2)
Monitoring carbon dioxide levels is one way to make sure the ventilation in tight buildings is optimal. Lack of ventilation leads to high CO_2 levels, which causes fatigue. Crowded rooms are full of CO_2. In addition to CO_2, lead, asbestos, radon, mold, and other hidden contaminants can be detected through testing (epa.gov 2012).

IAQ Solutions and Best Practices
- Use green building materials.
- Avoid toxic chemicals.
- Have good ventilation.
- Use HEPA (high efficiency particulate air) filters.
- Change air filters regularly.
- Control humidity.
- Clean and dust often.
- Monitor CO_2 levels; these are measured in parts per million (ppm).
- Check the location and efficiency of external vents; separate intake/outlet vents.
- Check HVAC systems for sturdy ducts and good filter systems (check for duct leaks and mold).
- During construction/remodeling: cover vents/ducts, replace filters, clean, air out and flush the building; test air quality before occupancy.

Filters and Particulate Matter
Check the MERV rating for filters: MERV is the *minimum efficiency reporting value* for filters. For ventilation guidelines see ASHRAE Standard 62. ASHRAE is the American Society of Heating, Refrigeration, and Air Conditioning Engineers. Particulate matter of less than 10 micrometers (PM_{10}) can be inhaled into lungs. Fine particles smaller than 2.5 microns can be inhaled deeper into lung air sacks. PM_{10} particles can carry other contaminants such as pesticides into carpets, etc. Small particles can be suspended for days and are re-suspended by walking, sitting, and vacuuming (ashrae.org 2012).

What makes a building material green?

Certain products are not necessarily green but can be used in ways that enhance the energy performance of a building. Globalgreen.org (2012) notes that a dual-pane, low-E window may not be green in terms of its material components or manufacturing process, but it can reduce energy use by maximizing winter sunlight and blocking out the summer sun. Perhaps the most sustainable and affordable materials are salvaged, reusable materials but they should be checked as they may contain lead, asbestos, or radioactive residue as many old materials do. There are tradeoffs with every material that should be evaluated in terms of what the goals and priorities are for the material.

> For more information on Operations and Maintenance (O & M), see the Building Owners and Management Association (BOMA) facility manager educational resources at boma.org.

WATER CONSERVATION

This section includes operations and best practices, some of which were included in corresponding chapters.

Indoor Water Conservation Solutions for Spas
- Train the staff to not leave the water running full blast unless necessary (low hanging fruit).
- Fix leaky faucets and toilets.
- Install high-efficiency plumbing fixtures and appliances that save about 30% of indoor water use and yield substantial savings on water, sewer, and energy bills (Figure 24-6).
- A high efficiency washing machine can save over 50% in water and energy use.
- Look for low water use appliances.
- Install on-demand water heaters on taps for instant hot water.
- Reduce linen use and laundry.
- Turn off and monitor hot tubs and steam rooms when not in use.
- Consider greywater systems to reuse sink or laundry water for landscaping or outdoor use.
- Look into alternatives for chlorine in pools and soaking tubs. Many spas are switching from harsh chemicals to saline for health reasons.
- Install 1 gallon per minute bathroom faucet aerators: an aerator reduces the amount of water that comes from the tap without impacting water pressure. An aerator uses only 1.0 gallon per minute (gpm) and is very effective in rinsing so even less water is used.
- Use faucet sensors and automatic shut-off valves.

High-Efficiency Water Specifications
- Toilets (tank-type): 1.28 gpf (gallons per flush)
- Toilets (flush-valve): 1.3 gpf
- Urinals: 0.5 gpf
- Shower heads: 2.0 gpm (gallons per minute)
- Lavatory faucets: 1.5 gpm at 60 psi

Look for the WaterSense label on products such as faucets, showerheads, toilets. Each product has met performance standards set by the EPA (www.epa.gov/WaterSense 2012).

Figure 24-6: High-efficiency plumbing fixtures and appliances save about 30% of indoor water use.

Commercial Best Practices for Water Conservation

Check out the epa.gov website for more information on the recommended commercial practices.

General Practices:
- Designate a water efficiency coordinator.
- Develop a plan with specific efficiency targets.
- Educate and involve employees in water efficiency efforts.

Equipment

- Install ultra low-flow toilets, or adjust flush valves or install dams on existing toilets.
- Install faucet aerators and high efficiency showerheads.
- Eliminate "once-through" cooling of equipment with municipal water by recycling water flow to cooling tower or replacing with air-cooled equipment.
- Detect and repair all leaks.
- Minimize the water used in cooling equipment in accordance with manufacturer's recommendations. Shut off cooling units when not needed.

Kitchens and Laundries

- Scrape rather than rinse dishes before washing.
- Use water from steam tables to wash down cooking areas.
- Do not use running water to melt ice or frozen foods.
- Handle waste materials in a dry state whenever possible.
- Wash only full loads or select the appropriate washing cycle provided on the washing machine (use a rinse water recycle system).

(Source: WaterSense, US EPA, epa.gov, 2012)

LANDSCAPING DESIGN

The most wasteful use of water is from landscape maintenance (Figure 24-7).

Landscaping Best Practices

- Retain the soil quality.
- Use native and pest resistant plants; group by water needs.
- Fill bare soil with plants and mulch to avoid weeds, erosion.
- Put conifer trees to the north, deciduous to the south for sun and shade purposes.
- Leave clippings on grass as mulch, use organic fertilizers.
- Minimize water use: compost, mulch, use water zones, drip systems, reuse water, and use xeriscaping.
- Use natural pest management.
- Install a water retention pond.
- Aim for zero-runoff: pervious paving, rain gardens, and swales.
- Use buffer zones for waterways.
- Research green roofs.
- Reduce chemical use.
- Water wisely outdoors with appropriate systems (drip or sprinklers).
- Install rainwater catchment systems off roofs.
- Use greywater systems.
- Use low impact development to catch more water on site and use less storm water infrastructure.
- Match water source to appropriate use. For example, if you can use reclaimed water or catchment systems for irrigation and save cleaner potable water for drinking, that would be a better design.

Figure 24-7: The most wasteful use of water is from landscape maintenance.

(Source: epa.gov 2012)

GREEN BUILDING WORKSHEETS

Table 24-1: This worksheet is an outline of building considerations and can be expanded to include additional components and choices not specified here.

TABLE 24-1: PROJECT PLANNING WORKSHEET			
Project Outline	**Considerations and Options** (can include specifications and goals)	**Action Steps**	**Timeline Schedule**
Project Goals and Vision			
Type of Building Design			
Budget, Funding, ROI			
Choose Designers and Contractors			
Hold Integrated Design Meetings			
Choose Third-Party Certification			
Review the Design and Research Materials			
Document Requested Specifications			
Get Written Bids with Specifications			
Sign Contracts including Change Order Agreements			
Track and Document Certification			
Permits and Zoning			
Utilities			
Infrastructure and Roads			
Site Design Aspects			
The Building Envelope	Roof: Frame: Walls: Floor: Doors: Windows: Insulation:		

TABLE 24-1: PROJECT PLANNING WORKSHEET *(continued)*			
Project Outline	**Considerations and Options** (can include specifications and goals)	**Action Steps**	**Timeline Schedule**
Energy Systems and Renewable Energy	HVAC: Fireplace: Solar:		
Daylighting and Lighting	Windows, skylights: Light fixtures:		
Green Building Materials	Flooring: Paint, wall coverings: Cabinets: Countertops: Furnishings: Window coverings: Other materials:		
Appliances and Equipment	Washer/dryer: Dishwasher: Refrigerator: Treatment rooms: Electronics:		
Water	Plumbing: Sinks: Toilets: Showers: Fixtures: Equipment, tubs: Water fountain: Pool:		
Landscaping	Design: Plants: Irrigation:		
Transportation Aspects	Location: Parking:		
Construction Waste	Recycling:		
Train Staff to operate systems and use Best Practices	Training manuals: Meetings:		

Table 24-2: An expanded version of interior choices would include a worksheet for all building categories such as fixtures and lighting for each area in the spa. You could also design your own sheet and make it as detailed as you like, or you can use the contractor's specifications sheets.

TABLE 24-2: SPA FACILITY INTERIORS WORKSHEET			
Spa Area	**Interiors**	**Equipment and Appliances**	**Green Materials**
Private Treatment Rooms			
Open Stations			
Client Lounges			
Changing Rooms			
Front Desk			
Reception			
Retail Area			
Office Areas			
Staff Break Room			
Bathrooms			
Fitness Center			
Water Therapies			
Other			

References

CHAPTER 1

BSR/Globescan. 2011. *The State of Sustainable Business Poll,* http://www.bsr.org/en/our-insights/report-view/bsr-gobescan-state-of-sustainable-business-poll-2011.

Environmental Leader. 2011, http://www.environmentalleader.com.

Green America. 2012, http://www.greenamerica.org/about/.

Green Spa Network. 2011, http://www.greenspanetwork.org.

ISPA. 2011, http://www.experienceispa.com.

LOHAS. 2011, http://www.lohas.com.

Sustainable Building Advisor Institute. 2010, http://www.sbainstitute.com.

CHAPTER 2

Athena Sustainable Materials Institute. 2012, http://www.athenasmi.org/resources/about-lca/technical-details/.

Elkington, John. 2012, http://www.johnelkington.com.

Hollingworth, Mark. "Building 360 Organizational Sustainability." *Ivey Business Journal.* Nov/Dec, 2009, http://www.iveybusinessjournal.com/topics/global-business/building-360-organizational-sustainability.

McDonough Braungart Design Chemistry, LLC. 2012, http://www.mbdc.com.

McDonough, William, and Braungart, Michael. *Cradle To Cradle: Remaking the Way We Make Things.* New York: North Point Press, 2002. http://www.mcdonough.com/cradle_to_cradle.htm.

The Natural Step. 2012, http://www.naturalstep.org.

United States Environmental Protection Agency. 2012, http://www.epa.gov/nrmrl/std/lca/lca/lca.html.

CHAPTER 3

Arjen Y. Hoekstra, Ashok K. Chapagain, Maite M. Aldaya, and Mesfin M. Mekonnen. *The Water Footprint Assessment Manual: Setting the Global Standard.* Earthscan Ltd.: Dunstan House, 2011. http://www.waterfootprint.org.?page=files/WaterFootprintAssessmentManual.

Global Footprint Network. 2012, http://www.footprintnetwork.org/pt/index.php/GFN/page/world_footprint/.

International Sustainable Development Foundation. 2012, http://www.sustainableschools.org/discover-sustainability/understanding-sustainability#EcologicalFootprint.

State of California Biodiversity Council. 2008, http://www.biodiversity.ca.gov/Biodiversity/biodiv_definition.html.

The Nature Conservancy. "Carbon Footprint Calendar." 2012, http://www.nature.org/greenliving/unf-carbon-calculator/index.htm.

United States Environmental Protection Agency. 2012, "A Student's Guide to Global Climate Change." http://www.epa.gov/climatechange/kids/glossary.html.

United States Environmental Protection Agency. 2012. "Water Trivia Facts." http://www.water.epa.gov/learn/kids/drinkingwater/water_trivia_facts.cfm.

Water Footprint Network. "Corporate Water Footprints." 2012, http://www.waterfootprint.org/?page=files/CorporateWaterFootprints.

CHAPTER 4

B Lab. 2012, http://www.bcorporation.net.

Fuller, Sieglinde. 2010. "Life Cycle Cost Analysis." *National Institute of Standards and Technology (NIST), Whole Building Design Guide.* http://www.wbdg.org/resources/lcca.php.

Global Reporting Initiative. 2011. *Sustainability Reporting Guidelines.* https://www.globalreporting.org/resourcelibrary/G3.1-Guidelines-Incl-Technical-Protocol.pdf.

Goal Setting Guide. 2012. "SMART Goal Setting: A Surefire Way to Achieve Your Goals." http://www.goal-setting-guide.com/smart-goal-setting-a-surefire-way-to-achieve-your-goals.

International Organization for Standardization. 2012, http://www.iso.org/iso/home.html.

NaturalCapitalDeclaration.org. 2012, http://www.naturalcapitaldeclaration.org.

Network for Business Innovation and Sustainability. SIGMA Project, Sept. 2003. *The Sigma Guidelines—Toolkit: Sustainability Accounting Guide.* http://www.nbis.org/nbisresources/accounting_and_green_banking/signma_sustainability_accounting.pdf.

US Environmental Protection Agency. 2012. "Improved Academic Performance: Evidence from Scientific Literature." http://www.epa.gov/iaq/schools/student_performance/evidence.html.

Water Footprint Network. 2012, http://www.waterfootprint.org.

WebFinance, Inc. 2012, http://www.businessdictionary.com.

CHAPTER 5

Answers.com. 2012. "Social Responsibility." http://www.answers.com/topic/social-responsibility.

International Organization for Standardization. 2012. "Guidance on Social Responsibility." ISO 26000:2010(en). http://www.iso.org/obp/ui/#iso:std:iso:26000:ed-1:v1:en.

Socially Responsible Shopping Association. 2012, http://www.srsassociation.org/library.

CHAPTER 8

Biodynamic Farming and Gardening Association. 2012, http://www.biodynamics.com/.

Campaign for Safe Cosmetics, The. 2011, http://www.safecosmetics.org.

Environmental Protection Agency. 2012. "Phthalates: US EPA, Toxicity and Exposure Assessment for Children's Health." http://www.epa.gov/teach/chem_summ/phthalates_summary.pdf.

Environmental Working Group. 2011, http://www.ewg.org/reports/bodyburden2/execsumm.php.

Hatter, Ila. 2012. Ironweed Productions. http://www.wildcrafting.com/.

Organic Monitor. "CSR & Sustainability: How the Beauty Industry is Cleaning Up." (May 18, 2010). http://www.organicmonitor.com/r1805.htm.

CHAPTER 9

COSMOS. 2012, http://www.cosmos-standard.org/.

EcoCert. 2012, http://www.ecocert.com/en/ecoproducts.

European Chemicals Agency. REACH. 2012, http://www.ec.europa.eu/environment/chemicals/reach/reach_intro.htm.

Green Seal. *Green Seal Standard for Personal Care and Cosmetic Products*. 1st ed. Washington, D.C.: Green Seal, 2011. http://www.greenseal.org/Portals/0/Documents/Standards/GS-50/GS-50_Personal_Care_and_Cosmetic_Products_Standard_Fifth_Edition.pdf.

Green Spa Network. 2010, http://www.greenspanetwork.org.

Organic Monitor. March 8, 2011. "Natural & Organic Cosmetic Standards Proliferation Continues." http://www.organicmonitor.com/r0803.htm.

Quality Assurance International. 2012. "USDA/National Organic Program." http://www.qai-inc.com/about/usda_nop.asp.

The Campaign for Safe Cosmetics. 2012. "European Laws." http://www.safecosmetics.org/article.php?id=346.

Wikipedia.com 2012, http://www.wikipedia.com.

Wuttke, Mark. Oct. 31, 2011. "The Importance of Certification Standards—It is What it Says It Is?" http://www.dayspaassociation.com/docs/news-items-library-articles/2011/10/31/Certification%20Standards797D950634E7.pdf?Status=Master.

CHAPTER 10

CANCERactive. 2012, http://www.canceractive.com/cancer-active-page-link.aspx?n=3148.

Environmental Working Group. 2012. EWG's Skin Deep Cosmetics Database: Formaldehyde. http://www.ewg.org/skindeep/ingredient.php?ingred06=702500#.

Gerson, J., Lotz, S., et al. *Milady Standard Esthetics, Fundamentals*, 11th ed. New York: Cengage Learning, 2012.

Green Spa Network. 2011, http://www.greenspanetwork.org.

Greer, Beth. "10 Ways To Tell If A Product Is (Or Isn't) Really 'Natural.'" Oct. 28, 2011, http://www.huffingtonpost.com/beth-greer/natural-products-labels_b_1024143.html.

Organic Monitor. 2011, June. *The North American Market for Natural & Organic Personal Care Products*, 2nd ed. (Report #3002-60). http://www.organicmonitor.com/300260.htm.

CHAPTER 11

Big Room Inc. 2012. Ecolabel Index. http://bigroom.ca/.

Textile Exchange. *2010 Global Market Report on Sustainable Textiles: Executive Summary*. http://textileexchange.org/sites/default/files/te_pdfs/2010%20Global%20Market%20Report%20on%20Sustainable%20Textiles-Executive%20Summary.pdf.

Sustainable Building Advisor Institute. 2010, http://www.sbainstitute.com.

Zaroff, Marci. 2012, http://www.marcizaroff.com.

CHAPTER 12

Ecology Center. 2012. "Reduce, Reuse, and Recycle and Eliminate Plastic. http://ecologycenter.org/factsheets/eliminate-plastic.pdf.

——— "Plastic Task Force: Seven Misconceptions about Plastic and Plastic Recycling." http://ecologycenter.org/ptf/misconceptions.html.

Matusow, Jamie, April/May 2011. Beauty Packaging. "Green With Envy." http://www.beautypackaging.com/articles/2011/05/green-with-envy.

——— April/May 2012. Beauty Packaging. "Sustainable Packaging in the Beauty World." http://www.beautypackaging.com/articles/2012/05/sustainable-packaging-in-the-beauty-world.

Mintel Group Ltd. 2011, Feb. *Green Living Report—US*. http://oxygen.mintel.com/display/542922/.

National Geographic Society. 2012. "Great Pacific Garbage Patch." http://education.nationalgeographic.com/encyclopedia/great-pacific-garbage-patch/?ar_a=1.

US EPA. Dec. 2011. *Municipal Solid Waste Generation, Recycling, and Disposal in the United States: Facts and Figures for 2010* (EPA-530-F-11-005). http://www.epa.gov/osw/nonhaz/municipal/pubs/msw_2010_rev_factsheet.pdf.

CHAPTER 13

ASHRAE. 2012. *The Indoor Air Quality Guide: Best Practices for Design, Construction and Commissioning.* http://www.ashrae.org/resources--publications/bookstore/indoor-air-quality-guide.

Bergs, John. "The Effect of Healthy Workplaces on the Well-being and Productivity of Office Workers." Amersfoort, The Netherlands. 2011, http://www.plants-in-buildings.com/documents/Symposium-Bergs.pdf.

Centers for Disease Control and Prevention. 2012. "Indoor Environmental Quality." http://www.cdc.gov/niosh/topics/indoorenv/.

Centers for Disease Control and Prevention. 2003. *Second National Report on Human Exposure to Environmental Chemicals*. (NCEH Pub. No. 02-0716). http://www.cdc.gov/exposurereport/.

eHow.com. 2012. "Other Feng Shui Tips." http://www.ehow.com/other-feng-shui-tips/.

Multiple Chemical Sensitivity Organization. 2012, http://www.multiplechemicalsensitivity.org/.

The Safer Chemicals, Healthy Families Coalition. 2009. "Reproductive Health and Fertility Problems." http://healthreport.saferchemicals.org/reproductive.html.

US Department of Labor, Occupational Safety & Health Administration. 2012. "Carcinogens." http://www.osha.gov/SLTC/carcinogens/index.html.

US Department of Labor, Occupational Safety & Health Administration. 2012. "Health Hazards in Nail Salons." http://www.osha.gov/SLTC/nailsalons/chemicalhazards.html.

US EPA. 2012. "An Introduction to Indoor Air Quality (IAQ): Volatile Organic Compounds (VOCs)." http://www.epa.gov/iaq/voc.html.

World Health Organization, Regional Office for Europe. 2010. "WHO Guidelines for Indoor Air Quality: Selected Pollutants." http://www.who.int/indoorair/publications/9789289002134/en/index.html.

CHAPTER 14

American Council for an Energy-Efficient Economy. 2012, http://aceee.org/glossary/9#lettere.

David Suzuki Foundation. 2012. "Climate Change Basics." http://www.davidsuzuki.org/issues/climate-change/science/climate-change-basics/climate-change-101-1/.

International Energy Agency. 2011. "World Energy Outlook, 2011." http://www.worldenergyoutlook.org/.

TerraPass, Inc. 2012. "How Carbon Offsets Work." http://www.terrapass.com/about/how-carbon-offsets-work/.

US Census Bureau. "Statistical Abstract of the United States: 2012." http://www.census.gov/compendia/statab/2012/tables/12s0930.pdf.

US Energy Information Administration. 2012. "Energy in Brief." http://www.eia.gov/energy_in_brief/major_energy_sources_and_users.cfm.

US Environmental Protection Agency. 2012. "Causes of Climate Change." http://www.epa.gov/climatechange/science/causes.html.

US Environmental Protection Agency. 2012. "Sources of Greenhouse Gas Emissions." http://epa.gov/climatechange/ghgemissions/sources.html.

CHAPTER 15

Clean Water Action. 2012. "Bottled Water is Not the Solution." Power Point presentation by NJ Environmental Federation & Clean Water Fund. http://www.cleanwateraction.org/files/publications/nj/bottledwaterpowerpoint.pdf.

Cruz, Ramon. Environmental Defense Fund. March 26, 2008. "Bottles, Bottles, Everywhere." http://blogs.edf.org/climate411/2008/03/26/bottled_water/.

Environmental Working Group. 2009. *National Drinking Water Database—Executive Summary.* http://www.ewg.org/tap-water/executive-summary.

National Service Center for Environmental Publications. 2012, http://nepis.epa.gov/Exe/ZyNET.exe/.

Olson, Erik D. April, 1999. "Bottled Water: Pure Drink or Pure Hype?" *National Resources Defense Council Report*. http://www.nrdc.org/water/drinking/bw/chap4.asp.

SpaFinder Wellness, Inc. 2012. "A Brief History of Spa." http://www.spafinder.com/spalifestyle/spa101/history.jsp

United Nations. 2012. "Water for Food: How Much?" http://www.unwater.org/worldwaterday/downloads/WWD2012_VW_FRIEZE.pdf.

United Nations Environment Programme. 2012. "Global Water Resources." http://www.unep.org/training/programmes/Instructor%20Version/Part_2/Activities/Economics_of_Ecosystems/Water/Supplemental/Global_Water_Resources.pdf.

US Environmental Protection Agency. 2010. "Pharmaceuticals and Personal Care Products (PPCPs)." http://www.epa.gov/ppcp/faq.html.

US Geological Survey, US Department of the Interior. 2012. "Effects of Human Activities on the Interaction of Ground Water and Surface Water." http://pubs.usgs.gov/circ/circ1139/pdf/part2.pdf.

World Water Council. 2012, http://www.worldwatercouncil.org/index.php?id=25.

CHAPTER 16

ISPA. 2011, http:// www.experienceispa.com.

CHAPTER 21

About.com. 2012. Geography. http://geography.about.com/prb.org/Publications/PopulationBulletins/2009/20thcenturyusgenerations.aspx.

Johnson, Meagan, and Johnson, Larry. *Generations, Inc.* New York: AMACOM, 2010.

Kenyon, Tim. October 26, 2010. "American Consumers Lead the World in Environmental Skepticism." GFK Trend Talk. http://www.gfkroperpulse.co.uk/2010/10/26/american-consumers-lead-the-world-in-environmental-skepticism/.

LOHAS. 2012, http://www.lohas.com/about.

Mills, Nancy. 2010. "Natural Products Outperform the Overall Personal Care Market: More Double-digit Growth on the Global Horizon. http://www.klinegroup.com/reports/emailings/newsletters/consumer/november2010/timely_trends.asp.

Mintel Group, Ltd. Feb. 2009. "Mintel Finds Fewer Americans Interested in Going "Green" During Recession." http://www.mintel.com/press-centre/press-releases/325/mintel-finds-fewer-americans-interested-in-going-green-during-recession.

LOHAS Consumer Trends Database™. 2012, http://www.lohas.com/Lohas-Consumer.

ReportLinker. 2012. "Organic and Natural Toiletry Industry: Market Research Reports, Statistics and Analysis." http://www.reportlinker.com/ci02148/Organic-and-Natural-Toiletry.html.

SpaFinder Wellness, Inc. 2012, http://www.spafinder.com/.

TerraChoice Environmental Marketing Nov. 2007. *The "Six Sins of Greenwashing™": A Study of Environmental Claims in North American Consumer Markets.* http://ftc.gov/os/comments/greengudesregreview/533431-00040.pdf

Williams K. , Page, R. 2011. "Marketing to the Generations." *Journal of Behavioral Studies in Business*. http://www.aabri.com/manuscripts/10575.pdf.

CHAPTER 22

Macy, Beverly, and Thompson, Teri. *The Power of Real-time Social Media Marketing: How to Attract and Retain Customers and Grow the Bottom Line in the Globally Connected World.* McGraw-Hill Companies, Inc., 2011.

CHAPTER 23

American National Standards Institute. 2012. "Overview of the US Standardization System." http://www.ansi.org/about_ansi/introduction/introduction.aspx.

Ander, Gregg D. 2012. *Whole Building Design Guide: Daylighting*. http://www.wbdg.org/resources/daylighting.php.

Athena Sustainable Materials Institute. 2012. "Athena Research Teams Follow Common Building Materials From Cradle-to-Grave to Calculate the Environmental Effects at Each Stage in the Product's Life Cycle." http://www.athenasmi.org/our-software-data/lca-databases/.

Biomimicry Institute. 2012. "What is Biomimicry?" http://biomimicryinstitute.org/about-us/what-is-biomimicry.html.

BRE Global. 2012. "What is BREEAM?" http://www.breeam.org/about.jsp?id=66.

Building Green, Inc. 2012. Green Building Products. http://www.buildinggreen.com/menus/.

Centers for Disease Control and Prevention. 2012, http://www.cdc.gov.

Database of State Incentives for Renewables and Efficiency. 2012, http://dsireusa.org/.

DesignLights Consortium. 2012. "Combining Quality Design and Energy Efficiency for Small Retail Lighting." http://www.designlights.org/downloads/retail_guide.pdf.

Energy Star. 2012. "Lighting." http://www.energystar.gov/index.cfm?c=business.epa_bum_ch6_Lighting.
Fosdick, Judy. Aug. 30, 2010. "Passive Solar Heating." US Department of Energy Federal Energy Management Program (FEMP). http://www.wbdg.org/resources/psheating.php.
Global Green USA. 2011. "What Makes a Building Material Green?" http://globalgreen.org/competition/pdfs/03_green_material.pdf.
Green Building Advisor. 2012. The GBA Glossary. http://www.greenbuildingadvisor.com/glossary.
Healthy Building Network. 2011, http://pharosproject.net/about/faq/.
Heschong Mahone Group, Inc. 2012, "Windows and Offices: A Study of Office Worker Performance and the Indoor Environment—CEC PIER 2003." http://h-m-g.com/projects/daylighting/summaries%20on%20daylighting.htm#Daylighting%20in%20Schools%20%E2%80%93%20PG&E%201999.
Low Impact Development Center, Inc. 1999. *Low-Impact Development Design Strategies: An Integrated Design Approach.* EPA 841-B-00-003. http://www.lowimpactdevelopment.org/pubs/LID_National_Manual.pdf
National Institute of Building Sciences. 2012. "Whole Building Design Guide." http://www.wbdg.org/design/envelope.php.
National Institutes of Environmental Health Sciences. 2012. "Electric & Magnetic Fields." http://www.niehs.nih.gov/health/topics/agents/emf/.
National Institute of Standards and Technology (NIST). 2011. BEES: Building for Environmental and Economic Stability. http://www.nist.gov/el/economics/BEESSoftware.cfm.
Pike Research. May 18, 2010. "Green Building Certifications to Cover 53 Billion Square Feet of Space by 2020." http://www.pikeresearch.com/newsroom/green-building-certifications-to-cover-53-billion-square-feet-of-space-by-2020.
Smart Growth Network. 2012, http://www.smartgrowth.org/.
Sustainable Industries. 2012. "Fast Facts: Building Energy Use." http://energyguide.sustainableindustries.com/fast-facts-building-energy-use/.
Sustainable Industries. 2012. "How to Use Your Lease as a Green Office Tool." http://energyguide.sustainableindustries.com/using-your-lease-as-a-tool/.
Sustainable Sources. 2012. Guidelines. http://passivesolar.sustainablesources.com/#guidelines.
UNESCO, the United Nations World Water Assessment Programme (WWAP). 2012. "World Water Development Report." http://www.unesco.org/new/en/natural-sciences/environment/water/wwap/.
US EPA. April 22, 2009. "Buildings and Their Impact on the Environment: A Statistical Summary." http://www.epa.gov/greenbuilding/pubs/gbstats.pdf.
US EPA. 2012. "Low Impact Development." http://water.epa.gov/polwaste/green/index.cfm.
US EPA. 2012. "Renewable Energy." http://www.epa.gov/statelocalclimate/state/topics/renewable.html.
US Green Building Council. 2012. "Green Building Facts." https://www.usgbc.org/ShowFile.aspx?DocumentID=18693.

CHAPTER 24

American Lighting Association. 2011. "Types of Light Sources and Light Bulbs." http://www.americanlightingassoc.com/Lighting-Fundamentals/Light-Sources-Light-Bulbs.aspx.
ASHRAE. 2012. "The Indoor Air Quality Guide: Best Practices for Design, Construction and Commissioning." http://www.ashrae.org/resources—publications/bookstore/indoor-air-quality-guide.
Building Owners and Managers Association (BOMA) International. 2012. "BOMA Energy-efficient Program." http://www.boma.org/trainingandeducation/beep/Pages/default.aspx.
Dines, Nicholas T. "Sustainable Site Design." n.d., https://www.usgbc.org/Docs/SBTM/part3.pdf.
Efficient Windows Collaborative. 2012. "Energy Star Windows." http://www.efficientwindows.org/energystar.cfm.
Energy Star, US EPA. 2008. "Heating and Cooling." http://www.energystar.gov/index.cfm?c=business.EPA_BUM_CH9_HVAC.
Global Green USA. 2012. "Green Globalism Program: What We Do." http://www.globalgreen.org/greenurbanism/whatmakesgreen/.
Los Alamos National Lab. "Sustainable Design Guide." Dec. 2002. LA-UR 02-6914. http://nnsa.energy.gov/sites/default/files/seis/LANL%20sustainable%20design%20guide.pdf.
Low Impact Development Center, Inc. 1999. "Low-Impact Development Design Strategies: An Integrated Design Approach." EPA 841-B-00-003. http://www.lowimpactdevelopment.org/publications.htm#LID_National_Manuals.
RenewableEnergyWorld.com. 2012. "Geothermal Energy." http://www.renewableenergyworld.com/rea/tech/geothermal-energy.

Sustainable Industries. 2012. "Reduce Your Energy Use." http://energyguide.sustainableindustries.com/reducing-energy-use/.

US EPA. 2012, "An Introduction to Indoor Air Quality (IAQ): Volatile Organic Compounds (VOCs)." http://www.epa.gov/iaq/voc.html.

WaterSense. 2012. "Using Water Efficiently: Ideas for Commercial Businesses." http://www.epa.gov/WaterSense/pubs/businesses.html.

ADDITIONAL REFERENCES

Bachman, Glenn. *The Green Business Guide: A One Stop Resource for Businesses of All Shapes and Sizes to Implement Eco-friendly Policies Programs, and Practices*. Franklin Lakes, NJ: The Career Press, 2009.

Borkowski, Liz. Jan/Feb 2006. "Real Green Living." http://www.greenamerica.org/livinggreen/plastics.cfm.

Coming Clean. 2012. "Phthalates." http://www.chemicalbodyburden.org/cs_phthalate.htm.

Cosmetics Business. 2012, "Organics: What the Future Holds." http://www.cosmeticsbusiness.com/technical/article_page/Organics_what_the_future_holds/49393.

Organic Consumers Association. 2012. "The Story of Cosmetics." http://www.organicconsumers.org/bodycare/index.cfm.

Fosdick, Judy. Aug. 30, 2010. "Passive Solar Heating." http://www.wbdg.org/resources/psheating.php.

Green Building Advisor 2010. "Windows, Glass, Ratings, and Installation." http://www.greenbuildingadvisor.com/green-basics/windows-glass-ratings-and-installation-0.

Horvath, Arpad. "Life-cycle Assessment." University of California, Berkeley. http://www.berkeley.edu/lectures/L12_lifecycle_assessment.pdf.

National Toxicology Program. Department of Health and Human Services. 2012, http://ntpsearch.niehs.nih.gov/query.html?qt=phthalates&col=001main.

O'Connor, J., Lee, E., et.al. 1997. "Tips for Daylighting with Windows: The Integrated Approach." Ernest Orlando Lawrence Berkeley National Laboratory, LBNL-39945. http://windows.lbl.gov/daylighting/designguide/dlg.pdf.

Payne, Craig. June 14, 2011. "North American Natural & Organic Personal Care Market Exceeds $5 Billion." *Natural Cosmetic News*. http://www.naturalcosmeticnews.com/recent-news/north-american-natural-organic-personal-care-market-exceeds-5-billion/.

Sitarz, Daniel. *Greening Your Business: A Hands-on Guide to Creating a Successful and Sustainable Business*. Carbondale, Illinois: EarthPress, 2008.

United Nations Environment Programme. 2009. *Buildings and Climate Change: Summary for Decision-Makers*. http://www.unep.org/sbci/pdfs/SBCI-BCCSummary.pdf.

US Department of the Interior Bureau of Reclamation, Southern California Area Office. July 2012. *Weather- and Soil Moisture-Based Landscape Irrigation Scheduling Devices, Technical Review Report—4th ed*. http://www.usbr.gov/waterconservation/docs/SmartController.pdf.

US DOE Energy Efficiency And Renewable Energy. 2012. "Low Energy Building Design Guidelines." http://www1.eere.energy.gov/femp/pdfs/25807.pdf.

US EPA. April 22, 2009. "Buildings and Their Impact on the Environment: A Statistical Summary." http://www.epa.gov/greenbuilding/pubs/gbstats.pdf.

World Health Organization, Regional Office for Europe. 2010. *WHO Guidelines for Indoor Air Quality: Selected Pollutants*. http://www.who.int/indoorair/publications/9789289002134/en/index.html.

PHOTO CREDITS

Figures: Shutterstock.com

Figure 7:1: aceshot1 / Shutterstock.com

Spa photos courtesy of featured spas.

Figure 2-2: Cradle to Cradle. Schulz, A. 2012. CC-BY-SA-3.0, creativecommons.org

Figure 3-3: Earth image: www.nasa.gov

Figure 23-5: Passive Solar Design: Billery-Schneider, P. 2012. CC-BY-SA-3.0, creativecommons.org/licenses/by-sa/3.0, via Wikimedia Commons.

Figure 24-3: Passive Solar Design. 2012, www.eere.energy.gov, United States Department of Energy, via Wikimedia Commons.

SPA AND SALON RESOURCES

abmp.com
amtamassage.org
beautyschools.org (American Association of Cosmetology Schools)
cidesco.com
dayspaassociation.com
dayspamagazine.com
experienceispa.com
gcimagazine.com (cosmetic and beauty industry)
globalspaandwellnesssummit.org
greenspanetwork.org
healinglifestyles.com
lneonline.com
lohas.com
medicalspaassociation.org
milady.com
modernsalon.com
ncea.tv/ (National Coalition of Estheticians, Manufacturers, Distributors, and Associations)
organicspamagazine.com
probeauty.org (Professional Beauty Association)
skininc.com
spaclique.com
spafinder.com
spamanagement.com
spatrade.com (American Spa magazine)
thespabuzz.com

BUSINESS RESOURCES

bcorporation.net
bsr.org (globescan.com)
ceres.org (sustainability leadership)
ecogreenhotel.com
environmentalleader.com
gfk.com (GFK Roper consumer reports)
globalreporting.org
greenbiz.com
greenhotels.com
greenlodgingnews.com
iso.org (International Organization for Standardization)
lohas.com
marketingpower.com (American Marketing Association)
nmisolutions.com
socialmediatoday.com
sro.org (social responsibility)
worldometers.info (world statistics)

SUSTAINABILITY RESOURCES

carbonfootprint.org
carbonfund.org
davidsuzuki.org
edf.org (Environmental Defense Fund)
environmentalhealthnews.org
epa.gov
fao.org (Food & Agriculture Organization of the United Nations)
footprintnetwork.org
greenfacts.org
iea.org (International Energy Agency)
ipcc.ch (An Inter-governmental Panel on Climate Change)
johnelkington.com/TBL
myclimate.org
environment.nationalgeographic.com
nrdc.org
ntp.niehs.nih.gov (National Toxicology Program)
poodwaddle.com (Earth Clock)
sustainabletravelinternational.org
terrapass.com
unesco.org (United Nations education)
waterfootprint.org
who.int/ (World Health Organization)
worldwatch.org

PERSONAL CARE PRODUCT RESOURCES

ams.usda.gov
cir-safety.org (Cosmetic Ingredient Review)
cosmeticscop.com
cosmeticsdatabase.org
cosmeticsdesign.com (cosmetic news)
ewg.org
fda.gov
gcimagazine.com
gsn.org
medscape.com
notjustaprettyface.org
nsf.org
safecosmetics.org
toxicfreelegacy.org
universalcompanies.com

STANDARDS AND CERTIFICATIONS RESOURCES

ansi.org
biodynamics.com
cosmos-standard.org
ec.europa.eu (REACH)
ecocert.com
eco-control.com
greenamerica.org
greenseal.org
kontrollierte-naturkosmetik.de/ (BDIH)
natrue.eu
npainfo.org
nsf.org
oasisseal.org

organicmonitor.com
soilassociation.org
tilth.org
usda.gov

GREEN MATERIAL RESOURCES (LCA, HEALTH, PACKAGING, RECYCLING)

athenaSMI.org
beautypackaging.com
cdc.gov
ecolabelindex.com
ecologycenter.org
fairtradeusa.org
globalgreen.org
global-standard.org
goodguide.com
greenamerica.com
greenbuildingpages.com
lcacalculator.com
life-cycle.org
mintel.com
oeko-tex.com
paperrecycles.org
senseclothing.com
stopwaste.org
sustainableindustries.com
textileexchange.org
threaddocumentary.com
underthecanopy.com
who.int (World Health Organization)

BUILDING RESOURCES

aceee.org (American Council for an Energy-Efficient Economy)
americanlightingassoc.com
arcsa.org (rainwater catchment)
ases.org (solar)
ashrae.org
athenasmi.org (Athena Sustainable Materials Institute)
biomimmicryinstitute.org
boma.org (Building Owners and Managers Association)
buildinggreen.com
carpet-rug.org/ (CRI: Carpet and Rug Institute)
cdc.gov
conservationtechnology.com/rainwater_documents.html
dsireusa.org (Database of State Incentives for Renewables & Efficiency)
earthadvantage.org
eere.energy.gov (energy efficiency and renewable energy)
efficientwindows.org
eia.gov (Energy Information Administration)
energystar.gov
epa.gov
ftc.gov
greenbuildexpo.org
greenbuildingadvisor.com/greenspec-product-guide
greenbuildingpages.com
greenexpo365.com
greenglobes.com
greenguard.org
greenseal.org
hbelc.org (International Institute for Bau-Biologie & Ecology)
iccsafe.org (International Code Council)
ilbi.org/lbc (International Living Future Institute: Living Building Challenge)
irha-h2o.org (International Rainwater Harvesting Alliance)
lbl.gov (Lawrence Berkeley National Lab)
masterspec.com
mbdc.com (Cradle to Cradle)
nahbgreen.org (National Association of Home Builders)
nibs.org (National Institute of Building Science)
newurbanism.org
nist.gov/el/economics/BEESSoftware.cfm
nrel.gov
ntp.niehs.nih.gov
passivehouse.us
pharosproject.net
pikeresearch.com
sbainstitute.org
scscertified.com ((SCS Scientific Certification Systems)
seia.org/ (solar energy)
smartgrowth.org
sustainableindustries.com
usgbc.org

BOOKS

Johnston, David, and Gibson, Scott. *Green from the Ground Up: Sustainable, Healthy, and Energy-Efficient Home Construction.* Newtown, CT: The Taunton Press, 2008.

Gerson, Joel, et al. *Milady Standard Esthetics: Fundamentals,* 11th ed. New York: Cengage Learning, 2012.

Michalun, Natalia, and Michalun, M. Varinia, *Milady's Skin Care and Cosmetic Ingredient Dictionary,* 3rd ed. New York: Cengage Learning, 2009.

Ottman, Jacquelyn. *The New Rules of Green Marketing: Strategies, Tools, and Inspiration for Sustainable Branding.* San Francisco: Berrett-Koehler Publishers, Inc., 2011.

Winter, Ruth. 1999. *A Consumer's Dictionary of Cosmetic Ingredients: Complete Information About the Harmful and Desirable Ingredients Found in Cosmetics and Cosmeceuticals.* New York: Three Rivers Press, 1999.

Index

(Note: index is simplified for main topics locations and definitions)

360° sustainability, 19

A
accounting practices, 37
acoustical elements, 128
action planning, 200
action steps, 208
ANSI 305, 83, 236
assessments, 185, 189

B
B corps, benefit corporations, 39
BDIH, 83
BEES assessment tools, 18, 232
best practices, 4
biodynamically grown, 75
biomimicry, 227
body burdens, 130
bottled water, 134, 151
brainstorming, 187
building envelope, 229, 241
building materials (see green building)
building toxins, 130

C
carbon dioxide, 25, 130, 141, 246
carbon footprint, 25
carbon offsets, 142
certifications, 84
chemicals, in products, 72
    exposure, 72
    in buildings, 130, 245
chemistry, green, 74
chief sustainability officer (CSO), 6
climate change, 26, 140
color therapy, 128
commissioning, building, 229
community, 45, 181
contractors, choosing, 226
core and shell, 241
corporate social responsibility (CRS), 4, 44
cosmetics, 98
CosmoBio, 83
COSMOS, 83
Cradle to Cradle, 17
culture, local, 45, 61

D
daylighting, 231, 241
demographics, 216

E
Ecocert, 83
eco-charettes, 226
EcoControl, 83
eco footprint, 25
eco-friendly, 6
ecolabels, 84, 108
ecological product, 84
ecology, 24
economic benefits, 33
economics, 32
ecosystem, 24
EMFs, EMRs, 230
employee productivity, 34
energy benefits, 138
    concepts, 140
    conservation, 33, 138, 244
    practices, 139, 175, 240
    sources, 141
    systems, 229
    tracking/assessments, 190
energy management system (EMS), 139
equipment purchasing, 169
ethanolamines, 99
ethics, 218
ethoxylated compounds, 99
EWG, 72

F
fair trade, 75
feng shui, 132
filters, MERV, 246
fitness centers, 63
food production, 150
food service, 63, 180
formaldehyde, donor preservatives, 98
full cost accounting, 38
functional ingredients, 97

G
generational demographics, 216
global reporting initiatives (GRI), 39
global reporting standards (GRS), 6
global warming, 26, 140
goals, 185, 201
GMOs, 75, 107
GOTS, 107
green, 15
    materials, 104
    planning, 185
    practices, 52, 165
green business, 3, 5

green building, 225, 240
    assessments, 190
    certifications and standards, 235
    construction waste, 233
    materials, 129, 232, 244
    planning, 238, 249
    practices, 238
    process, 228, 239
    trends, 234
green leases, 235
green materials, 104
    criteria, 105
    interiors, 244
    purchasing, 104, 173
green teams, 160
    training, 160, 186
green seal, 84
Green Spa Network, 8, 54
greenhouse gases (GHG) 25, 142
Greenwashing, 6, 69, 82, 93, 218

H

hair products, ingredients (see personal care), 98
harvesting ingredients, 75
healthy design, 126
heating, ventilation, air conditioning
    (HVAC), 127, 139, 230, 243
hormone and endocrine disruptors, 130

I

ICEA, 83
indoor air quality (IAQ), 9, 129, 245
Indoor environmental quality (IEQ), 34, 126, 235, 247
    practices, 174
implementing green practices, 208
INCI, 83
ingredients, personal care, 90
integrated design, 227
interiors, materials, 173
    planning, 251, 244
**International Organization for Standardization
    (ISO), 39,** 238
ISPA, 6

L

landscaping design practices, 179, 248
Life Cycle Assessment (LCA), 6, 16, **17,** 38, 105
Life Cycle Cost Analysis (LCCA), 38
lighting, 128, 138, 231, 243
Leadership in Energy and Environmental Design (LEED),
    109, 236
local culture, 45, 61
LOHAS, 1, 214
low impact development (LID), 228, 240
low hanging fruit, 33

M

makeup, ingredients (see personal care)
manufacturing and sourcing ingredients, 75
marketing, 213, 220
    assessments, 220
    checklists, 223
    planning table, 224
    tools, 220
massage, body care ingredients (see personal care)
materials, green, 35
measuring sustainability, 6
menu, design, 62
    services, 60
mixed-use development, 228
multiple chemical sensitivity (MCS), 130

N

nail products, ingredients (see personal care)
nail salons, chemicals, 131
Natrue, 83
natural ingredients, 71
natural pigments, 98
natural resources, 17, 27, 33, 108, 120, 141, 149
natural step, 18
nature-identical, 71
net zero, 16
nonpoint source pollution, 150
NOP, 83
NPA, 83
NSF, 83

O

Oasis, 83
occupancy, health, 127
    tracking 190
operations and maintenance (O&M), 231
Oregon Tilth, 83
organic ingredients, 71
organic monitor, 85, 90

P

packaging, 75, 119
    practices, 172
pacific gyre, 121
passive solar design, 229, 241
performance ingredients, 96
personal care, 94
pesticides, 7
**pharmaceuticals and personal care products as
    pollutants (PPCP's), 150**
Pharos Project, 232
photovoltaic (PV) systems, 141
phthalates, 73
pigments, natural, 98
planning, 37, 185, 201

plastic, 104, 121
polylactic acid (PLA), 75
precautionary principle, 83
precycling, 54, 117
printing, 6
products, personal care, 69
    choices, 90, 167
    criteria, 91
    standards/certifications, 82
public relations, 36
purchasing guidelines, 35, 53, 104, 118, 168

Q
QAI, 85

R
rainwater catchment/harvesting, 234
REACH, 84
recycling, 118, 120, 170
renewable energy, 141, 242
retail products, 92
    practices, 167
return on investment (ROI), 6, 32

S
service menu, 60
    ideas/practices, 166
site design, 230, 242
skin care products, 69, 90, 95 (see personal care)
smart growth, 230
social equity, 44
social media, 222
social responsibility, 44
society, 46
Soil Association, 83
solar power, 141, 230
    thermal systems, 141
spa industry statistics, 63
spa trends, 215
staff care, 45, 158, 181
staff training, 46, 160
stakeholders, 36
standards, natural and organic, 82
supplies, 53
    purchasing, 168
sustainability, 2
    benefits, 5
    goals, 200
    planning, 37, 185
    planning tables, 202
    principles, 15
    tools, 7

T
temperature control, 127
textiles, 107
three E's, 3
toxins, environmental, 150
    in buildings, 130, 245
    in products, 72
transportation, 36, 228
    practices, 180, 228
treatment menu, 52, 60
trends, spa, 217
Triple Bottom Line (TBL), 6, **16**, 38

U
USDA, NOP, 83

V
vendors, 76
visual aesthetics, 128
VOCS, 131, 246

W
waste management, reduction, 36, 117, 170
water conservation, 33, 148, 233
    assessments/tracking, 194
    benefits, 148
    concepts, 149
    impacts, 149
    practices, 150, 177, 236, 247
    quality, 149
water footprint, 26
wildcrafting, 75
windows, 241

X
xenoestrogen, 98

Z
zero net (or net zero) energy, 141

www.ingramcontent.com/pod-product-compliance
Lightning Source LLC
Chambersburg PA
CBHW080727230426
43665CB00020B/2652